Sir Clement Freud gra... ...Sigmund, was born in Berlin, 1924. With is Jewish family, he fled to Britain from Nazi Germany, and during the Second World War served with the Royal Ulster Rifles. His varied career in entertainment started when he become one of Britain's first 'celebrity chefs', owning a restaurant and soon becoming a food and drink writer for many national newspapers and magazines.

Freud's mournful voice and melancholy expression made him a familiar face on television and in 1973 his dream of being more than an entertainer came true when he won the Isle of Ely parliamentary by-election. He served as a Liberal MP for fourteen years, and on his departure was awarded a knighthood.

Freud will also be remembered as a much-loved panellist on the long-running Radio 4 show *Just a Minute*. After being a guest on the very first episode in 1967, he appeared in every series until his death, on 15 April 2009. He is survived by his wife, Jill Raymond, their five children and seventeen grandchildren.

Emma Freud, Clement's younger daughter, has worked as a TV presenter for the BBC, ITV and Channel 4 and a radio broadcaster on BBC Radio 1 and Radio 4. She is a trustee and director of Comic Relief and helped to run the Make Poverty History campaign and Live 8 concerts. She is also credited as script editor in many of her partner Richard Curtis's films, including *Four Weddings and a Funeral*, *Bridget Jones's Diary* and *Love Actually*. Emma and Richard have four children together.

A feast of
FREUD

The wittiest writings of
CLEMENT FREUD

Foreword by
EMMA FREUD

BLACK SWAN

TRANSWORLD PUBLISHERS
61–63 Uxbridge Road, London W5 5SA
A Random House Group Company
www.rbooks.co.uk

A FEAST OF FREUD
A BLACK SWAN BOOK: 9780552776554

First published in Great Britain
in 2009 by Bantam Press
an imprint of Transworld Publishers
Black Swan edition published 2010

A CIP catalogue record for this book
is available from the British Library.

Addresses for Random House Group Ltd companies outside the UK
can be found at: www.randomhouse.co.uk
The Random House Group Ltd Reg. No. 954009

The Random House Group Limited supports The Forest Stewardship Council (FSC),
the leading international forest certification organisation. All our titles that are printed on
Greenpeace approved FSC certified paper carry the FSC logo. Our paper procurement
policy can be found at www.rbooks.co.uk/environment

Typeset in Minion by SoapBox.
Printed in the UK by
Cox & Wyman, Reading, RG1 8EX.

2 4 6 8 10 9 7 5 3 1

Contents

Editorial note

The pieces included in A Feast of Freud come from a very wide variety of sources, and are here reprinted essentially as they were when first published. The original texts have been changed only to apply some stylistic consistency; to correct a very few trifling errors; and to avoid repetition – though the repetition of the reaction of Freud's wartime adjutant on learning that he could not drive, and thus was not the ideal man to take the wheel and deliver a lorry-load of Belgian collaborators from Ostend to Brussels (pages 6 and 240), has been allowed, as to have it surgically removed would have been to the detriment of either piece in which it here appears.

Some of the articles are more resonant of a particular period than others, and not every reader will pick up every allusion in the earlier pieces. For example, when on page 89 Freud is in the Cavern Club in Liverpool in 1963, 'the walls shook with the voice of a man's amplified deliberations as to the best deployment of a hammer, which he did not appear to possess' – a reference to the Trini Lopez hit song of the time, 'If I Had a Hammer'. To offer an explanatory gloss of such allusions, and of people who were household names forty or fifty years ago but might no longer enjoy that status, would be too much of a distraction from the artless magic of Clement Freud's prose.

It is a measure of the longevity of Freud's career on the journalistic front line that this book contains so many transactions in 'old' money. For those young enough (or old enough) to need reminding: before the introduction of decimal currency in 1971, one pound (£) was divided into twenty shillings (s.), and one shilling was divided into twelve pennies (d.). A guinea, then as now, is one pound plus an additional 5 per cent: £1 1s. in old money, £1.05 in new.

Sean Magee

Foreword *by* EMMA FREUD

MY FATHER WAS a fabulous, complicated, unusual, gifted, glorious, difficult, riveting man. Adrian Gill said the thing he loved most about him was that he didn't just 'not suffer fools gladly', but that he would go out of his way to find fools 'not to suffer enthusiastically'.

He was perhaps the definition of a modern polymath, impossible to contain in one occupational category. He was a writer and an author, a performer, broadcaster, restaurateur and cook, gambler and horse owner, university rector, business consultant, Member of Parliament, shadow minister for Northern Ireland, knight of the realm, charity fundraiser and very long-lasting panellist. But most importantly, in his own eyes, he was a columnist.

For fifty-five years he was a working journalist. His first commission came from Chris Brasher in 1954 when, as a thirty-year-old ex-soldier, chef and nightclub owner, he was asked to write about none of that and instead was commissioned to do a match report of a Portsmouth home game.

He went on to become an undercover investigative journalist for *Queen* magazine – his 'Mr Smith' persona stitched up the pompous and self-important institutions of Sixties London – and in his writing life he played many parts: food correspondent, racing correspondent, travel correspondent, free-ranging interviewer, restaurant reviewer, columnist on being young, on being elderly, on meeting celebs, on being a celeb, on going out, on staying in, on life, on death, on everything. He was eventually sacked as chief football writer of the *Sun* by the incoming proprietor Rupert Murdoch, but was later forgiven when my brother helpfully married Murdoch's daughter. He went on to write about 8,000 articles during his life, a tiny fraction of which have been lovingly chosen by Sean Magee and are published here. A month before he died, I think he must have been the only octogenarian to have pieces running in three separate national newspapers on the same day.

Being the child of a columnist isn't always easy. Roughly twice a week for the whole of my adult life my Dad would send through to my fax or computer the column he'd just written. He would generously allow me around seven minutes to get through it, given that I might be reading slowly that day, but if I didn't reply after that, there was trouble. There would be a phone call to say, 'Did it not come through?'

'It came through.'

'Have you read it?'

'Not quite yet.'

'Why not?'

'I am cooking my children their tea.'

'So when will you read it?'

'When I've finished.'

'Oh really, not till then?'

Then later, if I forgot to call, he would assume I had read it and hated it, and there would be a measured amount of sulking. I haven't checked with my siblings, but after a few decades I certainly got into the habit of waiting seven minutes and then ringing to say, 'It's the best article you've ever written,' while often not having yet read a single word. His need for reassurance extended beyond the world of his children. He was at one point the highest paid journalist in the country, yet if the editor didn't call within an hour of his filing copy to say that it was fine, he presumed he had been fired.

My brothers and sisters will attest to the frustration of a visit to see Dad on deadline day – which was most days. It was always dominated by him sitting at the kitchen table next to his typewriter and reading us his latest piece, instead of chatting, as word had it that normal fathers did. And while we sometimes resented sharing him with his readers, I think we all recognized that the real Clement Freud was often more reflected in his writing than in any other form of expression. The man you are about to meet in this book – funny, erudite, obscure, witty, perceptive, campaigning – is the very best version of my father.

The subjects he covered in his articles span the key social and cultural topics of the last fifty years. But this book is rightly titled *A Feast of Freud*, because reading through the pieces here (many for the first time), it's clear to me that if words were his kitchen, then food was indeed his favourite ingredient. It became the constant theme in virtually everything he did, and not just in his articles. If he was stumped in a round of *Just a Minute*, he simply won by finding a way to justify reciting a long, long, long list of ingredients. Food was how he saw the world; it made him happy, it was his best thing. While he never mentioned to any of my children that he had spent fourteen years as an MP, they sure knew how to make his bread and butter pudding.

I'm endlessly told about classic encounters people have had with my father. Most of these stories end in my having to apologize for his behaviour, but my current favourite was hearing of an acquaintance who had had lunch with him. Quite late in the meal, my father reached over for a third sausage roll. His friend said, 'Clay, I thought you were trying to get into shape.' My father instantly replied: 'I am. The shape I have selected is a triangle.'

So you'll find quite a lot of food in this book. And some travelling. A bit of complaining, a lot of anecdoting, some tiddly-winks and a game of conkers, his learning to drive a racing car and to fly a small plane ... and, crucially, a generous serving of gambling. I'm not sure that there is any fraternity that will miss him more than the trainers, bookies, jockeys, stewards and racegoers of England and Ireland. He was a racehorse owner, gambler and follower of the Turf who championed the Sport of Kings on behalf of every punter who he felt deserved a reasonably priced parking space, honest odds, an adequate measure of alcohol and a sandwich containing ingredients of appropriate quantity and quality. And his racing columns gave him more pleasure than almost anything bar egg sandwiches.

Being famous irritated my father during his life, as will become obvious in his writing. But when he died there was such a response that one commentator described it as a Spontaneous National Round of Applause. At the time my mother said to me, 'Apparently Dad was a national treasure ... Who knew?' Even Nicholas Parsons noted that 'Clement was admired by everyone, even those who did not enjoy his company.' If Dad had had any idea of the outpouring of affection, media tributes, twitters, blogs and postings that were to surface on his death, I think he would have gone years ago. And I think a huge amount of that affection was based on these articles, which gave his life meaning.

His final article was written on the day he died, a week before his eighty-fifth birthday. It was in many ways the death he would have hoped for – at home, with my mother, to whom he'd been married for fifty-nine years, after a day's racing at Exeter. He was in his study, writing an article about the Exeter meeting for the *Racing Post*, when his heart stopped. And that was it. It felt fitting that the winnings found that night by the undertakers in the pocket of his suit ended up paying for half his funeral.

When we woke up his computer the next day, we read the words he'd been writing at the moment he died: 'in God's good time ...' My mother said it was the only reference to God she had ever known him make. The Almighty had waited fifty-five years for a mention, and having finally got one, it was all over.

But Clay was still typing when the final whistle blew ...

The Barometer Story

I WAS FOR six years rector of the University of Dundee. As rector, one would chair the court of the University. There was one occasion when a physics student came to us with a complaint. He had, in the course of his final-year physics exam, been asked the question, 'How would you gauge the height of a skyscraper, using a barometer?'

He had answered that he would take the barometer to the top of the skyscraper. He would tie a piece of string to it, and lower it to the ground. He would then measure the elapsed string, add the length of the barometer, and that would be the height of the skyscraper. He was failed for showing a total ignorance of physics. He appealed to us on the grounds that he had given a correct answer and received no credit for it. And the marks were important to the quality of his degree.

We considered, and then accepted he had a point and so appointed an external examiner to ask the question again. When the examiner met him, he said to the student, 'You've had plenty of time to answer it, so come on, what is your answer?'

The student said, 'It isn't as simple as that. I could of course go to the top of the skyscraper, and drop the barometer. And then with an accurate stopwatch record the length of time taken for it to hit the ground and then, bearing in mind the falling speed of the object, I could give you a pretty good idea of what the height of the skyscraper is. Or, and this is I imagine what you had in mind, I could measure the barometric pressure at the top of the building, and then again at the bottom. But on consideration, what I think I would do would be to go to the janitor and say to him, 'If you tell me the height of this skyscraper, I will give you a barometer.'

Sir Clement Freud, *That Reminds Me*, **BBC Radio 4**

1
FREUD
IN PRIVATE

'In 1945 I was asked by my company commander to drive thirty Belgian collaborators from Ostend to a Brussels prison in a five-ton truck. I said I was sorry; I didn't drive. That, said the major, serves the bastards right.'

A piece of my mind
***News of the World*, 28 February 1965**

MY NAME IS Clement Freud – the surname is pronounced
Freud. I am 5ft 10in tall, though very much smaller when I walk
on all fours: temporarily I weigh 13st.

I have temporarily weighed 13st for fifteen years so that the
thin man inside me is suffering from acute claustrophobia and
has, as far as I can tell, given up trying to get out.

I am in my late thirties … or to put it another way, I am forty.
Moreover my wife understands me and to prove it we have
five children of assorted sexes; they wait until I have to write
something and then race round the house shouting: 'Be quiet,
Daddy is working.'

As this sort of background is limiting to literary output, I tend
to work away from home, scribbling in railway carriages and
sitting at tables in sheds at the bottoms of other people's gardens.

We have no shed at the bottom of our garden; in fact our
garden is so small that it only just has a bottom, where there are
eleven daffodil bulbs (what is called a gardener's dozen) which
my wife is cultivating for some blue and grey vases she bought
in the sales.

The vases were a bargain, a 25s. line reduced to 12s. 6d.; she
bought one last January, and when she came out of the shop there
was a 40s. parking ticket stuck on the windscreen of her car. So
she went back and bought two more vases and worked out that
we were only 2s. 6d. down on the entire deal.

Thanks to a number of such transactions, we are now very
rich. We can afford to go out to other people's houses and eat
huge meals which we were never asked to do when we were poor
and lived on doughnuts.

Opulent living is a many splendoured thing. For instance, I
have a self-winding watch.

It is kept going, said the kindly Japanese shopkeeper from whom I purchased it, by the movement of your body.

He did not say that unless I wake up every few hours during the night and wave my arm under the bedclothes, I am called at 3.30am with a cup of tea and seem to be six hours out of true for the rest of the day. This displeases people with whom I have appointments.

I started writing rather late in life, about the time I started losing my hair.

There is no actual connection; for years people sent me back what I had written; no one has yet sent me back my hair which is scattered widely over the countryside of Britain.

A writer's job is very serious and very responsible. He sits down every morning with a pile of newspapers and reads them diligently then an Editor rings him up and says, 'How do you feel about South Vietnam?'

Of course the chances are that he does not feel either way about South Vietnam and is wondering whether he is going to get rich tea or squashed fly biscuits with his coffee, but it is more than a job is worth to say no.

Therefore he grunts a bit and at length professes to feel very badly about South Vietnam. Warming to the theme, he goes on to say: 'I feel terrible about Laos, too.'

By midday he is good and ready to write a strong piece about the whole of Malaysia.

As the piece is going to be read by millions of people who will, as a result of his writing, bore millions of other people, he writes carefully – remembering that General Khanh is the new strong one, and General Phat the other one who went away when Khanh khame.

He also has to keep in mind that there are in this land people who write letters at the slightest provocation. He must put into his articles the odd phrase or sentence that is going to make these people feel that he is the sort of man with whom correspondence will be fruitless.

'Some of my best friends are becoming Black Muslims' is one I have found useful in the past. 'As the Coroner keeps telling me' is another.

The aim is to make people feel that while you are basically nice, you are also unreliable; the sort of person who steams stamps off franked self-addressed envelopes.

But not everyone is put off: a few days ago I received a letter from a man in County Durham who said that he used to admire me on television.

However, he continued: 'Last Saturday at Sunderland station I went up to you, touched you on the arm and said, "You are Clement Freud." You walked on without taking any notice, brushing your coat where I had touched it.'

Now I don't remember the man, I don't own a coat, but I was on Sunderland station last Saturday morning so presumably it was I.

But if someone you don't know comes up to you and says, 'You are Marmaduke Ponsonby,' and on careful consideration you decide that you are, what on earth do you do next?

How do you know whether he is going to say, 'In that case take this!' and give you a left-arm jab in the kidneys, or ask for your autograph for his little niece?

If you do nothing, it is clearly a terrible affront.

My correspondent finishes his letter with the words: 'I will continue to watch television, but when the name Freud appears it will be simply "nowt" to my family and me' (he little knows that he might watch television for years before seeing me again).

But to treat the incident sanely, if I had heard him I would have replied, as I tend on these occasions, 'Yes, I am Clement Freud, actually' and look embarrassed; which does not exactly spark off the conversation of the year.

Perhaps the best solution is to deny the whole thing, so that the conversation goes like this:

'You're Clement Freud.'

'Certainly not, but I know who you are, you swine!'
Attack, they say, is the best form of defence.

* * *

How to become an Advanced Driver
Sunday Telegraph, 14 June 1964

IN 1945 I was asked by my company commander to drive thirty
Belgian collaborators from Ostend to a Brussels prison in a five-ton
truck. I said I was sorry; I didn't drive. That, said the major, serves
the bastards right.

I heard later that some of my charges, before being sentenced,
pleaded for mitigation on the ground that they had received their
punishment on the journey from the coast.

When I left the Army in 1946 I was given a brown and white
tweed suit, a little money and a wealth of documents, among them
one stating that I was able to drive a motor vehicle. I have driven
ever since.

I lean my right elbow on the window ledge, normally hold the
wheel at the quarter past six position and tend to listen to the Light
Programme with my left foot on the clutch, although I can get the
Home more loudly (I have two speakers, one at the back of the car,
so that the sound is very nearly stereophonic).

I have four endorsements on my licence – the last one barely
legible as it has had to be printed on the inside back cover; and I
have had three accidents – none very recent. The thin scar on the
bridge of my nose is now but a fading reminder of the night I hit
the roundabout on the Chiswick by-pass. All things considered, the
time had clearly come for me to take the advanced driving test.

There are a number of reasons why one should take the
examination: the comforting knowledge that an independent judge
of proven integrity endorses your own high opinion of yourself as
a motorist and the pretty badge they give to members are only two.

Fringe benefits such as the respect of the jury when an advanced motorist is accused of killing a Mensa member on a zebra crossing are countless.

There is no syllabus for the test; a booklet describing the non-profit-earning aims of the Institute says that the test offers an incentive to develop that extra skill and concentration ... There is a paragraph headed 'careless habits' and elsewhere one is reminded of the correct positioning of hands on the wheel, feet off clutch and arm free of window; also a little warning that excessive use of the electric starter will be noted, as would unintelligent use of the gear lever.

I filled in a form, sent £3 13s. 6d. (a guinea of which is the first year's subscription, returnable if you fail) and was given an appointment at 9.30am on Wednesday.

Now I am reasonably certain that the very minimum number of mortals drive with their hands permanently in the 10 o'clock–2 o'clock position while they sit alertly upright watching the speedometer, keeping an eye on the driving mirror, and using their handbrake to 'secure' the vehicle for each minor stop. On the other hand, it does seem to me to be essential for a decent motorist to be able to do just this, for a protracted length of time, in differing road conditions.

So I drove to Chiswick at a time when I am normally having breakfast in bed, parked where the secretary had told me to, was shouted at by a tough lady employee of the Institute and waited for twenty-five minutes under a sign which proclaimed 'skill with responsibility'. At length an examiner appeared and said we should be on our way.

We went down to the car and I told him that I had never taken a driving test. He said if there were any questions I should ask now; once the test started he could say nothing.

Hands here?, I asked. He nodded.

Foot off this? He nodded again.

I took great trouble to under-use the electric starter, looked in all mirrors, used the gear lever intelligently and eased safely – progressively is a word they like to use – into Chiswick High Road.

Now you have only my word against his, but I drove quite beautifully for an hour and forty minutes. I reversed downhill with skill and executed a noble three-point turn; my gear changes were smooth and silent; my foot left the clutch pedal at the slightest provocation and I tugged at my handbrake as I had never tugged at it before. Moreover, I negotiated such hazards as Brussels sprouts falling from a vegetable lorry, and a drunk towing another drunk.

On one occasion a woman, who may or may not have been an agent provocateur of the examiner's, jumped on to a zebra crossing as I passed. I pointed out to my companion that I could have stopped but was concerned for his safety when his face hit my windscreen. He nodded.

I tried to make conversation. It was to no avail. In silence we drove along the Oxford Road, through Uxbridge and on out towards Iver, with the only communion between us his instructions as to the direction I should take.

On his lap he had a pad on which he made notes. The first one, under the heading of STEERING, declared: 'No hands,' written in a handsome copperplate. It did nothing to make me feel at ease.

When we finally returned to the car park, he told me that he would put me straight out of my misery. I had failed. The reason was that I had faults with which the Institute were not prepared to put up. I had persistently coasted up to traffic lights and other compulsory stops, where I also under-used the handbrake; otherwise I was 'undoubtedly a very experienced driver with good driving ability; I should have no difficulty correcting my faults.'

I pointed out to the examiner that I always coasted up to lights out of gear. Nowhere in his book did it say that I shouldn't. The fault, if it was a fault, was consistent not persistent. Consistency should be rewarded. He went off to take his next prospective member in the cause of advanced motoring.

I switched on the car radio, put my elbow comfortably on the window ledge, gave a long and unintelligent pull at the electric self-starter and with foot irrevocably engaged on the clutch pedal shot through the amber lights. I must have done all of a mile before I noticed that my handbrake was still on.

* * *

I'm always one of the Don't Knows
Daily Herald, 13 August 1963

AS A BOY, I was told not to talk to strangers. As a man I find this advice practically impossible to follow.

First, I have the sort of face that makes me the obvious target for any stammerer who wants to know the time, and Eskimos with English phrase books who have lost Tottenham Court Road have an uncanny habit of consulting me.

Secondly there are the people who come to the door on behalf of opinion polls or market research organizations. 'Do you think,' asked a tremendously smartly dressed lady the other day, 'I could have a rummage in your dustbin?'

I told her to help herself.

I did not mind her so much but we get men who come to ask what brand of petrol I use, when anyone in his right mind fills up at the first filling station on the left when the petrol gauge is about an eighth of an inch from E.

Men come to ask how we vote and I once came home to find a young man pumping our *au pair* girl on whether or not she thought President Kennedy was doing a good job.

'Not a good job,' I heard her say to the youth who was writing feverishly, '*Mein Gott,* what a job.'

I am fairly certain she was referring to her own position in our household.

Yet a few days later when the figures had been churned in and

9

out of a computer I read in a paper that 61 per cent of the British public were satisfied with the present American administration.

I showed this to the German girl who said: '*Mein Gott*. To be satisfied with 61 per cent.'

And it's not only in the home.

Some time ago I was walking quietly along the seafront at Lowestoft when a middle-aged woman in a shiny silk dress gripped my arm, thrust a packet of detergent in my face and addressed me in the following manner: 'You,' she said to me, 'are the green OMO man.'

(I wasn't.)

'In accordance with the rules of the easy-to-enter competition I hereby claim the prize of one year's supply of washing powder and a handsomely bound volume entitled *The Easy Way To Softer Hands*, value 5s. 9d.'

I told the lady that actually I was waiting for the bus to Kessingland.

She said: 'That's as may be, I claim the prize.'

Realising that this was a tricky position I wrote her name and address on the back of an envelope and told her that she would hear from us.

I think it was the 'us' that did it, for she ungripped me and went down the steps to the beach.

All things considered it seemed the easiest, cleanest way of getting rid of her and I did in fact enter her name and address on a card which stated that 'you can have £3,597 at the age of 62 or £16 a week for life. Write in for more details without obligation.'

So she heard from someone.

Frankly, this whole business of stopping people in the street and asking them questions or telling them answers is getting out of hand.

Last week I was driving along the A12 when I was stopped by three civilians and two policemen on the by-pass some two miles outside Wickham Market.

'This is a survey,' said one of the civilians. (I already knew this because a notice board had said, 'Stop. Survey.')

'Where are you going?'

I told him I didn't know.

He said I must know.

I told him to look at any statistical chart – there were always about 17 per cent of people who didn't know.

He asked me whether he should put 'touring'.

I said I would prefer it if he told the truth. He had asked me a question. I had given him an answer. If he wanted to answer his own questions, he would have had no need to stop me.

'All right,' he said, 'I have one more question. Are you stopping in Wickham Market?'

'No,' said I.

He said thank you, I could drive on now.

In Wickham Market there was another board saying, 'Stop. Survey.' More policemen, more civilians.

They flagged me down. I drove on.

A police car raced past me, skidded across the road in front of me.

'Didn't you see the sign?', asked the policeman belligerently.

I said I had seen it.

'Why didn't you stop?'

I told him that I had promised the policemen on the by-pass that I wouldn't stop in Wickham Market. I was trying to keep my promise.

'This is a survey,' said the policeman, pulling out a notebook. 'Where are you going?'

* * *

Are you sure it's only once a year?
Daily Herald, 17 December 1963

IF PARENTS WANT to be really kind this year, please would they desist from asking my children to attend their offspring's Christmas parties?

The invitations come addressed to the Misses Nicola and Emma Freud.

Lindsay Tutte-Handful, it proclaims, requests the pleasure of your company at a party; we shall have fun; you simply must come; oh goodie!

Actually everything on the card except the Tutte-Handful part is pre-printed, available at all good stationers, price 8d.

The party is from 3.30 to 6. Only about four miles away, fractionally the other side of London ... quite near, really.

If I can possibly intercept such communications before they reach the addressees I tear them into small pieces and eat them. If they do reach the children then there is nothing for it but to accept.

It is now simply a question of buying two presents for Lindsay; taking the children to the party (3pm), coming home (4pm), taking the boys – who weren't asked – out; buying them a balloon each and making them as sick as the girls are going to be when they get back; leaving home (5.30) to collect the girls and return them to the bathroom (6.30).

What is so monstrous is that at 6pm one is expected to smile at Lindsay's mother as one says: 'Thank you so much for asking them. It was awfully good of you.'

Or could it really be that they are getting their own back for the children's parties we keep having to give?

The woman beside me in a Fleet Street pub ordered a small port and a glass of shandy. The woman standing behind her said: 'Let me pay for them, Elsie,' to which Elsie replied: 'Oh, no, Louise, dear, you paid for them last year.'

The season of unwanted, reciprocal entertaining is upon us and the office party is now only four days away. Upon the way I treat Mrs Golightly at the Boomerang Hotel next Saturday evening is going to depend my telephonic frustration of 1964.

The switchboard, I know, has each extension annotated with such messages as: 'Let him wait five minutes before answering; he took the last egg sandwich and snogged all night with the girl from Classified.'

Come the middle of December there are those who ring up and say in their own inimitable tone of nasal ingratiation: 'We're giving a little Christmas party ... do try to come ... bring a bottle.'

You say yes, and your troubles really begin.

First there is that moment of truth in the off-licence. You have to decide whether anyone would notice if you brought cider ... or do they really expect you to bring whisky and drink beer like everyone else?

And then you start wondering about Mongolian Spanish-type Claret; might it not be rather nice ... for other people?

I deplore bottle parties. I feel that if people can't afford to give parties the solution is so very simple. When I go, and if there is one thing I dislike more than a bottle party it is no party at all, I now take a small bottle of beer, half a bottle of whisky and a candle.

I give the well-wrapped beer to my hostess with an expansive smile; I then enter the room, open the whisky, stick the candle into the neck of the bottle, light it ... and provided I help myself very carefully it's all mine for the rest of the night.

It's the same every year at about this time. There comes an evening when I am sitting in one corner addressing the Christmas cards, my wife sits in another wrapping presents, the baby (there always seems to be a baby) cries into the baby alarm system which amplifies a gentle chortle into a fierce universal death rattle, and one of the other children – we have four of these – is not only sick but comes down and tells us all about it.

Just about then I turn to my wife and say: 'Let's give it all up. No cards, no presents, pack off the children to granny, send a cheque to Oxfam so that no one can say we did it for the money, and we'll go to bed with the electric blanket switched to a permanent HI which we have found over the years to be slightly less cold than the alternative setting called LO.'

It may not sound like a very happy Christmas, but it seems at the time to be the only solution if we want to survive to enjoy the prosperous New Year that everyone is talking about.

* * *

The giver of blood
Daily Herald, 24 December 1963

THIS CHRISTMAS, I thought, I'd give blood. In America tramps sell the stuff for 10 dollars a pint: in Ireland they trade it, quart for quart, with Guinness. In London the only incentive to be bled is love for humanity.

With only a handful of blood-giving days before the holiday, there was no time to be lost. I telephoned Blood Transfusion Service Edgware 6511. 'I should like,' I said to the lady who answered, 'to give a little blood.'

Engaged, she said; please hold on: and hold on I did, as if it were congealed as well.

After nine minutes I was put through to an extension and repeated my offer.

Are you a donor?

I am, I said, a prospective donor.

You are over twenty-one, she said … (it was not a question). Have you had jaundice?

Ah, I said, haven't we all?

I'm sorry said the woman, we can't use your blood if you've had jaundice.

I only had a little jaundice, I lied; a long time ago, a sort of pastel shade.

I was told that I would be put through to a doctor.

It appeared that there is a virus in the blood of those who have had jaundice which makes transfusion undesirable. However, small quantities of my second-rate type of blood were needed from time to time for research and things: was I prepared to give it?

With the uneasy feeling that I might be helping the black pudding industry, I said that I was.

I was in tremendous luck, the doctor said. If I could get along to the fracture clinic of the Middlesex Hospital at 4.30 they would bleed me there ... yes, even me. Would I ask for Dr Lecher? I said I'd rather not, not Lecher.

Dr Rogers, then?

That, I told him, was more like it.

I arrived at the fracture clinic punctually at 4.30pm. A nurse arched an eyebrow into a question mark.

I have come to give blood.

Do you know Maund-Sutton?

I said that if it was the village in the North Riding of Yorkshire, near Saltburn, I had once passed through it on my way to taking afternoon tea with the Marquess of Normanby.

She said she meant Maund-Sutton round the corner. Out of the front door, turn left and left again, and it was at the bottom of Cleveland Street. There were three of us who had all been told to go to the fracture clinic and now made our way to Maund-Sutton.

I must say it would have been easier to find if the building had not been clearly marked 'Courtauld Institute'. We told a nurse that we had come to give blood; she told us to sit down.

Ten minutes later Dr Lecher appeared and said: 'Good heavens, three of them. I was only expecting one.'

Having ascertained that one of us had not had jaundice, he asked an elderly lady and me whether we knew the fracture clinic. Out of the door, turn right and right again ...

We arrived back at the fracture clinic at 4.50.

The nurse who had sent us away had sensibly disappeared. We were met by a lady who apologized prettily and ushered us into a ward.

Dr Rogers met me, ascertained that my blood was 'not fit for people,' and a nurse gave me a chair and asked me to get ready. I fumbled with my shoelaces.

Just loosen your collar, take off your jacket and roll up your sleeve, she said.

I retied my shoelace and did as she requested.

Dr Rogers said that he would begin by taking a sample, just to make sure that my need was not greater than his.

He took a needle and jabbed it solicitously into the middle finger of my left hand. I was marvelling at his skill when he jabbed again harder. The first jab had failed to draw blood.

He then took my blood pressure, gave me a small injection by way of a local anaesthetic in my right forearm and then forced a great needle with attached tube into the vein.

It was ugly to watch, though entirely painless. In my right hand I held a plastic toilet-roll, which I was required to press and release to make the blood flow; out of sight, somewhere under the bed on which I lay, was the bottle.

After seven minutes the needle was withdrawn, a plaster fitted over my arm and I was advised to rest for half an hour.

I pronounced my inability to do this.

Dr Rogers inquired the reason.

I told him that my parking meter ran out at 5.26.

The doctor said that hospitals had a way of dealing with that sort of problem … did I want a cup of tea?

I said I'd prefer coffee, so coffee I got. Hot Maxwell House with the offer of biscuits.

After twenty minutes, ten lying, ten sitting, I asked whether I might now go. The doctor said goodbye, and delegated a nurse to see me to the front door in case I fainted.

Apart from the feeling that my right arm had gone to sleep and taken a long time waking up, I felt no worse than I had when I arrived.

At the door the nurse said goodbye, and thank you; that was it.

They have a pint of my inferior, jaundiced blood and I had a cup of their coffee, two jabs in the middle finger of my left hand, a plaster on my right forearm and a ticket from Traffic Warden No. 349 requesting me to send 10s. 6d. to St. Pancras Town Hall within seven days.

On the face of it, it sounds like a pretty poor exchange, but this is the season of giving and as Wordsworth said:

High heaven prevent the lore
Of nicely calculated less or more.

Didn't he? Or was it Milton?

* * *

Jokes I can live without
Daily Herald, 16 June 1964

SOME YEARS AGO my wife telephoned the laundry to ask about a pair of my pants which had not returned.

The woman who answered the telephone said: 'Now would that be Mr Freud's pants with the frayed elastic at the waist or the ones with the green ink stain on the left leg?'

It was entirely as a result of this that we bought a washing machine.

While I am a great believer in personal attention, the thought that somewhere in north-west London there existed a community of people who knew when my nose bled and how currently buttonless were my shirts, was an intrusion of my personal privacy with which I was unprepared to put up.

Also I shall not go back to the restaurant in Chelsea in which a very slim young waiter with particularly tight-fitting trousers brought me a plateful of lunch and then inquired whether I would like the beans facing the other way ... 'You know – pointing towards the cutlets.'

There is a point at which solicitous service gives way to a gratuitous mateyness at which I draw the line.

As with hairdressers who feel that one is genuinely interested in the state of their health, and then expect a tip when it is so clearly they who should slip you sixpence for twenty minutes of enforced therapeutic listening.

And jokey grocers – inspired by television serials – are my noirest bêtes of all.

I care not a damn whether I am called Sir, Tosh or You.

I do mind, very much indeed, when I am served out of turn, when I have to wait while the grocer has a cup of tea or find myself at the receiving end of such compulsive shop japes as being asked to repeat my order, only to be told: 'That's what I thought you said; we haven't got any,' for the delectation of the queue.

I have no more than a lukewarm affection for policemen who say: 'You shouldn't have done that.'

'It is inadvisable to park here.'

'I have a good mind to ask you what you are doing.'

'Weren't you going a bit fast?'

There was a time when I looked them straight in the eye and said: 'Will you either arrest me or shut up?' ... Until I found one who took me at my word.

I am wary of chummy policemen. I also distrust deaf piano-tuners and church-going atheists.

It seems extraordinary that our public image of 'national inefficiency camouflaged beneath a thin patina of suspect charm' has not infuriated more people.

He's a bit of a character, they say, when the publican starts to clean his fingernails on the bar counter.

It's just his little way when a taxi-driver belches the smoke of age-old socks through a pipe into the back of a cab.

What is surprising is that it seems to take newcomers absolutely no time at all to get into the swing of things.

'The dining car is at the other end of the train, but surely you've already eaten?', said a shining Jamaican ticket-clipper at Liverpool Street last weekend.

I walked to the far end of the train. No dining car. 'Never no dining car on Sundays, man, but other days that's where you'd find it.'

I suppose if one has to have inefficiency, charm is better than nothing.

I recently travelled by air from Glasgow to London. The plane was due to leave at 1pm. It left at 1.30. It was due to take an hour and five minutes. It took an hour and twenty-five.

Now one would have put up with all this quite cheerfully if someone had told us what was going on. The fourteenth screw from the left is loose might have explained the first delay; a headwind the second.

But no one said a word and it took us twenty-eight minutes at London Airport to become reunited with our luggage.

The girl behind the buffet tried hard to re-establish the balance. 'What's this then?' she said, as I handed her a Scottish pound note.

I told her. 'Never seen one like this,' she said, suspiciously, 'what's it meant to be worth?' And then, just to show that there was no ill-feeling, she added:

'We get a lot of queer people in here trying on all sorts of things.'

Goodness, I know what she means. Rotten old foreigners with 100 dollar notes and travellers' cheques.

* * *

How baby Matthew was undefeated
Daily Herald, 4 August 1964

BANK HOLIDAY MONDAY reared its ugly head over my part of East Anglia with all the fringe benefits attendant to the midsummer frolic – like no bread, no mail, no buses and, reasonably enough, closed banks.

In the Freud household the fact that this was a special day would have escaped any but the most observant.

A two-year-old Freud known as the Demon Emma arrived in the marital bed at her statutory hour of 5.45am waking an eight-months-old Freud called Matthew who sleeps in a cot by our side.

Soon after 6.30 fighting broke out between Dominic (5) and Ashley (8). Was stopped by the doyen of the nursery, a Freud called Nicola, aged 12; there was a two minutes' silence from 6.34 to 6.36 but it never looked like anything more substantial than an empty ceasefire.

Tea, made with water that was pleasantly warm, arrived via its conceptor – one serious-minded, culture-seeking, twenty-year-old female from Hamburg who occasionally answers to the name of Anneliese and joined our household closely followed by a Foreign Office document entitled, I seem to recall, 'Au Pair Girls – and how not to misuse them.'

After breakfast, with Emma watching the opening ceremonies of the National Eisteddfod on television, the boys fighting in the garden and Nicola huddled in a corner with a horsy book, it was decided to enter Matthew for the baby show at the village fête to be held on the common at 2.30pm.

I have always been against this sort of contest. It is the clearly advertised intention of fêtes to raise money for political parties with which the baby in question is not necessarily in sympathy.

To jeopardize a child's future by indelibly casting his lot with, say, the Conservatives before he reaches the age of reason seems to me a negation of the rights of man.

However, as our fête is in aid of the village sports club I did not demur; in fact I set off for the Common to find out something of the requirements for entry and the judges' terms of reference.

The Common was thick with public-spirited members of the community banging nails into pieces of wood. They were, on the whole, vague about what might be required of the winning babe.

'A well kept baby is what they will be looking for,' thought Mr Samuel, unloading giant onions on to the produce stall.

'Teeth, hair and initiative is what they're after,' said Tom the builder.

'It's general condition they want,' said an Australian lady who is staying the week with one of the vice-presidents of the sports club.

As this left me with no clear idea of whether Matthew would benefit from a bath, a tin of Bob Martin's powder or a course in Pelmanism, I returned home little wiser, but suggested that he might be spruced up a bit.

We looked the child over for blemishes. He has always appeared to us to be all that one desired in a baby. But then we had to admit that the judges would look at him with different eyes.

He has no obvious faults. No dandruff or anything.

His two teeth are white and straight – as far as they go.

His eyes are enormous, his nose small and cold, his ears neat, his complexion possibly on the pale side of bouncing, ruddy health, with a small bruise on the right cheekbone where one of the boys had got him with a mallet.

We decided to let him take his chance.

The contestant was given a light, early lunch and put to rest in his pram.

The contestant's father, the while, adjourned to the Anchor Inn and had a drink with a Member of Parliament who knew all about baby shows.

According to him the requisite qualities for success were personal freshness, lack of dribbles, clearness of eye and absence of paunch.

Winners, he assured me, tended to be female offspring of left-wing, intellectual parents.

Undeterred, we wheeled the contestant to the Common, left him outside the cricket pavilion and went in to enter him for the show.

Matthew Freud. Eight months. Two teeth.

A doctor was to head the judges – rumoured to have seven children and no local connections. The ideal man for the job.

With twenty minutes to go a nappy was changed, hair brushed, hands wiped, blankets straightened. Five minutes before the off and stable confidence was ebbing.

He seemed surrounded by female children of advanced babyhood with abundant teeth, flowing hair and indelibly Marxist parents with beards and sandals.

While they looked calm and sun-tanned, Matthew, and for that matter Matthew's connections, were strained, apprehensive, going rather yellow.

'This way,' said a man, 'this way for the baby show.'

Drained of confidence by the arrival of yet another ten-month beauty with golden ringlets, we decided to scratch him. Far better, we thought, never to have run at all than to have run and lost.

Because one day there will come a form requesting full details of his life and one of the questions will be:

'Have you ever failed to win a baby show?'

It will be nice for Matthew to be able to write the word 'No' clearly and honestly in block capitals.

* * *

It really is bad form
Saga Magazine, June 1989

IT COULD HAVE something to do with having got my free bus pass, or possibly the mild spring weather is the cause of my being inundated with forms: requests for single payment policies before some law changes; new life assurance to reflect that Lady F. is going to have a personal allowance next year, just as if she were a real person. There is a claim-form for flood damage, an application for off-street parking permits … and each time they send a questionnaire to fill out.

It begins harmlessly enough: name, age, sex are the first things about which they ask. Freud; sixty-five; not very often, I answer. Then there is a line for occupation: altogether more difficult, especially within the space provided. In my dictionary it explains that occupation is 'a way of spending time'.

Well, what I do quite a lot (and have done for many years though you cannot fit this into one line) is to take rolls of toilet paper from their housing and turn them round. I have this conviction that loo paper should be accessible from the back of the roll, NOT hang over the front, and while I am sitting comfortably I decide I might as well leave the fitting as I expect to find it. That accounts for some of my time, though I fail to understand what business it is of anyone else.

Also I trim my beard a lot. When I first began growing it I did not fully appreciate the available options: a beard can be square, spade like, rounded, pointed, triangular, forked, cover only one side of your chin ... so I get these good scissors that my secretary always blames me for taking away from her desk, and have little sessions in front of the mirror. (Avoid doing this in the bathroom for shreds of beard in the basin look unappetizing, whereas they disappear totally into the drawing-room carpet; especially my beard in my carpet.)

Why is it that they want to know my occupation when I claim for a new drainpipe after my old one got struck by lightning? Could it be that someone who turns round toilet rolls is a better-or-worse risk than one who leaves them as they are?

I believe there are two reasons. Firstly 'they' like to know as much as possible about us, because the more information they have, the weaker does our position become. Write and say, 'Dear Sir, It is now six weeks since I sent you the glazier's bill for my front window and I await the courtesy of a reply ...' And they write back and say, 'As a sixty-five-year-old amateur interior designer of bathrooms, you are fortunate that we accepted your policy.'

The second reason is more sinister: 'they' have actuaries who have access to all information and compile records as to which age range, in which profession, in what locality, of which sex is the most prone to have accidents, get mugged, stick their fingers up a fuse, or whatever.

It would be so much more reasonable if they said 10,000 people of your sort of background (sixty-five, SE England, sex not very often) had heart attacks last year, therefore we consider it unlikely that any more will suffer the same fate; have this policy on us. That would be decent. What they do is to lumber teenage public relations workers, riding motorbikes, with the cost of paying out for others in that calling. This is hogwash. Lightning does not strike twice in the same place. I always try to take flights on airlines which have recently had major accidents on the route I want to fly; to date no one has crashed twice on the same route on consecutive days.

The good news is that 'occupation' is no longer an essential item on all forms: post-1984 passports make no mention of this, which is going to be welcomed by some and regretted by others, and save the passport office much correspondence from folk wishing to amend 'housewife' to 'Prime Minister'. There was never any check on the veracity of the answer provided; my friend Len Deighton, when a cookery writer before he became a famous author, described himself on his passport as 'international lawyer'. He maintained that it impressed hotel receptionists when he complained about his bill on departure, and quite often got him better accommodation at a keener price on arrival.

When I became a Member of Parliament I used to have surgeries on Saturday mornings and because a lot of people came to see me, my agent decided it would be helpful to the overall atmosphere of the waiting room if the customers were given something time-consuming to do. So they got forms to fill in: that way no one said, 'Disgraceful, I had to wait thirty-five minutes to see my MP'. They said it was really well organized: by the time I filled in the form the MP was ready.

Every now and then the system backfired. I was ready and half a dozen constituents insisted on completing their forms before they came into my surgery office.

'Occupation' featured on the sheet and I was steadily surprised how many people wrote retired or unemployed, neither of which are occupations; both are predicaments. Perhaps we should have had a separate entry for predicaments. Next time you are asked to fill in a form and they ask your occupation, you might consider putting in 'filling in forms'.

* * *

Statistics that really wind me up
Saga Magazine, **November/December 1990**

I READ IN a serious Sunday newspaper's colour magazine that the average Briton breaks wind 13.4 times a day. My first reaction was relief: it must be all right if everyone does it so often. Then I started to think about the medic's claim, wondered who composes these statistics? Do learned societies place advertisements in Situations Vacant columns offering 'An opportunity to research human behaviour; must be numerate and have good hearing. No previous experience necessary.' And I wondered how we, the wind-breakers, subjects of the researcher, manage a .4? I tried. My wife came into my study and said, 'You are looking odd; are you all right?' I told her I was fine. She said, 'Don't overdo it.' I promised not to; overdoing it would be upwards of 18.5 per diem – on average.

One of our worst national faults is to believe implicitly in 'averages' and organize our way of life accordingly. That is why things go so terribly wrong when it rains more than the average however-many-inches-a-month or snows more than it is meant to, or, as last summer, doesn't rain the requisite amount. Other countries seem to manage when these extremes occur. Not us.

Sir W.S. Gilbert, he who penned the lyrics to the music of Sullivan for the Savoy Operas, and is the author of the *Bab Ballads*, wrote to the Station Master at Baker Street on the Metropolitan Line earlier this century:

'Sir,

'Saturday morning, though recurring at regular and well-foreseen intervals, always seems to catch your railway by surprise.'

You smile. On average you hear 2.8 unhappy stories about London underground trains each day and statistics show (there we go again) that the average number of railway accidents involving damage to staff or passengers in our country is 98.5 per annum. Some of these are minor. A train shunting into another resulting in a buckled guards-van, a dislocated ankle. 'An inquiry will take place,' says a spokesman.

A man leans out of a railway carriage, is decapitated by an oncoming train with an open door. Tragic accident. It is not just on railways. A lifeboat coxswain is swept overboard, body washed up two days later. Grievous accident: collection by the local lifeboat institute, wreaths sent by well-wishers. The difference between a serious accident and a catastrophe is one of volume. The entire crew of a lifeboat; the passengers on a cross-channel ferry, the revellers on a Thames pleasure cruiser, the fire at Bradford, the Hillsborough disaster – there you have catastrophes with questions in Parliament, weeks of newspaper coverage, senior Judge to conduct public hearing and the reaction by the public is to send money.

The widow of the decapitated man gets nothing, though he is very dead and she totally widowed. There is a whip-round for the coxswain washed overboard ... but when more than one or two people are involved there is a national appeal. Hundreds of thousands, often millions of pounds are sent by citizens who feel sorry and also greatly relieved that it was someone else, not them.

It is plum unfair that if life is lost under one set of circumstances – say a coach crash with a single victim – public reaction is so very different from that when a whole coach crashes over a mountain and kills all the occupants. Then do you get serious coverage, and news bulletins telling you which banks will accept money for the survivors' family fund; all that.

You might feel that the lesson to be learnt from these musings is that if you are going to be involved in an accident, you would be better off being part of a catastrophe ... that way you are remembered and your family is secure.

There is a further matter to consider: let us call it the The Towyn Syndrome: a disaster in which something tragic happens WITHOUT LOSS OF LIFE in an unfashionable part of the country. Like other disasters, people were left homeless, such belongings as remained were stolen; houses were looted. Hard-bitten news editors give it a few column inches on an inside page. No one dead, never heard of Towyn. MP hasn't made a fuss that anyone noticed. Forget it.

If you believe that a disaster is a disaster – regardless of how 'fashionable' the accident – then it might be worth investigating a national insurance scheme in which the government picks up the damage and compensates the bereaved. This would also spell an end to insurance policies which use small print to exempt the insurers from liability for most things that are liable to happen.

* * *

Over the decades my photograph ceased to be a true likeness
Saga Magazine, **January 1996**

I HAVE NEVER willingly posed for a photograph. I empathize with aboriginal tribes who believe every click of the lens deprives them of some persona – a possible explanation for why so few Page Three models win academic honours or the Booker Prize.

Some years ago, a man in Builth Wells took a very good photo of me opening a local restaurant, and I asked if I might buy from him a few dozen copies so that I could send them to people who had hired me to make after-dinner speeches and needed my picture on the programme in order to frighten the waiters.

Over the decades, something happened to that photograph: it ceased to be a true likeness. For instance, it had a smooth face while mine

27

brandished a beard; it had on its scalp hair, which I did not. And the cheekbones were a different shape, the eyebrows a different colour. So I stopped sending it out and countered occasional requests for a picture with a polite note explaining that I had none, not much demand.

The other day, my passport expired and in order to obtain a replacement (mine had served its maximum stint of twenty years via renewals), 'they' asked for two photos.

Not 'Will you be kind enough to send me ... with an appropriate message of goodwill to Granny Gladys' but 'Enclose two passport-size photographs with a cheque and completed form; then wait four weeks or more and desist from wasting our time by ringing up and asking about progress.'

The actual form was more straightforward than it used to be. 'Special Distinguishing Marks' has been expunged. My elder daughter's best friend had a terminal row with her live-in partner, stormed out of the house to go home to Mummy and, on the way to the door, saw her lover's passport on his desk. She snatched it up and under 'Special Distinguishing Marks' wrote 'No Penis'.

My previous passport picture had been supplied by a friendly man on the picture desk of a newspaper for which I worked; I no longer have friends in high places. I thought of the Earls Snowdon and Lichfield, and Messrs Bailey and Duffy, and, being ignorant of their present form, I asked my wife which of these good men was currently considered best. She said there is a Photo-Me machine at Marylebone Station.

You would think that after forty-five years of marriage I should receive a more up-market response to a courteous question. You would think wrong.

The following day found me at Marylebone. I discovered the machine, sat down where indicated and inserted £2.50 in the appropriate slot as instructed by the illuminated message.

Sitting there, quietly minding my own business, there was a sudden flash, causing me to close my eyes; and, as I opened them, there was another flash, then a third and a fourth.

'Wait five minutes' was the advice on the noticeboard in the booth, so I settled down with the *Sporting Life* and about twenty minutes later a man disturbed the curtain on my booth and said, 'You waiting for pictures?' I nodded.

'Are they these?' He held up a strip of four photos of an old boy with his eyes closed. 'They were in the drawer outside the booth,' he explained.

We examined them and decided they could easily be of me.

There is a note on the passport application form to the effect that 'If you have changed significantly since the last photo was taken, you would be advised to get a new one.' There is little doubt that those pictures will see me out. In fact, I doubt there is an immigration officer in the world who would put his hand on his heart and say, 'This is not a true likeness of any bald, bearded *Saga* reader with his eyes closed'.

As I needed only two pictures and the man who had come into the booth was not dissimilar, give or take twenty-five years, five inches in height and a *retroussé* nose, I gave him the couple I did not require and saved his sitting fee.

I wonder whether Snowdon ever does that?

* * *

Freud on phones
Nine Hundred Megahertz, **Autumn 1990**

'BUT WHEN I became a man, I put away childish things ...' wrote Paul in his letters to the Corinthians. (Why did the Corinthians never write back?) Well, I did that also. Put away my bath toys and stuffed giraffe and now hold on only to an electric razor, television remote control zapper and mobile telephone: these three, but the greatest of these is the mobile telephone. The Millicom salesman said it calleth all things and receiveth all things and my purchase clearly profiteth him and his masters, for he left rejoicing. It also cheered me up a lot and continues so to do.

When I was a child I spake as a child. I remember all those years ago we had an apparatus with a horn to catch the sound. 'Hawo', I shouted into the speaking tube, not knowing that I might have more advantageously positioned my ear for a response.

Now this thing I have, this third black technological object which neither shaves me nor changes channels on the TV set, keeps me in touch with the outside world. The machine lies quietly in my brief case, a spare battery by its side, just waiting for me to activate the 'on' switch. It is a brilliant addition to the contents of any briefcase – takes up hardly any space – and if you want a compartment to yourself on, say, the 16.50 to Lowestoft, turn on the phone, get someone to ring you at 16.52 and as it burrs, feign alarm and ask your fellow passengers whether they know where that buzzing is coming from? Lead the exodus, give it a few minutes and then return to the empty compartment, lower the blinds and have a happy peaceful journey.

My current life necessitates much rail travel and it is only fair to point out that tunnels and mobile telephones are not mutually compatible. There are also social drawbacks. Initially, when you board the train for Inverness and put the mobile on the table in front of you, people take notice: lip readers can distinguish words like 'whiz kid' and 'yuppie'; they are impressed. However, if by the time you pass Fort William the damned thing has not rung, it makes fellow passengers feel that you may not be the important person they thought you were when you got on at King's Cross. On careful consideration and bearing in mind your lifestyle, you might prefer to leave it out of sight.

The Kokusai KE101 is small. Its makers advise users that it will fit into a man's trouser pocket. And they are correct, though when you walk with it *in situ*, you tend to lead with the foot beneath the pocket in which you carry the mobile. In Spring, you see a lot of men walking like that, possibly – it now occurs to me, though I may be wrong – because they want others to think they are carrying a telephone about their person.

Road-testing the Kokusai got me into an embarrassing situation. On the train to Leicester I went to the buffet car, KE101 in pocket as I was expecting a call. I queued at the counter, moving ever closer to the corned beef with tomato chutney sandwich, when there was a beep. Assuming a resigned look of 'We tycoons are never left alone', I pulled the thing from my pocket and announced my identity. A second beep. 'Hello, Yes,' I said impatiently. There was yet another beep and the man in front of me in the queue told me that while he did not know what noise my phone makes, the three *recent* beeps were, in fact, the microwave doing his bacon roll.

One of the Kokusai's strongest selling points is the 99-number storage facility. Before a recent trip I made to the West Country, my secretary used the upper registers of the mobile's memory to key in hotels and restaurants in the area. She also included Devonshire AA offices, plus the homes and office numbers of those people with whom I had appointments. Item 82 was an hotel on Dartmoor that did cream teas. From its gardens I dialled numbers one to four in the memory bank to glean whether Ladbroke, Hill, Coral or Tote Investors gave a better price on the horse I wanted to back for the Ebor Handicap.

For a politically motivated, itinerant Intercity sandwich designer, freelance journalist, broadcaster and family man who tries to keep up with his wife and children, this is a great and wonderful toy. Even if – and the BR tunnels are in part responsible – my folks think I have changed my name to 'The number you have rung is unobtainable.' I can always ring them. I have ever tended to be less phoned against than phoning.

* * *

Why I'm happy to be a grump
Daily Mail, 1 March 2002

MAN IS, BY nature, a grump. A good man should have no time for twitty small talk, for folk who expect him to react politely, for

31

people asking him questions, giving him opinions, telling him tales of joy or woe (*their* joy or woe).

Good men, in my view, are gruff and grumpy, quick to take offence, sullen, cranky, crabbed and cross.

I consider myself to be a good man and I am all of the above. I am also acerbic, waspish, sour, belligerent and very occasionally shrewish.

Meet me in the street, ask whether I am Clement Freud and I am also deaf.

Am I kind to my neighbour, do I hear you ask? The answer is in the negative; I have always felt that were it natural to love your neighbour they would not have had to make an issue of it in the Scriptures.

But now, instead of accepting that grumps are exactly the sort of chaps we need, scientists have this week come up with a theory that describes our natural irascibility as Irritable Male Syndrome.

They blame it on stress which produces a sudden drop in testosterone levels. I rather thought testosterone was like Marmite, or Vegemite, but my dictionary says not.

It is to do with testes, which I personally consider to be balls. Though if they are right, my level has been down among my Chelsea boots ever since my voice broke.

And only last month we learned of the existence of the 'grumpy gene', controlling a postage-stamp-sized area of the brain, that determines a constantly negative outlook on life, irritability, anxiety and anger.

What I find so totally pathetic is that scientists feel the need to search for an explanation for irascibility, for tetchiness, for anger.

Anger is good, necessary, a trait devoutly to be sought. Go to a restaurant, be angry and you get terrific service. Shout at bus conductors and you don't need to buy a ticket.

Get on a plane, claim someone else's seat loudly, then tell the person sitting next to you that you have no desire to engage in conversation, and travel is smooth and peaceful and the stewardess brings you an extra helping of mango ice-cream.

Heaven, apart from having really good dessert trolleys, is going to be filled with those who won't stand for nonsense, who – far from turning the other cheek – will bite the hand that feeds them and send the hand's owner off with a flea in his ear. If that is not how you want it, go to hell.

'Nice' people are our enemies. They who go out of their way to manifest kindness and understanding to others. Customers who tell people that 'everything was lovely' because 'no one wants to make a fuss', they explain in a whisper.

Well, we grumps do. Making a fuss is absolutely the right way to treat poor service, incompetence, slugs in your lettuce, rancid chicken, burnt custard.

'Is everything all right?' is a question that deserves considered assessment, though even grumps need to bear in mind who is to blame.

You don't undertip the waiter because the food was bad, or late, or cold. Leave him nothing and tell him why, if he forgot to bring the cutlery or spilled soup on the tablecloth.

Train rage is good, too. Find out the name of the chief executive of the railway company and go for him. Hitting the station manager might make you feel better, but it lets down the grump team.

The important thing about anger is to keep it going and especially not to forgive.

I remember having lunch with Ted Heath after some memorial service. It was on a day that Ted had been particularly beastly about Mrs Thatcher and the papers were being very bitchy about him, calling him fat and useless and spoilt and incompetent and past his sell-by date.

Do you forgive?, I asked him. He said that he forgave but never forgot.

That is not a sign of a grump. I, who am a tried-and-trusted, 40-carat grump, forget, but I never forgive. There are people I hate, I cannot remember why, but I will never forgive them; I walk out of parties to which they come, seat myself at another table if I find them sitting near me on a table plan.

Lack of forgiveness is an important part of our characters and has, in my view, absolutely nothing to do with sudden drops in testosterone levels.

We grumps are designed not to suffer people gladly. On being introduced to someone new, our first reaction is one of apprehension and distrust.

At Goodwood racecourse last year, a man came up to me to claim we had been at the same school, he rather thought in the same class. I told him that had we been friends, I would doubtless have kept up the relationship.

Non-grumps would have asked such a man to have a drink and engaged in the most tedious of conversations in which you recall something the other person does not.

Non-grumps, unfortunately, also fail to understand our honesty. I was making a speech in the Midlands when my host asked me whether I would like to meet the Sheriff of Nottingham. I said, No thanks. Umbrage was taken. I explained that had he told me he would *wish* me to meet the Sheriff, that would have been another matter.

Ask a question and you have to be prepared for both a positive and negative reply. Grumps find negatives more attractive, though we make exceptions if the question is: 'Would you like another glass of Château Lafite 1961?'

I often wonder whether non-grumps realize how tedious their lives become? Responding to people who ask them the time, helping old ladies across the road, ringing members of their families for anniversaries, high-days and holidays, asking after the health of those about whom they care not a jot.

Grumps, in contrast, may say: 'Is everyone all right? Good. Now about that money you owe me ...'

When you go to bed tonight, stop to consider how much trouble and inconvenience have befallen you because, like a good little boy scout, you smiled and whistled through difficulties, listened to people who did not deserve attention, said 'please' and 'thank you' as if nanny were still alive and prodding you.

I suppose the only good news that can follow scientists' identification of Irritable Male Syndrome is that if you want to join us whose normal reaction is to scowl, grimace and snarl, others will no longer say, 'What a rude bastard' but sympathize with your condition – and suggest a visit to the chemist or, worse still, an expensive specialist.

* * *

Glorious insults
Daily Mail, 11 August 2005

RATHER AS DUSTIN Hoffman playing an autistic savant in the film *Rain Man* read the telephone directory and remembered the waitress's seven-digit number from the name tag pinned to her blouse, so there is a scholar lurking somewhere in a provincial library who has carefully appraised the contents of the *Oxford English Dictionary*.

The latest edition, out yesterday, has led him to publish the news that for every word which assesses people's good qualities – nice, kind, patient, charming, warm, helpful – there are nine that put them down.

From chump, clot, thicko, ass and moron to a whole new category of verbiage such as ning-nong and fribble.

How times have changed since I was a Boy Scout and learned The Scout's Law created by the movement's founder Lord Baden-Powell.

In those days – admittedly, some decades ago – the qualities I was told to ascribe to my sniffly, foul-mouthed, rude, grubby, thieving, skiving, scowling fellow Scouts who wore shorts and silly hats were: honourable, loyal, dutiful, brotherly, courteous, kind, obedient, smiling, thrifty, and clean in thought and mind.

But I always knew what they were really like.

Why should we be surprised that the *Oxford English Dictionary* contains ten times as many ways to insult someone as to laud them? There have always been more words in our language that condemn than praise.

Look at our politicians: what mileage is there in speaking well of an MP when you can call him/her a crooked, ignorant, illiterate charlatan, and be considered a great judge of character?

There are several dozen TV interviewers: but the ones who spring to mind are those few who practise insults, ask people the same question nine times, won't take yes for an answer and bring up mistresses, bastards and abortions.

In the early Fifties, I opened a nightclub in Chelsea. I always believed that the saying 'The customer is always right' was invented by a customer who was almost certainly wrong.

If people complained that 'The soup is too thin; the chips are the wrong size', I would kick them out.

'Go away, get out of here, don't pay your bill, just consider yourself banned for life.'

And invariably within the next few days, people would come in and say: 'Are you the man who bounced Freddie Smith out of this club? I would like to join.'

I once considered having my tombstone inscribed with the words: 'He never insulted anyone unintentionally' (it is now going to be 'best before' followed by the date of my demise).

To have insults in your armoury has always seemed to me to be advantageous, and I am not the only one.

In Las Vegas, I heard a cabaret artist round on a heckler saying: 'When your face comes to a head, have it lanced.' That shut him up and deterred any further interruptions.

For the record, it was also too major an insult for a minor transgression, and the comedian lost his audience whose sympathy now lay with the heckler.

Insults have to be geared to the occasion.

On another stage, I heard a comic asking a heckler whether he would like to come on to the stage and join him in a double act.

When the man agreed, he was told: 'What I have in mind is, I'll play the front part of a horse, and you can play yourself.'

Being pedantic or honest is often conceived as insulting. A man once came up to me at a party and said: 'Would you like to meet my mother-in-law?' I said: 'No, thank you.'

The man took a terrific offence and said I was the rudest man he had ever met. I pointed out that he had asked me a question to which there were two possible responses of which I had given him one. He replied, through clenched teeth: 'She was your biggest fan; now I'm going to sell the radio.'

Tell people the truth and they accuse you of rudeness, and the accusation sticks.

I have a certain reputation because I don't tell white lies.

'How was the dinner?' – 'Disgusting.'

'Did you enjoy the show?' – 'If I had sat on the aisle, I would have walked out after ten minutes.'

'Do you find my wife very attractive?' – 'Not really.'

Thirty-five years ago, I featured in a dog food commercial. People still come up to me and say: 'How's your dog?' I say: 'Dead.' What the hell do they expect me to say?

Perhaps I should reply: 'Sadly, the many dogs and their understudies who appeared with me in the 1968 TV commercial died of old age or were run over by a bus/put down by a vet; let us go and have a cup of hot chocolate and talk about this at length.'

If that is what not being rude is about, I'll carry on the way I am.

Trouble is, that if you have the least reputation for overt unkindness, people take offence even before they have heard you out ... and never forgive.

The good thing is that you can abandon attempts at being politically correct and tell it like it is: just as Anne Robinson hates the Welsh and said so in an interview, I don't see the point of Belgium, and when I mentioned this in some random article, I was showered with abuse.

I still don't see the point of Belgium, also I can't stand people who wear therapeutic sandals manifesting ill-shapen toes for all to see.

I believe that if you have trouble with your feet it should be a matter strictly between you and the digits on your foot.

I can't take the smell of tobacco and when someone lights up in my vicinity, I leave. Is that ruder than explaining that I'm on my way because of their filthy habit?

Probably best not to reply to invitations at all. 'How rude,' say the folk who invited me, especially when the function is eight months hence and I explained that on that day I am attending a funeral.

No wonder then that our dictionaries provide more nasty words than nice ones. We live in a nasty world.

On TV we watch nasty cricketers and dirty footballers and blind umpires and bent referees.

There are incompetent weather forecasters who lie to us, and in newspapers there are City pages commending the purchase of shares that lose us money.

And I haven't even mentioned estate agents, lawyers, tax inspectors – or journalists.

If someone leads a blameless life we never hear about him.

But if we catch them dogging or watching pornographic material on their mobile phone or lying about reasons for going to war, we writers rush to our dictionaries to find new and more compulsive words for disgusting, shameful, vile, heinous, immoral, degenerate, sinful and infamous.

Why do we do it, I hear you ask. My reply is shut up and get on with your own business, you witless creep.

* * *

Analysing Sigmund Freud:
the reflections of a grandson
The Times, 28 April 2007:
review of *The Interpretation of Murder* by Jed Rubenfeld

SIGMUND FREUD DIED in September 1939, a few days after the outbreak of the Second World War. He was eighty-three, had suffered from cancer of the mouth for many years, been in constant pain, chain-smoked cigars. The headmaster of my school in Berkshire heard the news on BBC Radio and called me to his study to tell me that my grandfather had died, adding: 'He was a great man.'

I told him that he had been a very nice grandfather. 'Have you read any of his books?', he asked. About a year earlier, when I had gone to the Freud house for tea and to collect my fourteenth birthday presents – an Egyptian relic from him and a white silk nightshirt from my grandmother – I had asked whether I should read his books and he had thrown up his hands and explained that he wrote for the medical profession, not schoolboys; I should read Robert Louis Stevenson. This grieved me, for among the books on the shelf behind his desk was a copy of *Lady Chatterley's Lover*, signed 'respectfully to Sigmund Freud from D.H. Lawrence'.

In my youth, 'Freud' was not a household name in Britain, as it was in the United States. At prep school, I was once called to the headmaster's study to be beaten for talking during class, told to take off my trousers 'and your pants, you stupid little boy', and lay across the man's knee as he fondled my bum with his gnarled hand, whereafter he said: 'I am not going to smack you because your grandfather would disapprove.' When people ask whether being related to a famous man is a help or a hindrance, I think of that.

I was called up in 1942. Having been born in Berlin, schooled in Devon, London and Berkshire, and lived in Suffolk, I ended up in the Highland Light Infantry. I was sent a third-class rail ticket to

Glasgow, and stood in the corridor of a packed train for six hours, chatting to another eighteen-year-old also bound for Maryhill Barracks. On arrival, we had a coffee then took a tram down the Garscube Road. At our destination we were told to hand in our call-up papers, wait until our names were called, come to attention, call out 'sergeant', and move to the quartermaster's office to get our uniforms. After a while, the sergeant called 'Frood'. Too tired to argue, I came to attention and shuffled towards the designated location, when the man called 'Jung'. My new friend, with whom I had travelled from London, was following and I gripped him by the shoulder and said: 'This is the most amazing coincidence: you heard him call me Frood; well, my name is Freud and Freud and Jung, I mean, what an extraordinary thing.' He said: 'My name is Young.'

Jed Rubenfeld, an American law professor, has written a meticulously researched thriller, *The Interpretation of Murder*, based on my grandfather's only visit to the US, in 1909. Freud was accompanied by Jung, then his pupil and friend, to lecture at Clark University. Freud hated the US from the moment he stepped off the gangplank of the SS *George Washington* in New York; he was unwell and Jung went to some lengths to publicize the fact that he had gone to his master's room and found him unconscious on the bed. There was also an occasion when the demands of the Freud bladder caused him to ask Jung to walk very close to him while he urinated in the street, down his trouser leg. Nicer men would have kept quiet about this. Jung did not qualify under the 'nice man' appellation.

Freud feared that the world regarded psychoanalysis based on sexual awareness as 'Jewish psychiatry', and believed that a Swiss Christian was a good person to lead the science forward. Jung used his position to undermine Freudian thought, to revoke his belief in the Oedipus and castration complexes, to deny that sexuality was the animal part of human nature and to denigrate his teacher whenever he could. They fell out big time. Jung was a snake, Jed thinks, although he does not quite say so in the book.

A faction in US psychiatry attempted to stop the 1909 lectures on the grounds of prurience, but they were attended by prominent philosophers and psychologists and received considerable acclaim in the local papers. Freud continued to hate the US with renewed vigour: the food, the lifestyle, the noise ... the fact that his wife's cousin, Edward Bernays, who lived in New York where he was the first PR man in the land, had agreed to meet him and did not turn up.

Then there was the presence in his retinue of A.A. Brill, who had translated his books into English with so little skill that we (to whom Freud left the copyright) had them re-translated by John Strachey – these were brilliant translations and convinced the world that Freud was a great writer as well as a great scientist. I learnt from my Aunt Anna that he had dreamt of winning the Nobel Prize for Literature.

Anna had a house in Skibbereen, Co. Cork, where she celebrated her eightieth birthday. Every couple of hours, the postmistress would arrive on her back porch with another clutch of congratulatory telegrams. At one point Anna asked: 'In the last lot there was one which must have been a mistake; could you have another look?' 'Would that be the one from Philadelphia?; I thought it odd but there is no mistake; I checked.' The message had read: 'The rapists from Philadelphia send their congratulations and good wishes.' There should not have been a gap between 'the' and 'rapists'.

Jung visited brothels and was known to have had sexual relations with his patients. Not so Freud, although Jung disclosed that my grandfather – whom he had analysed – had a relationship with my great aunt Minna, grandmother's sister. I remembered her as a tall, almost blind, angry old woman who walked with a stick and had lived with them since the death of her fiancé during the First World War.

My father, an architect and the youngest Freud son (there were three boys and three girls), took me to Vienna to meet him. My eldest brother had gone two years earlier and said that it had been all right. My second brother came back from his visit to tell me that in the flat in 19 Berggasse was a waiting room full of raving lunatics, worth observing for their wild speech and insane behaviour. When it was my turn to go, I was delighted because it was about the only time that I can remember doing anything other than in the company of my two brothers. I had pillow fights with Paula, the Freud maid, I sat dutifully at meals and was taken for a walk by my grandfather, me holding one hand, the leash of his Alsatian dog in the other.

He told me what a very smart dog the Alsatian was: once he had been out for a walk and the dog had run away and could not be found. Grandfather went home and the Freud dog is said to have gone to a taxi rank, waved the identity tag that was around his neck at a driver and was driven back towards the address. At the corner of the street, my grandfather said, the dog, knowing that there was business to be transacted at the destination that would be beyond him, jumped out of the window and raced home. The driver, deeply impressed, went to the flat to express his admiration for the dog. Even then, I did not believe his summation of events, but small boys did not argue with their elders and betters.

On that walk, we came across a man having an epileptic fit in the street. We stood and watched; the man's hat had fallen from his head and, as he twitched and salivated, people placed small sums of money into the hat as a token of sympathy. We walked away, grandfather, the dog and I. Why did you not give him any money?, I asked. Grandfather looked at me and said: 'He did not do it well enough.'

Back to Jed Rubenfeld: I invited him to lunch at my London flat. He arrived as the clock struck the hour and could not have been a nicer, more forthcoming interviewee. I cooked him a Viennese meal, which seemed appropriate – not that one eats particularly well in Vienna, now or ever; one just eats a lot. Should you, in a restaurant, tell the waiter that your meal has been disgusting, he is likely to say: 'Have some more.'

We had a strong chicken consommé, celeriac in chervil mayonnaise, Wiener schnitzel with asparagus, Lyonnaise potatoes and tomato salad. I had tried to buy a Sacher torte, but our Marylebone patisserie explained that it was using all its chocolate for Easter eggs ... would I like apple cake? We had that, a bit heavy on cinnamon but saved by Guernsey cream spiked with Calvados, and we drank a Grüner Veltliner 1985 Auslese. Then we went out for coffee, to talk more and get someone else to do the washing-up.

Jung, Jed says, first repudiated Freud in the US in 1909 and was never forgiven. To have worked as closely as the two had, then to deny sexuality and continue to analyse patients, was unforgivable. Freud continued his dislike of America and all things American throughout his life: 'Americans embraced psychoanalysis but they did not understand it.' I asked whether Jung was brilliant. Jed didn't think so. He believes that Freud was one of the all-time great men, and my thoughts went to the frail, cancer-ridden old man, revered by so many, of whom I was so proud and whose name got me invited to all the right parties, even if for all the wrong reasons, and by whose will – in which he bequeathed his royalties to his grandchildren – I was never completely broke and always had a little more money than my fellow scholars, fellow soldiers, fellow workers.

In 1978 I was on a parliamentary delegation to Japan and returned via China during the Cultural Revolution, a choice also made by young Winston Churchill, then the Conservative MP for Stretford. On my final day, I was debriefed by the minister for information, who asked if there was anything at all I would like to ask. I said: 'Yes. Everything you do, you do with extreme care and precision. When I ask questions that your government does not like, my driver calls for me five minutes later than arranged. When I ask if there are any blind or handicapped children in China, I get cabbage soup for dinner. Now I am in your country with a colleague, than whom I am older, have been in parliament longer, have held higher positions in our respective political parties: we are both staying at the Peking Palace Hotel and his suite is bigger than mine. Why?' The minister, very embarrassed, finally said: 'It is because Mr Churchill had a famous grandfather.' It is the only time that I have been out-grandfathered.

2
FREUD
IN PUBLIC

'"On the telly, with a face like that?"'

Official spokesman on a bicycle
Daily Herald, 25 February 1964

I AM NOT unaccustomed to public speaking. When I had been in the army for about two weeks our Scottish platoon sergeant said: 'You, over there, with the lah-di-dah voice,' and I came smartly to attention and said: '3533 Freud, your obedient servant.'

Then he said: 'What were you going to do for the next sixteen evenings?' and gave a rather unpleasant laugh.

Within hardly any time at all it transpired that there were in Glasgow – where we were then stationed for our initial training – an ever-increasing number of clubs, societies and institutions prepared to offer soldiers temporary hospitality in respect of their wooden boards, their gramophones, their rock cakes and their daughters.

When the welfare sergeant had delegated, say, forty-eight men to the ladies' bowling club pavilion in Shettlestoun, and sixty to the YWCA in Milngavie, my job would be to leave the barracks on a bicycle and call in upon each gay centre of entertainment.

Fifteen minutes after my arrival I was to detach myself from the others, rap a nearby table with a NAAFI soup-spoon (for which I would be asked to sign) and in the ensuing silence make a speech of thanks on behalf of the chaps.

The speech which was given to me was printed on khaki blotting paper and contained in an envelope marked SECRET/ NORTHERN.

I honestly feel that full publication cannot now prejudice either the war effort nor yet undermine national morale and intend to give you the full text:

'My friends,' it ordained that I was to begin, 'on behalf of all of us here today/tonight/this week I should like to thank you for your abundant (optional) generosity/hospitality. We from the South/ West/East had little idea of the warmth/friendship that we could expect to find in the North/North East/North West/Scotland nor of the spontaneous kindness that you have so ungrudgingly extended to us/my men.

'In expressing my/our thanks I should particularly like to mention – *see AF 729 to be supplied prior to departure by welfare corporal* – and God bless you all.'

Thanks to the blackout regulations this speech was usually made by the light of one 15-watt bulb; consequently I could ask any other soldier under fifty with dark hair to take over and pedal off to my next function.

If this does not make compulsive reading, it does explain why it is that I am not unaccustomed to public speaking.

The ninety-one speeches that I made in and around Glasgow have stood me in good stead.

Although I only spoke once more during my military career – briefly to a major who demanded to know whether I had any complaints with regard to the tapioca pudding – I have since consumed innumerable indifferent dinners at no more personal cost or inconvenience than travelling a few hundred miles, talking for half an hour and coming home to a bucket full of Alka Seltzer at 3am.

Around this time of year, and again in October, the telephone rings two or three times a week to announce, say, Mr Brashlick, secretary of the Cucumber Cricket Club.

'You wouldn't know me but I once just missed seeing you on television,' he begins. 'I'll tell you what it's about.' (The fool; I know what it's about.)

'A friend of a friend heard you speak the other evening at the Dragonfly Club dinner and I wondered whether we might have the honour of having you with us as our guest speaker … Trevor Bailey will be there.'

It's an odd thing but they always say that Trevor Bailey will be there. (I have never met Trevor Bailey though he did once telephone to ask me to speak at a dinner which he, himself, would unfortunately be unable to attend.)

For some unaccountable reason I always seem to say yes, and on the appointed day I drive to Chatham or Runcorn or Macclesfield and it's Tomato Soup and Chicken and Ice-Cream again, and Trevor Bailey isn't there again and my name is spelt Frued again and an anxious man comes up and says: 'We did get it right ... didn't we?'

And there's the problem of how much one can drink before one's speech and still speak – and how much drink is going to be left to drink after it if one stays sober; and you know damn well that if you don't laugh at what the idiot on your left says he isn't going to laugh at you.

So you hear yourself saying things like: 'No, I hadn't heard that. That's very good, I must make a note of that ... the man said that isn't a lady that's ... my wife will enjoy that.'

And then it's my turn to speak. The ideal speech begins with something fantastically topical – like a comment on the dinner, or on something that a previous speaker has said – so that everyone says to himself: 'Well, he didn't rehearse *that* in front of the bathroom mirror before he came out.'

It is followed by something devastatingly apposite – like 'Cricket's a funny game' at a cricket dinner, or 'Football's a funny game' at a football do.

One then finishes with thirty-one lewd jokes if it's a stag party or one long, clean story if there are women present or the waitresses are still there, listening.

I suppose psychologists would say that I accept the invitations because I hanker back to those carefree wartime blackout days when bombs were falling on the civilians of London and I was safe in the army in Scotland, and it was just me and my bicycle and my speech and all those nice Glaswegian ladies clucking over their knitting as we dallied with their daughters.

And I suppose psychologists would be right.

* * *

Unaccustomed as …
Financial Times, 9 December 1967

THIS IS THE banqueting season. Nightly now, in ballrooms up and down the land, inevitable chicken is preceded by predictable soup, followed by uncontroversial ice-cream which is garnished with sweet nasties in order to qualify for the name of Bombe Maison. If the guests have paid in guineas rather than in pounds, there is also an item marked Petits Fours: this covers a multitude of sins but tends to be segments of mandarin orange tackily set in caramel.

When, oh when, will people realize that, in compiling a banqueting menu, the ambition should be to please the majority of guests instead of aiming at the fewest complaints?

If you examine the writing opposite the assembled gastronomic delights, you will as often as not come upon the toast list. The first is The Queen ('Oh, is she here?', asked my sixteen-year-old daughter at a recent luncheon).

The loyal toast is now drunk after the soup, not so much from a greater striving for patriotism but to enable guests to smoke into their chicken.

Other toasts are drunk at the end of speeches, one of the purposes of speakers being to drown the noise of waiters clearing tables.

The change that man undergoes when rising to his feet in order to address his fellow humans is quite remarkable. I have sat by the side of pleasant, rational people who have punctuated the meal with balanced and articulate conversation. Comes the tap of a hammer, a request for silence and that same individual is up on his feet and turns into a monstrous Hyde.

'This reminds me,' he says, looking at no one in particular, 'of the Duke of Devonshire who came into his club in 1919 and was given a napkin and a napkin ring.'

One would have thought that if we really reminded him of that occurrence, he might have had the courtesy to have mentioned it to us, his neighbours, before getting up. Not a bit of it.

'Do you really mean that there are people, in England, who use a napkin ... twice?'

'I am afraid so, Your Grace; post-war austerity,' said the club servant. 'Poor devils,' said the Duke.

Of course the speaker is an out-and-out liar. We did not in any way remind him of that story. If we had simply sat there and belched, he would have related it regardless – for it was written on his notes. He had heard someone else tell it who had heard it from someone else, all the way back to 1919 when it happened, or did not happen, as the case may be.

Minor dishonesties like this do not worry him now that he is on his feet. He is power-mad. No joke is old enough or bad enough, long enough, or cheap enough to be discarded from the repertory. If someone told it to the Rotarians of Wigan, he reasons, then it is good enough for the WVS executive of Plymouth. Why not indeed?, as Mr Macmillan was so fond of saying.

'My Lord Mayor, gentlemen. For the second time today I rise from a warm seat clutching a piece of paper. I was asked to come here and break down the audience ... and you are the most broken down audience that I have ever come across ...

'Which reminds me of the story of the man who was beating his wife when the vicar passed the window ...' and as the vicar came storming into the house the man gave his wife an especially brutal kick and shouted: 'Now will you go to church?'

What is so depressing about after-dinner speakers is that the occasion demands votes of public appreciation or the broadcasting of interesting or important information – while custom requires the telling of an amusing anecdote. By and large people who can manage one of these functions are unable to achieve the other – as a result of which you get a comedian pontificating about the effects of devaluation on Cheshire while an economist tells a bawdy joke about an Irishman, an Englishman and a Jew.

It seems to me time that something was done about the whole business – a major rethink.

To begin with, if the dinner is official and the speech significant, it ought to be got out of the way before the meal. A speaker gains nothing at all from performing on a full stomach and going easy on the Châteauneuf du Pape for fear of slurring his words.

Also a pre-dinner speech would give the guests something to talk about instead of the interminable: 'How's your wife?'... to which one feels like answering: 'Compared with whom?' If the speech is solely to be made for its entertainment value, then let it be billed as such and let the speaker be paid a fair rate for the job; because the making of an entertaining after-dinner speech is a job like any other job needing preparation and understanding.

I am not against the Prime Minister, in closing, paying his respects to the ladies of the raffle committee or the banqueting staff. I am all in favour of a witty speech. What I cannot take is the 'This reminds me of ...' followed by badly told old jokes, in the middle of a report on the results of the past cricket season.

What I particularly resent is when the local Member of Parliament takes on the portmanteau functions of dignitary, humorist and master of ceremonies. The reasoning seems to be: 'I am standing up and you are sitting down; let's keep it that way ...' and he goes on for thirty-five boring minutes. This was never meant by the term 'good food and fellowship'. Goodness knows that our banqueting food is bad enough; let us try to do something for the fellowship.

I recently heard Mr Bob Monkhouse make a brilliant after-dinner speech – in the light of which, memories of the bland baked battery bird paled.

He was employed for his entertainment value and deserved every guinea he got. Preceding him was the export manager of the company, who punctuated a stirring report of achievements with badly told, unamusing stories; he should have been shot.

Now that might have been entertainment.

* * *

My all-conquering chestnuts
The Times, 29 March 1990

WOGAN SAID NEVER do it on a boat – never, that is, unless they give you a cabin and you can lock the door when it is over. We were talking about public appearances. When the deed is done, and the performer has nowhere to go, people feel they must come up and say: 'I liked your dyslexic Afrikaner who blew up C&A; have you heard the one about the man who went on holiday to the Channel Islands and asked his best friend to look after the budgerigar?' Well, this man went on holiday to Jersey and he had a friend who was a plumber and played in a heavy metal band ...'

Most people believe that after-dinner speaking is a doddle; that speakers have but a single oration which they tote around the country in search of audiences who have not heard it. This is some way from the truth.

What we have is a format, which we adapt to suit the punters. At a legal dinner, 'Why did the solicitor cross the road?' goes down a treat. For local authority functions, 'There was an English environmental health officer, a Scottish environmental health officer and an Irish environmental health officer ...' makes them feel you have really done your homework.

'Who was that travel agent I saw you with last night?', is one to keep in mind when speaking to Thomas Cook's people. Our aim is to have audiences believe that the speech is bespoke, designed for this and no other occasion.

Some of us, at the top of the profession, have multi-discipline anecdotes, like the man in the Gobi Desert who, because of geographical miscalculation, finds himself and his dog without food and water, three days' march from the nearest mirage ... You can tell that to canine clubs, planners' associations, Weightwatchers and the Society of Motor Manufacturers and Traders. Actually you can tell pretty well anything to the Society of MM&T.

Last week, I was asked to speak at a clients' dinner given by a prestigious firm of glassmakers. There were about 100 guests, most of whom sold the company's produce to licensed victuallers. During the meal, I thought again about Vatel, Louis XIV's major-domo, who killed himself with a carving knife when His Majesty's fish course was late in arriving from the kitchen.

He was thirty-four, about the same age as the waitress who explained that a half-hour wait after the prawn cocktail was standard. I thought perhaps I should hide my cutlery.

My brief stipulated that I should talk about my connection with catering and discuss the merits of fine glassware, stressing the desirability of investment in the company's products between reminiscence and anecdotes. I began with the story of this liquor glass salesman who went to heaven and St Peter asked him what made him think he had come to the right place, and moved smoothly to the half-grapefruit dilemma. Restaurants cannot serve half grapefruits, delicious though they are, because too many people know the price of a whole grapefruit, are able to divide by two and could then glean how substantial is the profit on which the caterer works.

As a consequence, you get grapefruit cocktail, fashioned of nasty tinned segments and two green maraschino cherries, three thin slices of Cape gooseberry in a frosted glass, the rim of which is rubbed with lemon and dunked in caster sugar. No one knows how much that costs, so the caterer feels he might as well charge twice as much as he would have done for the half grapefruit.

I moved smoothly to the good reasons why restaurants should purchase large glasses: to shame parties of four into buying more than one bottle; and why they should have a good stock of small ones: so that they can use less wine when selling it by the glass.

I ended by telling the assembled company about the glass-blower who went to his doctor for a check-up and learnt that he had only twelve hours to live. The story ends with his wife saying: 'It's all right for you, you don't have to be up in the morning.'

And after I had sat down, a man came by and told me he had heard that self-same story about a racehorse trainer: 'There was this racehorse trainer who went to his doctor for a check-up ...'

I asked him where he had heard it, and he said at the Royal Lancaster Hotel's Derby Night Dinner.

'Who told it?'

'Come to think of it,' said the man, 'I believe it was you. But I preferred tonight's version.'

* * *

On the telly, with a face like that?
Sun, 2 August 1965

SPORT, LIKE BEAUTY, is in the eye of the beholder – and if you get round to thinking that my sporting Saturday was nothing of the sort, we come back to the question of 'it all depends what you mean by sport.'

It started in Oldham at two o'clock in the afternoon. The Oldham Carnival, the organizers had assured me, was the biggest in Britain.

Sixty thousand people lined the streets and thousands of pounds were collected for charity.

If I could possibly sit in a car which would have my name on it and take part in the parade and select a beauty queen they would all be terrifically grateful ...

So I said yes.

And I sat in an open car which crawled behind a galaxy of tiny hip-swinging majorettes.

I was goggled at for two hours by people who had instantly recognized Jimmy Saville, Billy J. Kramer and the dishy girl in *Coronation Street*, but were less certain about me.

They looked worried, the way I look at that face in the 'How Good Is Your Memory?' advertisement.

Every now and again a mother despatched a reluctant child to collect my autograph. The child would approach trotting behind the car, almost hand me her book, look back to Mum for reassurance that she had got the right person, get the OK and then say, 'Sign please.'

I signed gratefully.

There were frequent stops, during which I was stuck in the middle of the road sitting up on the back seat of the Triumph Spitfire being stared at by the populace who happened to have chosen that part of the pavement for a vantage point.

'Who's this then?', they said.

I scowled.

'It's the one on the telly,' said someone.

I smiled.

'On the telly, with a face like that?'

The one highlight of the motorcade was a steward who had clearly been overbriefed by the organizers.

He had distinguished himself throughout by caring for our comfort far beyond the call of duty.

As we approached the end of our tour his great moment came. He came up to me earnestly and said that the screaming thousands in the park would probably tear me to pieces as I got out of the car.

He had therefore prepared a plain van, hidden by the side of the road, into which I should dive – preferably with a blanket over my head for anonymity.

Fortunately, the van was so well hidden that we never found it and in spite of the man's fears I reached the judging platform unharmed.

At 5 o'clock I left the carnival for sporting pastures of a less challenging nature. Ninety-one miles to the West of Oldham there was billed to take place an international trotting event.

The meeting was at Prestatyn raceway, first race 7.40pm, and the first six people from whom I sought directions did not know they had a raceway in the town.

I found it at length, a half-mile oval circuit on the beach side of the town. A good stand held 700 to 800 people; a dozen bookmakers graced the rails and a Welsh-Canadian voice asked the drivers for the first race to come on to the track. There were three.

Compact ponies harnessed to light chariots, driven by men in long white trousers, coloured tunics and crash helmets, preceded by a strangely out-of-place huntsman in full regalia.

The starter's car appeared on the course and opened up a wide starting-gate behind which the trotters trotted. When they were neatly in line the car streaked off the track and the race was on.

On the face of it, trotting is as unnatural a sport as road walking, high jumping in Wellington boots, or motor car racing with the brakes on.

In fact, trotters are bred by trotters expressly for trotting, and they are trained to trot, which they do most gracefully.

It is only when you see them break into a clumsy gallop – which they do every now and again by mistake – that you realize that trotting is a vocation rather than a curb.

Even so, and despite the fact that five favourites won the five races I witnessed, I found trotting less satisfactory than horse or dog racing. This was not so much because I laid the last three favourites to lose – and consequently lost – but because you get a definite sense of frustration when you urge on a trotter to trot faster.

Everyone else, however, punters, holidaymakers, both local peers, even the bookmakers, seemed to enjoy it all immensely.

There was also a Russian contingent, consisting of four horses, an interpreter, whom I could not find, and three available comrades whose combined English consisted of the word 'good'.

Fooled by this monosyllable, I backed the Soviet horse called Travnik at 6-1. Travnik made up fifteen yards in the home straight but failed to win by half a length.

I found the driver and taught him a new word.

At midnight I got back to my hotel in Manchester and, hearing

the noise of much merrymaking emanating from the ballroom, set
out to investigate.

Thus did I chance upon the party given to celebrate Manchester
United's championship of the Football League.

It's a hard life, a sportsman's life.

* * *

*Freud's most long-lasting public role was as a regular panellist
on BBC Radio 4's hugely popular panel game* Just a Minute.

The panel with flannel
Radio Times, **6-12 February 1993**

IT BEGAN 25 years ago ... and I cannot even claim that I was
very young when it happened. Ian Messiter rang me and asked if I
remembered Gerard Hoffnung.

'Cartoonist,' said I; 'played the euphonium, told that brilliant
story about a workman and a bucket; gave a party to which he
invited only people whose surnames contained the word bottom.'

'And was in *Just a Minute*, a panel game which I invented,' said
Messiter. 'It ran briefly some years ago [as *One Minute, Please*] and
I want to bring it back; would like you to be the argumentative,
pedantic, erudite member of the panel.'

Nicholas Parsons was chairman; I think the BBC needed
someone with fair hair. Over the first few recordings there were
some comings and goings, but among the personnel who stayed
were Derek Nimmo – chosen for his urbanity; Peter Jones to deflate
and Kenneth Williams to dazzle. We were the regulars: what we had
in common was that we all thought Parsons was totally the wrong
man for the job. Whoever heard of a lightweight chairman? (This
was five years before I won a seat at Westminster and found out.)

Over the years some of us progressed: Nimmo – who came to

the show as an actor, talk-show host, leading man to Anna Neagle – took to arriving in a Rolls-Royce, driven by a chauffeur wearing a cape with gold buttons.

I, who had been a nightclub owner, journalist and TV cook, became an MP and sometimes had to race away to vote. (The Paris Theatre in Lower Regent Street is within division bell distance of the Commons.)

Parsons, who had been a juvenile lead, impeccable straight man to Arthur Haynes, game-show host, kept getting younger.

Jones never changed – not even his clothes – but Williams, who started with a claque of half-a-dozen, built this up to such numbers that the rest of us (a) had trouble getting guests into the theatre and (b) steadily lost the vote when Parsons asked the assembled audience to 'cheer if you think Kenneth Williams's challenge is correct, boo if you don't.' Exactly why Parsons thought that 300 runcible folk, many of whom had only come into the place because it was raining outside, were qualified to give an opinion on whether Kathmandu is or is not 2,500 metres above sea level steadily mystified me.

It was not always the regular four; one or other of us would be unavailable – or there was an election in the offing and my opponents pointed out that the BBC charter demanded equal radio and TV time for all candidates, which put paid to me for a month. So the director, first David Hatch, later John Lloyd and then Edward Taylor, invited 'guests'. Parsons, voice charged with the breathless sycophancy of a toastmaster, announced, 'And to join this male bastion of our three brilliant, exciting, fascinating regulars, we welcome Aimi MacDonald ... Elaine Stritch, Sheila Hancock, Victoria Wood ...' whoever.

'We don't want women on the show,' said Kenny, till he was buzzed for repetition. When we had male guests on *Just a Minute* – Richard Murdoch, Tim Rice, Willie Rushton, Peter Cook – he would wait to hear what they had to contribute, nudge me or blow a kiss in my ear (we were always placed next to each other) and say, 'Listen to her.'

Over the years we tried the game for television (twice) and for one series we switched chairman: Parsons, as a panellist, asked me to explain exactly why I had disallowed a challenge. I explained that I was trying to emulate his inscrutable rulings. I do not think we were much good as chairmen – though we did find out that the Corporation pays panel-game chairmen more than panellists. We spent some years ribbing Parsons over the fact that, as he was getting more than us, he should work harder on his performance.

Williams was not only a genius, he had an absolutely unique ability of spreading gloom: we would arrive at the Paris fit and well and cheerful, happy to be together again, and Kenny would arrive in a deafening sulk; ignore some of us, chat intimately with others, shout, 'Get on with it' while the audience was being 'warmed'. When he was in this mood, the game took on a whole new dimension; you not only had to consider whether or not a buzz was justified or should be withheld lest it spoil a good story; you also had to bear in mind that a challenge might so annoy Kenny that he would not say another word until it was his turn to start a round. 'I am a cult figure. I have come all the way from Great Portland Street; you've interrupted my natural flow' were indications that trouble was ahead.

Just a Minute, we discovered to our costs, was not a good medium for telling stories: nearly all seemed to have about them an element of timing – which is disallowed as 'hesitation'. Repetition is customary in jokes and unless 'joke about a blind parachutist' is the subject on the card, you are likely to be buzzed for deviation also. If you did manage to get out the punchline unimpeded by fellow panellists (the blind parachutist was told that he would know when he was five yards from the ground because the dog's lead goes slack) the audience laugh – and unless you shout over their laughter you get buzzed for hesitation.

The show did not die with Kenny Williams: it changed. Paul Merton is the most regular of the occasionals; Wendy Richard is a frequent guest. Messiter, the inventor, no longer sits there and blows the whistle when sixty seconds are up, but now encourages us on the telephone. Also the director has changed sex.

Nicholas Parsons, absurdly, gets younger by the season, now looks to be about twenty-five years my junior. Odd thing, that; we were at school together.

* * *

Let's play spot the deviant
The Times, 14 December 1989

I AM CURRENTLY involved in recording more deathless instalments of *Just a Minute,* a long-running Radio 4 panel game in which contestants try to speak for sixty seconds on a random subject without repeating themselves, hesitating (an 'um' is enough to deprive you of your turn) or veering from the broad meaning of the word prescribed.

A little thought will make readers appreciate that thrown into a spontaneous monologue on say, Vapour Rub, the speaker is unlikely to come forth with a reasoned treatise on the benefits and defects which, in normal circumstances, could be gleaned after an hour or two of research.

This brings me to a letter just received from a man with a hyphenated name living in London E3 5AR:

'Reference *Just a Minute*: you should never, never put ginger in spotted dick. It is a travesty, a betrayal of all that is best and British. Yours sincerely.'

Even before the post arrived it had been a rotten day, with my shares under-performing and the Alka-Seltzer packet empty again. Hyphenated man takes me to task about a recent *Just a Minute* programme in which the chairman had said: 'Spotted dick for one minute, Clement.'

'It is a delicacy,' said I (the first few seconds are not crucial; whoever interrupts has to take on the subject and it is much more effective to let others do the donkey work before pressing the buzzer and being left with ten seconds and the ensuing bounty). 'Spotted Dick is a predominantly English confection' and, knowing how very helpful are lists when it comes to filibustering, I launched into 'usually made with some or all of self-raising flour, bicarbonate of soda, salt, suet, water, currants, raisins, sultanas, candied peel, crystallized ginger, milk, eggs and sugar blended together over heat, custard is a popular accompaniment to spotted dick (you can repeat the key word) as is single, double, or whipped cream – also the condensed issue of a cow's udder that may be purchased in supermarkets in red and white tins bearing the word Carnation.' One cannot take a breath between sentences nor pause for effect; one gallops on.

Well, hyphenated man from East London, I wanted you to know what caused me to mention these good products in one breath. I'm sorry about spotted dick and ginger. You are right; there *is* too much messing about with traditional receipts (though some have not much more than tradition and history to recommend them): an Irish stew made with herbs from Provence is delicious, but it is not strictly an Irish stew, any more than Olde Englishe Sherry Trifle is any of those things when fashioned of kiwi fruit.

Brandy butter is correct; rum butter is just permissible with Christmas pudding; Amaretto butter, excellent though it is, comes under the heading of 'betrayal of all that is best and British' – being best and Italian.

That distinguished chef Monsieur Anton Mosimann would be just the man for a filibustering panel game: he has published a Guest List – nine pages of customers who have eaten his food – which he could use for just about every *JaM* topic.

'The next subject is safety razors.'

'Here is a list of some people who did or possibly never used safety razors. I shall start with His Excellency Boukar Abdoul, Special Envoy and Ambassador of the Chad Republic ...'

As Mosimann was *chef de cuisines* of the Dorchester Hotel for many years, his list mentions most people of note, though I could not help noticing that the Kray brothers were not included. (My grand-twins Max and Harry auditioned to play Ronnie and Reg in a forthcoming film about the brothers and failed to get the parts 'because they did not take direction'. (My grand-twins are three years old.))

Mr Mosimann starts off with the Queen, followed by the Royal Family, and proceeds in alphabetical order through the palaces of Belgium, Denmark, the Hellenes, Luxembourg, their serene Highnesses of Monaco, pauses and lists the Shah of Iran, King Bhumibol of Thailand, Haile Selassie and continues via Personalities and Distinguished Figures, through World of Entertainment to Chefs, Food Writers and finally Journalists.

I appear as a distinguished figure – nowhere else. No repetition. The man is a natural.

* * *

Clement Freud was a Member of Parliament for fourteen years, winning the Isle of Ely seat at a by-election in 1973 and sitting as Liberal MP until defeat in the 1987 General Election. He began the 1973 by-election campaign as a rank outsider at 33-1 – and made a great deal of money by backing himself – but his odds shortened dramatically after a memorable public meeting ...

Sugar beet on the way to the House
The Times, 4 October 2001, extracted from his autobiography
Freud Ego, published that month

I WAS LUCKY fighting a by-election when I did, for neither Tory nor Labour had much going for them. As for us Liberals, our main attraction was that we were neither Labour nor Conservative.

In my first week of meetings in 1973 I talked a bit about making life better for the Third World, accepting Vietnamese refugees, saving public money by merging embassies (what is the point of having one in Luxembourg, Liechtenstein and Andorra?) and deprivatizing water authorities. Big yawns. So I sounded off about regional excellence – in Doddington there was a woman who made wonderful horseradish cream – and stressed the importance of the community, based on the cornerstones of the school, the church, the shop and the pub, all of which had to be fought for. Hands off our primary schools, long live small shopkeepers.

Those who actually attend public meetings are either supporters who applaud anything you say, however foolish, or enemies who sit sullenly silent and then bombard you with prearranged, complicated questions. The National Farmers' Union, a deeply Conservative organization, stalked me. At every meeting there would be representatives wearing blue rosettes, waiting for me to finish so they could start.

'Mr Freud, if you were elected to Parliament, what would you do about the quota for sugar beet?' (The fact was that if I got to Parliament, the Conservatives would still have their majority and the answer was 'nothing'.)

'Do you grow sugar beet?', I asked one such questioner.

'Yes, sir.'

'Do you grow much sugar beet?'

'Few hundred acres.'

'Well, what I would urge a Liberal Government to do is compulsorily purchase sugar beet crops from farmers stupid enough to ask MPs for their advice.'

My elder daughter had a relationship with *Playboy's* travel editor and, while with him in America, had been persuaded to pose naked with two large black gentlemen. A magazine whose name escapes me had published this under the heading 'Freudian dream' and a March Conservative, presumably a subscriber, went canvassing, showing voters the pictures, asking them: 'Would you want an

MP whose daughter appears in pornographic publications?' Two decent Tories telephoned me to apologize: it certainly did nothing to promote John Stevens, the Tory candidate and the enemy of un-British personal criticism.

Nor did Anglia Television's Friday-before-the-election political programme help their cause. The TV company had invited the three candidates, each with six supporters, to come to the Norwich studio. The programme's anchorman would pick a supporter of his choice to ask a question – either of his man or of one of the others – and get the other candidates to comment. There was to be time for four questions from each party, and before transmission we sat in a local hostelry debating what questions to put and to whom.

A Tory supporter chosen by the anchorman asked me about sugar beet, which was silly because by then I knew about sugar beet, quotas, profitability, et al. Halfway through, a Whittlesey supporter of mine was requested to put his question: he asked Stevens what, if he were elected, he would do about MAGPAS. Stevens was on the button. Very much in favour; underfunded at the moment but he would do his best to get Government to reconsider support.

Asked to comment, I risked such political future as I might have had, turned to Stevens and said: 'You are a liar. You don't support MAGPAS. You don't know what MAGPAS is. You are wholly bogus.'

Stevens lost his calm. 'Of course I know what it is.' He turned pale.

Me: 'What?'

He: 'It's one of those agricultural organizations.'

Me: 'It is the Mid-Anglian General Practitioners' Accident Service.' My supporters cheered. The Labour Party supporters cheered. The audience cheered.

On the drive home I asked Dr Pulvertaft, the originator of the question, how many voters would have watched the programme.

He said: 'All of them, and the ones who did not will be told.' He was right.

On the Monday Ladbroke's marked me down 6-1, Stevens 1-3.

* * *

Freud won the by-election, and early in the life of the new Parliament gave a new boy's impression of the House of Commons.

Around the world in 80 days – to save 2p on a phone call
Daily Express, 15 October 1973

THIS IS BY way of an interim report.

I have now been a Member of Parliament for eighty days ... and as it is you, the taxpayer, who sees to my salary, I felt it was time you were told how things were going.

I want to be completely honest with you, so I must admit that to date I have only been to the House of Commons (the House, as we call it) twice.

On the first occasion I drove into the forecourt, which looked like a demolition yard, and asked the policeman on duty where I might park.

He suggested I leave the car over by the seventh Irishman from the left, adding that he could see no reason why I should not enjoy full use of the car park under construction if I retained my seat at the General Election.

On that occasion, I went to visit our leader who has his own office; around the walls are pictures of Rt Hon. J. Thorpe with crowned heads, presidents, and others who have had the support of the electorate.

He gave me a conducted tour: ' … These are the private dining rooms, that the library, yonder the committee rooms and hence the speaker's robing apartment.'

In the actual chamber he pointed out the bench upon which we Liberals sit … second row up, halfway along … and when someone called him to speak to Afghanistan on the telephone, I said I would find my own way out.

This was a rash promise. In the course of half an hour I wandered around cellars and terraces, kitchen, sculleries and a shooting gallery without discovering an exit or a sign of humanity. Finally, in a small boiler room, I came across two men playing cribbage.

I told them that it had taken me weeks of total dedication and deprivation to get into the House of Commons: how the devil did one get out?

They guided me to a marble hall, at the end of which one turned right for an exit. I was free.

On the second occasion my aims were administrative rather than political. I had spoken to the Whips' Office to ask about pay. It's a bit embarrassing, I said; I am almost certain one gets paid for being a Member of Parliament, although I have had varying reports as to the actual amount.

The Whips' Office said that the Fees Office dealt with that side of life and, having arranged a visit, I found them to be quite especially helpful and pleasant.

It would appear that one is paid monthly; Members are treated as self-employed persons so that the only deductions are for a compulsory pensions scheme … 'and the money you contribute is, of course, repaid if you should spend less than four years in the House.'

He made this sound about as likely as being savaged by a dinosaur.

Then there were allowances, which you claim on a special form, also expenses.

For instance, you may travel from your home to Westminster as often as you like. Or you may travel from your constituency to Westminster as often as you like.

'And from your home to your constituency,' I prompted the man.

He said 'no dice', not actually using those words, but discussing the matter he opined that there was no reason why one should not go from home to constituency *via* Westminster.

I explained that this added 95 miles at 5p a mile to the taxpayers' bill, also 2½ hours to my travelling time. Apparently, that was 'one of those things', a bit like not being able to claim for a telephone call to a Ministry from your home or constituency office.

You can, of course, go to Westminster, which is apparently rotten with free telephones, and charge for the 200-mile round trip undertaken to make the call.

In the normal course of events, explained the man from the Fees Office, we would have nabbed you straight after you had taken your oath, before which we cannot, of course, pay you. Pity that.

I nodded sympathetically and went to keep my appointment with the Serjeant at Arms. I had expected to meet a Falstaffian character with three stripes on his arm who would tell me about a desk for my secretary, and direct me to suppliers of stationery, shoe polish and sealing wax.

In fact, the Serjeant at Arms is a noble knight, who had been a rear admiral in Her Majesty's Navy. After pledging total co-operation he advised me that it would be politic to carry my identity card at all times (stops the police from searching your briefcase) and advised me that it was pointless to ring the Ministry of Works if there is no loo paper; they would only get on to him.

He then informed me that I was entitled to two tickets for the Visitors' Gallery every fortnight – my first allocation is for 22 October – and gave me the key to locker 296.

This is my first and only tangible proof of being a member of what someone once called the most exclusive club in Britain.

After leaving the Serjeant at Arms, I went to inspect my locker. It is pleasantly positioned, hard by the Labour Whips' office, 2ft 6in from the floor, about 10in deep. There is ample room for books and sandwiches – and a bottle of whisky would fit in sideways.

Tomorrow, among what promise to be scenes of passionate apathy from the Government and Opposition benches, I will be walked towards the Speaker and officially received – after which, I understand, one goes out and comes in again.

And please do not think I have spent the 11½ weeks of my non-parliamentary career standing idly on the sidelines, waiting for the chaps to come back from their summer holidays. Far from it. Apart from travelling up, down and sideways in the Isle of Ely and elsewhere in Britain, my reading has been confined to eclectic works on Parliamentary procedure; the mechanics of amendments and protocol, the moving of adjournments, the mechanics of prayers and Private Members' Bills.

I learn, for instance, that it is technically out of order to cross the House between the Chair and a speaker, to read newspapers, books, or letters, or carry on a conversation; and that until my maiden speech one may be seen but not heard except for permitted exclamations of which 'Hear, hear', 'Oho', 'Shame' and 'Withdraw' are currently favoured.

I note from an admirable book called *The House of Commons at Work* (something I have yet to experience) that maiden speeches are treated with especial courtesy, although it records the sad case of Sir Wilfrid Lawson, who attempted to make his maiden speech just as the House was about to adjourn for dinner. He met with a very unfavourable reception.

Nowadays, the author goes on to say, the maiden speaker is usually congratulated from both sides of the House, but is expected to avoid controversial matters in his speech.

I am preparing something on the lines of: 'What I did during the holidays.' My wife has arranged to have some tuck put in locker No. 296.

* * *

Following defeat in 1987, Freud was awarded a knighthood
for public service.

What She said
The Times, 13 December 1990

AFTER AN INVESTITURE, 'What did She say?' is the most common question asked of participants. The most common answers tend to be some way from the truth: 'She said she wished it could have been a baronetcy – but the prime minister has abolished them,' I told enquirers. Also: 'She told me to be sure to let her know if she could be of help finding me another job.'

Show us the gong then, they said, and I opened the box and let them inspect the gold and red medallion hooked onto its wide scarlet and yellow ribbon – long enough to put *in situ* over a top hat. Three and a bit years after the event it occurs to me that there was something really useful that Her Majesty might have said.

Last week the Imperial Society of Knights Bachelor held a reception at St James's Palace in the gracious presence of Her Majesty the Queen. 'Neck badges will be worn,' it said on the invite; it was my first time. I took the thing from its box in my dressing room, slipped it over my head and heard a subdued clonk as it made contact with my penultimate waistcoat button.

I have been a member of the society since 1987. Among the flow of letters of congratulation on my honour – which started to arrive before the flow of letters expressing regret at the loss of my parliamentary seat had stopped – was one from its clerk. He welcomed me. He went on to state that knighthoods are the oldest rank and dignity known to Christian civilization and he enclosed a banker's order.

'Not much point being a knight if one doesn't join the Imperial Society,' I said to the newly ennobled Lady F. She thought perhaps there would be more in it for her than being an MP's wife – for

whom the only bounty is a room off Parliament's central lobby
where spouses can change from what they wear at home to clothes
to be worn in the Palace of Westminster: women would arrive in
startling designer gowns and leave the 'family room' in dull, dark,
dowdy dresses.

We got to the Palace at 6pm like it said we should. There was a
queue. We joined it, shuffled down a corridor nodding to those
similarly decorated. A man came and said: 'I am the registrar.' I
shook his hand, asked if I might pre-register my death there and
then, to avoid another queue later on. 'Registrar of the society,' he
explained; as he was limping noticeably I agreed when he asked me
to move aside while he made a run down the inside rail. He passed;
others followed; we joined them. 'Are you with this party?', asked
a belligerent lady as we passed her in the registrar's slipstream. (I
stopped calling females ladies after a reader wrote that they were
all women. This one was a Lady.)

I had rather thought that the queue was for wine. It was for a
desk where four women sat behind boxes bearing guests' name-
tags. As no one knew which of the quartet was in charge of what
letters, progress was slow. Palaces do not go in for notices like A-D,
E-K, etc.

Here is how the party works: there is a huge room, possibly
several rooms opening one into another. The 360 guests are divided
into groups of thirty each with a council member as shepherd and
an oval table as home base. The shepherd decides which of his flock
are to be presented and arranges them to form part of the front row
of a hollow square. First there was champagne, also canapés of the
kind served in American bars under an 'eat as much as you like'
notice: small puff pastry cases filled with minced polystyrene; a
slice of raw carrot mounted by an unhappy prawn. Nothing to get
the chaps excited.

At about 6.40 there was a hush. She had arrived; drink was now
harder to find and among those in the front row one observed
a modicum of curtsy practice as She made her way around her

people. Then it was our moment. Lady F. curtsied; I bowed, and because she exudes such dazzling charm I did not ask, as I had intended, why she had not advised me to buy a thinner, shorter, shinier ribbon for my medal and wear it tucked under the chin as do all her other knights.

* * *

Three years after leaving the House of Commons, Freud reflects on the pros and cons of being a celebrity MP.

Enter member from stage, left
The Times, 5 April 1990

A MAN FROM BBC television news rang last week to say that Glenda Jackson had been adopted as Labour candidate for Hampstead and Highgate. I asked why he was telling me this; he had not phoned when Lithuania declared its independence and I had had to find out the result of the Calcutta Cup match all by myself.

The BBC newsman said it was because Ms Jackson is a celebrity seeking election to Parliament and, according to their records, I was the last celebrity to win a seat. 'What is it like, can we send the cameras, will you talk about the sort of reception you got and Glenda Jackson is likely to receive if she gets in?'

We conversed at 11am; the cameras arrived at 11.45; the item was carried on the News at 1.20; impressive high-tech even if limited in viewer appeal. As I explained to the interviewer, there will be two major differences between Glenda Jackson's arrival at Westminster and mine; first, she will take her seat with a substantial number of other debutants, to the customary mutterings by established MPs that 'they look just like a Japanese trade delegation, can't tell one from the other'. I got in at a by-election, a new boy among 633 old hands.

Secondly, she will be welcomed by a substantial number of political allies. When I arrived, there were eight Liberals in the House – effectively seven, for one spent most of his time in Europe. Came the call of 'Division', the only way I knew I was voting in the right lobby was when I found the instantly recognizable figure of Cyril Smith and followed in his slipstream. A new Labour member will have all sorts of colleagues delegated to be of assistance.

But the BBC newsman had a good point: the great British public is deeply suspicious of celebrities who wish to go straight. Even the great East Anglian Liberal public in the 1970s was apprehensive. When I was shortlisted for the Isle of Ely by-election in 1973, there were only nine members of the association to decide between me and the other applicant. Embarrassed by this small number, the secretary was deputed to swell the crowd from an adjacent old people's home … who voted me in by 12 votes to nine.

Old people are in favour of faces they recognize from television. Political activists, on the other hand, feel that you cannot do better than plump for a university lecturer.

At the general election following my victory, both Conservative and Labour went around telling my constituents that it was ignominious for them to be represented by 'someone from television'. I quintupled my majority. For the next three Parliaments, however, I remained, to my political opponents, the MP who used to be on TV, did adverts, nudge-nudge, was a director of the Playboy Club, ho ho ho.

So what, said I; my Labour Party opponent is a prison officer.

'Hasn't been on telly,' said they. 'He's clean.'

I was an MP for five Parliaments, and then lost my seat in 1987. 'When we first voted for you,' said one of my local supporters, nibbling seed-cake at the wake, 'you were always on the box. The only time we see you these days is doing those boring political programmes; no wonder you didn't get in again.'

There is a lesson here for Ms Jackson – although, if she were to hold on for five Parliaments, she could be seventy-eight and might not want to continue.

As to physically taking her seat, she may be interested in what happened to the last celebrity to make it to Westminster. According to the papers of the day, 'following Mr Freud's arrival at the Bar of the Chamber, there were ribald [some broadsheets called it humorous] references to the fact that the new MP had been a cook and appeared on a TV commercial.' One particularly flat-brained Midlands member punctuated my progress towards the mace with fierce barking.

As Glenda Jackson is not averse to stripping in the interests of cinematic art, I wonder whether some Conservative member might mark the occasion by taking off his or her clothes. Now that the proceedings are televised, a parliamentary streaker is one of the few happenings we have not yet witnessed. Hearing a passionate female voice espousing support for the less fortunate people of this country will be welcome also.

* * *

Hair today – or not
The Times, 26 July 1990

MY AGENT PHONED to say she had had a call from an independent film company making a documentary about distinguished men who have lost their hair, and they had asked her whether I would take part.

My appointment book is fairly bare at this time of year, not a lot of action until our ruby wedding party in September, so I said, 'Yes, what sort of money can we expect?'

My agent suggested we ask for four figures, and descend to a high three. I advised her to become tetchy at two and refuse lesser sums. That happened a week ago. We arranged to shoot the interview this afternoon in my flat, this entailing a modest fee in compensation for their use of my electricity.

A short, snappy schedule: camera crew set up at 3.30, start rolling 3.45, all over (what is technically called 'wrapped') ten minutes later, 'which is why we cannot pay a lot of money', the producer had said, adding that she much looked forward to meeting me. Nothing personal in that; producers always look forward to meeting people who appear for v. little money.

The researcher, with whom I had discussed the content of the programme, was unable to provide names of the other participants; they were working on this. She expected Yul Brynner, Duncan Goodhew, Lord Longford; I looked like being a borderline case for inclusion in her cast list.

'When did you start losing your hair?' had been the initial question; 'Did you mind?' was next, then 'What difference did it make to your life?'

I told her that these were all matters that could be appropriately discussed in front of a camera, even as I wondered whether a handful of bald or balding coots would provide more compulsive viewing than, say, a similar number of victims of tooth decay.

I deplore philological euphemisms like 'I have lost a lot of hair' instead of 'bald' or 'I have put on much weight' to signify 'fat'. Also 'temporarily strapped for ready cash' meaning 'broke'.

Thinking about my contribution, I had decided to pursue the 'I have increased the amount of visible cranium' line; would admit that, given a free choice, more hair is better than less hair, but point out that bald is better than wig and what I do with the remains of mine (cut fairly short by Keith of Smile in the New King's Road and combed away from the crown), is better than *la méthode Scargilloise*. Odd thing about us bald people; we look at hirsute contemporaries with suspicion, point out to all who will listen that so-and-so now has a fuller head of hair than when we worked together in the 1960s. And there is Elton John to give us succour; went bald, had a painful and expensive transplant. Now wears a hat.

At Westminster, there was much opportunity for the examination of scalps, for we sat on tiered benches. Unlike so many parliamentarians who yo-yo from one side of the House to the other, I remained steadfastly on the same second-row opposition bench through five administrations. During Mr Heath's term of office, looking down upon the extroverts beneath the gangway, I was the first to identify Skinner's dandruff. Came Mr Wilson and I got a preview of Tebbit's receding hairline. When Mr Callaghan was PM, I witnessed the amazing sight of the honourable Member for Haltemprice not simply adjusting, but removing and repositioning his wig. The cameras would have loved that.

At 3.20, I went downstairs, asked the medical receptionist of the house in which I live to admit a film crew plus impedimenta, arriving imminently. I mentioned tripods. She looked impressed.

I went back to my flat to prepare for the interview; grey suit, striped shirt, Liberty tie, a few apposite touches.

The phone rang at 3.50. 'This is the film unit you were expecting,' said a woman. 'I am afraid we are running a bit late, see you shortly.'

I told her that I had another engagement at 4pm, to do with an up-coming family celebration. She said she was really sorry – perhaps we could reschedule? I said perhaps and ran a bath to shampoo the make-up from my scalp. Over to you, Yul.

* * *

And politics – to be precise, the size of the Prime Minister's pay package – played its part in one of Freud's most notable public roles, as dining companion of bloodhound Henry.

Freudian slips
The Times, 6 October 2001, extracted from Freud Ego

ONE DAY IN 1968 a man called from the advertising agency Collett Dickenson Pearce. 'Do you like dogs?', he asked.

'Not other people's dogs, I don't.'

'Do you eat dog food?'

'Not knowingly.'

'In that case, would you do a dog food commercial?'

I said that while I saw no reason not to, I would (a) be very expensive and (b) want to speak my, rather than the copy-writer's words.

Mr Tim Warriner, a dapper Australian, saw nothing wrong with that; explained that the theme would be 'You are the famous cook/gourmet who appreciates this or that amazing dish, while the dog (and you can choose a dog that looks like you or that you can look like) is hooked on the product'.

'What is the product?'

'It's called Minced Morsels.'

I apologized for wasting his time: 'Minced Morsels is not something I am prepared to say on television.'

Warriner suggested that someone else could say Minced Morsels, do the 'hard sell'. 'What do you mean by "a lot of money"?', he asked.

'What the Prime Minister gets.'

We left it there.

It took him an hour and a half to ring back and say: 'The deal is on. You do the dog food commercial, write your own words, not name the product, get paid what the Prime Minister is paid.'

We met and got on rather well. Warriner was an account executive and read the scripts the agency had worked on in a Clement Freud accent, made them sound more like me than I could have done.

The Quaker Oats people made Minced Morsels; no one I knew had heard of Minced Morsels. What harm could it do, and might it not help us send four children, plus Ashley, who was a nephew and had adopted us, to their expensive private schools? I asked Jill what she thought. She thought what the Prime Minister gets on top of what I was earning would be helpful ... 'But you don't like dogs.'

For £45,000 I am prepared to sit next to a dog.

Warriner and I chose a dog, were torn between a bloodhound and a basset hound, and he had me sit beside a number of brutes with a mirror behind the camera while I imitated his expression (which was quite like mine) and his stance. We finally picked a basset hound which smelt unpleasantly of dog and was managed by a woman who gave forth a similar odour.

And we agreed a first script. We were going to call the dog Henry. He would wear a bandage around his ear and sit beside me at a dinner table. 'As today is the second anniversary of Henry's operation, I thought we would celebrate. I bought a pound of Aberdeen Angus steak, marinated it in 1961 Château Beychevelle, dusted it in flour, simmered it in butter and added some double cream. And he hated it. Said he wanted this stuff.'

I held up a packet as the hard-sell voice said: 'Minced Morsels.'

I had 26.5 seconds for my part.

We filmed at a studio in Wandsworth. The set was dressed and lit, the table was laid, a platform was built on which the dog would sit so that his head came up to the height of my head. I went to make-up, as did the dog. We met later under the fierce lights.

A coordinator had prepared my plate with the steak, fine wine and a good-looking claret glass. The director looked at us through the lens, then the client looked through the lens, finally the cameraman took over. Action.

'Today is the second anniversary of Henry's …'

I was looking at the mirror behind the camera so that I could move if Henry moved. Henry was handsomely trained, hardly moved at all, but five seconds into the script the heat caused him to have so massive an erection that between suave me in a dinner jacket and soulful Henry wearing an ear bandage there came into picture an entirely gynormous, red and glistening penis.

'Cut,' said the director, rather unnecessarily.

The studio gaped at the erection in amazement. The client shook her head in disbelief, the men from the agency sat and stared, and the woman who had brought the dog said: 'I thought that might happen and have brought some bitches who look very similar.'

We went out to the pub, had a drink, came back and started over again. A number of bitches had been assembled, all of them Henry-like if you did not look down, and we selected one and got her in place and the clapper-boy said: 'Minced Morsel commercial Take Two.'

I always hoped that Denis Norden in his *TV Bloomers* programme would find Take One. It would have to be shown after 9pm.

There were a number of reasons why we went to Take 41. Henry had to sit still; I had to hit my allotted time. What tended to happen was that I got spot on 26.5 seconds and Henry barked or sniffed or played doggo: Henry behaved impeccably and I over-ran, under-ran or fluffed a line. Occasionally, we both did it perfectly and a helicopter flew overhead to Battersea heliport.

The commercial went out a few nights later; then, again, then again and again; three, four, five times each night. Packets of Minced Morsels stared at one from supermarket shelves. Rumour had it that the sales director of Kennomeat shot himself, Chum reduced its price, Spillers advertised for new personnel for its PR department. Minced Morsels became brand leader and wherever I went people who did not bark at me asked after Henry's health.

I continued to write about football; on a good day only 750 people came up to me and said: 'How's your dog?', expecting me to fall about with mirth.

On the credit side, I received a letter which I treasured:
'Dear Mr Freud

'Your address was given to me by a person in high place. [For the record, it was in the telephone directory.] This dog food you say is good, is not so very good; it smells bad and it don't go too well with green banana chips. I felt you should know.'

At around that time Harold Wilson gave himself a very large pay rise and, as my fee was geared to his salary, I became wealthier.

The commercials went on and on. Tim and I thought up new Henry situations and directors fell over themselves to lend their names to them: Dick Lester, Terence Donovan, Brian Duffy. 'I went on holiday to Provence and wrote to Henry about a place that serves a wonderful bouillabaisse. He sent me a postcard about a tin he had bought in Tunbridge Wells ...'

'Chunky Meat,' said the hard-sell voice: at some point during the campaign the product had changed its name. Sales soared.

The commercial made me virtually unemployable. *Panorama*, game shows, quiz shows, talk shows, even children's shows could manage without featuring someone of whom 99 per cent of viewers said: 'Where's his dog?' I grew a beard to avoid immediate recognition.

It hardly helped.

Henry's owners did well: Henry or one of her brothers/sisters opened garden parties and fêtes, became celebrity guests, received hundreds of letters asking for paw-prints. I became paranoiac, very hard to live with, accepted every invitation to work in foreign countries where I could be me rather than the two-legged half of a dog-food commercial.

3
FREUD
OUT AND ABOUT

'He was unimpressed. Have you been to an all-night launderette? I haven't even been to an all-day launderette, I said; I am just not a launderette man.'

My day with the Quorn
Sunday Telegraph, 10 November 1963

THE SECRETARY OF Quorn Hunt is given in *Bailey's Directory*; his name is Inglesant; he answers the telephone readily, and he said how glad he would be to have me join him for a day's hunting on Friday. The meet was at Beeby, near Melton Mowbray.

He also gave me the name of a livery stable, whom I telephoned. 'Having a day out with the Quorn,' I said, giving it just the right blend of boredom and bravado as I thwacked my pyjama trousers with my non-telephone hand. The livery stable thought I should have two horses.

I said yes, two or three. The livery stable said they would be pleased to oblige me. Old horse, I suggested. Sensible horses, they said. How well you put it, I told them.

The Brothers Moss suggested that their hunting wear hire department was temporarily rather depleted; this was the beginning of the hunting season. A pity I couldn't have come in the cricket season, but they promised to do their best.

They did splendidly. Over the course of an hour and a quarter, for the expenditure of £18 19s., I hired breeches and a jacket that made me look like the Michelin tyre man's younger brother; a silk hat, freshly ironed; a hunting crop with five feet of whip tied to the end (recently returned from contract hire at Sheffield), spurs and a stock; with this came an unvaluable pin.

It was not until we descended into the basement for boots that things became difficult. I wasn't actually misshapen ... Oh dear me no, sir. It was just that my feet were too long and my calves too thick for the shortness of my legs; an unusual combination, what we might call difficult. He tried my size 9 feet in size 7½ boots, with disastrous results, and we finally settled for the right length in feet, though the height of the boot covered my knee.

Having bought (you cannot hire) a pair of yellow gloves, I was complete. Not perfect from a sartorial point of view, for as the manager pointed out to me, a silk hat commands glossy, patent leather boots, but perhaps we were being pedantic.

I arrived at Beeby punctually at 10.45 – levered myself out of the car and crunched stiff-legged to a horse-box disgorging two tall horses.

'Mr Freud's mounts?' This was so. The brown would be my afternoon ride, I was told; the grey should see me through the morning. The grey and I looked at each other critically. With the slight exception of my silk hat–unshiny boots mélange, neither of us could be faulted.

I found mounting difficult. The normal procedure would appear to be for the rider to bend his leg while another grips him at the knee and hoists him aloft. Booted over the knee joint, I stretched my left leg like a man caught at the apex of a goose step, somehow engaged the toe in a suspended stirrup iron, and with some help I attained the summit.

Looking down, I picked out the lady who had brought the horses and offered to pay her. In the case of an accident I considered that it might cause her embarrassment to be seen going through my pockets for her hire charge. She accepted twelve guineas.

I pointed my horse towards the main centre of activity and arrived outside a large and handsome house where a man with a tray of glasses and fruit cake offered me some cold port. I accepted it, taking care to spill none on to my horse, and at length found a man to whom I descended the empty.

At the termination of this orgy I was approached by a rider wearing a leather money-bag strapped across his pink hunting jacket. He supposed that it was I who had telephoned him the other day.

Now I know nothing about hunting but my goodness I can tell when a man is waiting to be paid. 'You'd like some money?', I suggested.

'Five guineas, if that's all right with you.' I don't think that he meant it would have been less if it hadn't been all right with me, so I paid. There were no trading stamps.

At 11.15 the hunt moved off. No one had as yet spoken to me, but one man raised his hat. As I had purposely chosen a hat three sizes too small for me so that it would stay on my head under adversity, I had only begun to prise up one side by the time he turned and left. We – some sixty of us – walked and trotted for nearly an hour; it was fairly painful. On this excursion two men said 'Fine day' to me and a woman told me to keep away from her horse – 'it's a kicker.'

Shortly after noon we arrived at a wood which they called a covert, pronounced cover. A number of hounds who had preceded us were encouraged to snuffle among the trees while a huntsman gave us positions at ten-yard intervals around the perimeter. We stayed there for ten minutes, listening to the yelping of the hounds.

After a while people started galloping away into a field: so I said 'Tallyho' to myself in a very low voice and followed. I stood in the stirrups and we made quite a pleasant journey of it.

At the end of the field there was a fence; we walked up to it, examined it carefully, watched three or four others jump over, and then followed a tough-looking lady into it. Her horse refused just as mine was about to take off ... that appears to be the joy of being at the back of the pack. I waited while the tough lady refused three more times before I galloped at the fence and threw my arms round the horse's neck on the other side; this had to serve as my only means of support until I recovered the stirrup irons.

We galloped on, jumped several more times without actually physically parting company, and after about twenty minutes we were back in the cover spelt covert. Again we waited, broke rank, galloped, jumped and came back; once more we waited.

The third time we left the wood everyone seemed to go in a different direction; I followed a gaggle of eight men through fields and gates and when we approached a small hedge I, who hate exhibitionism, decided to jump last – unseen by the rest.

Thus it was that when we reached the gate at the end of the next field, the leading hunter opened it, the second rode through shouting 'gate' as he did so – a cry which was repeated by the third, fourth, fifth and sixth. The seventh man said 'gate' and galloped away. That was the last I saw of the Quorn Hunt.

Unable to dismount, I eased the grey into the gate and by leaning far down I eventually closed it, while my horse took protracted nibbles at the Brothers Moss's right boot. As I was about to ride off I found that I was minus a stirrup. I slid off the horse, picked the stirrup from beneath the gate, and walked a mile or so to a road where a man was persuaded to hold the horse during my ascent. Remounted, I jogged alone along the quiet roads.

I rejoined my second horse at 2.45pm I patted its back to get my money's worth and decided to call it a day, or as the local grooms say when they go home for lunch, 'Good night.'

I doubt whether I shall go hunting again. To pay £30 in order to be allowed to contribute five guineas for the convenience of men who order you to shut gates (before they say good morning) and then gallop into the middle distance is about as one-sided a sport as getting a pack of hounds to go after one single fox. Mind you, there was absolutely no sign of that.

* * *

In the Cavern where the Beatles were born
Daily Herald, 26 November 1963

SOME WEEKS AGO an enterprising travel agent urged his clients to spend their holidays in Liverpool. On the face of it this was a monstrous idea, comparable in unlikeliness only to the national newspaper which once held a competition for a first prize of one week's holiday in Manchester, and a second prize of a fortnight's holiday in Manchester.

The family who take a beach ball, bucket and spade to Merseyside are in for a long walk before they find the golden sands.

Not even the most bigoted Liverpudlian would deny that such attractions as the city has to offer are less visual than vocal.

The man who catches cockroaches in the kitchens of a West End hotel told me one wartime night that if the atmosphere is right, beetles will just keep coming up, irrespective of remedial measures.

In Liverpool the atmosphere is perfect and if it isn't actually genuine 100 per cent, gilt-edged Beatles that keep coming up, the insurgence of vociferous, long-haired, un-lapelled, string-plucking, fame-seeking young men with amplifiers is pretty well non-stop.

The Beatles themselves emerged into public life from a side-street cellar near the city's centre called the Cavern Club, annual subscription 1s.

They were followed in quick succession by musicians of similar orchestral persuasions, some of whom became better known than others, and consequently it was to the Cavern Club that I went for my instruction.

The pink local paper advised me in its classified advertising section headed 'Jazz' that it was time I swung over to the best: 'Have a rompin stompin week-end at the Cavern.'

The menu was The Mojos, PLUS The Tomboys PLUS The Panthers and Vince Earl AND The Talismen. 'Please,' they urged, 'be early for this Saturday night out.'

I arrived outside the Cavern at 7pm when the queue was already about 100 strong, stood quietly at the end, immediately behind three very small teenagers one of whom had recently given himself a going-over with a garlic-flavoured deodorant.

After a short wait a young man informed me that I was in the queue for the Cavern Club. (The intimation was clearly that I looked un-with-it.) I told him that I knew this.

'If you're meeting someone down there, you don't have to wait in the queue,' he said.

I thanked him, decided to meet someone, went down, was suitably received by the resident compère, purchased a lukewarm, non-habit-forming, sparkling drink the name of which escapes me, and within half an hour the queue had been admitted and my rompin stompin weekend had begun.

The Cavern is a dark damp cellar comprised of three arches about 15 yards in length. The centre arch has a raised stage at one end and rows of utility chairs all the way back to the unlicensed bar. The two other arches are used for dancing.

The place is replete with loudspeakers, and for the opening session the music was piped, punched out against the walls and curved ceilings, pulsating with ever-increasing volume through the crowded room.

A not dissimilar effect could be produced by hermetically sealing yourself in a telephone kiosk with five super-charged transistor radios. The compère announced the records in batches of three or four, some of his own choice, others requested in poems of only limited artistic merit, like: 'Dear Bob, play my request, this group I think is best.'

In the aisles, they danced. Boys with boys, or girls, but mostly girls with girls. It was not easy to see who was dancing with whom, or indeed who was what.

The dancers swayed in a sort of static Veleta, reacting to one beat in six, one arm swinging, legs moving without ever making any ground. In the first hour there were seven requests, all made to celebrate someone's eighteenth birthday.

The front two rows were occupied by girls, I think; the atmosphere was sweat, chewing gum and tipped Woodbines, and at length, after much moving of amplifiers, drums and other assorted impedimenta, we were asked to give a wild cheer for – yes – The Panthers.

The noise was deafening. Not so much the noise of the cheer:

the noise generally. Four of the Panthers had guitars to which they appeared to be wired.

Heavy currents clearly passed through their bodies and as they screamed in pain the fifth man, a drummer, percussed fiercely, regardless of their agony.

Sweat trickled down the walls and dripped from the arched ceiling and in the side aisles the Veleta was replaced by a viciously purposeful quake, a sort of asexual St Vitus quiver performed with hands outstretched, one hip thrust in front of the other, eyes closed in rapturous agony.

This, the compère told me, was the Cavern Stomp. No less. It was really more of a physical, sympathetic resonance.

Forty-five minutes later The Panthers left for pastures new – £8 the richer for their efforts. (A two-hour act is paid £15, £8 is the norm for the shorter spell.)

'And now here's a request from a little darling,' said the compère as The Panthers were unplugging themselves, and in a flash the walls shook with the voice of a man's amplified deliberations as to the best deployment of a hammer, which he did not appear to possess.

The Mojos came next, shouted at each other from different sides of one microphone and were replaced by requests from other little darlings, and at length by other groups.

After three hours I took my numb eardrums to the comparative quiet of the neighbouring pub. Many of my fellow drinkers were still shaking.

Over my third whisky, I asked a shiny-leather-suited youth where he had purchased his clothes; where, for instance, I asked him, could one get that sort of jacket?

He looked me over fairly carefully, and then pointing to my dark-grey, single-breasted suit he said:

'Where does one get *that* kind of jacket?'

* * *

On the subject of undress
Daily Herald, 23 June 1964

THE WAITRESS, WEARING sandals, sateen knickers and a striped shirt, said: 'You tell me what you want, dear, and I'll tell you whether we've got it.'

So I said: 'A toasted egg sandwich would be nice.'

'A toasted sandwich?'

'Yes.'

'You mean two pieces of bread toasted, with something put between them?' She made it sound slightly indecent – like wearing sateen knickers and a shirt.

'Exactly,' I said.

'Now,' she said, 'I've heard everything.'

In the kitchen, a woman who looked remarkably like the Beverly Hillbillies Granny was smoking into a saucepan, and behind me, in the restaurant part of the hut, two men wearing absolutely nothing at all drank tea and used their saucers to protect themselves from the hot drips.

Outside it was bitterly cold.

The advertisement had read: 'Nudist resort. The place for holidays long or short (all visitors must undress completely). Illustrated brochure: 5s.' There was a telephone number.

I rang up to say that I should like to come down for a day and the woman who answered the phone said: 'Are you keen on swimming and the open air?'

'Oh, rather.'

'Our standards of morality are of the highest,' she said.

'Goodness,' I assured her, 'so are mine.'

She said that in that case, all things being equal, she would be delighted to see me, any day from 8.30am onwards. And I, wondering how it felt balancing a cold plastic telephone on a soft warm thigh, replied that I, too, looked forward to our meeting.

It was, as I have mentioned, a bitterly cold day. I looked up at the gathering clouds, listened pessimistically to the promise of rain on the 9 o'clock news, thought of calling it off and then, feeling that an exclusively fine-weather nudist must be considered a pretty poor fish, drove off to the appointed place.

Up the motorway, off onto a main road, down a side street, along a lane, into a path and there was a notice saying 'Welcome' and a prefab office marked 'Reception.' All in all an unlikely pitch to attract much passing trade.

A fully clothed woman sat behind a desk.

She passed me a form, asked me to fill it in: name, address, nationality, profession … all to be treated as confidential. The price was 12s. 6d. for a day, 6s. 6d. had I been a lady, 2s. for parking the car on the mudflat outside her hut, or 5s. if I wanted to park farther down the path.

As it's rather cool, she said, her teeth chattering, you don't have to undress unless you want to. But please, one thing or another. Either take them all off or leave them all on. We do hate having people who are in between; and leave your valuables locked up in the car; and have you got a bath towel?

I walked down the gravel path to the dressing rooms, one marked gentlemen, one ladies, and wondered why they segregated sexes in the process of undressing and not when they were undressed. Ah well.

The place was a sort of shanty town of huts, chalets and tents, some for sale (apply at office), and there was a fair incidence of fully clothed nudists walking along the interconnecting gravel paths.

Two naked nudists, men, sat by a small swimming pool and another naked man watched them from a distant deckchair. A little farther on a naked man was repairing a motorbike in the drive of a cabin.

There was not a nude 6s. 6d. lady in sight.

So I went up to the two men by the pool and asked whether there was anywhere closer than yonder dressing rooms where I could leave my clothes.

They said no, there wasn't, but it's only a couple of hundred yards and do remember to lock up your valuables …

It wasn't the valuables that stopped me from taking off my clothes. It was the thought of the 200 yards of gravel path; carrying a towel held well away from my body to show that it was what the Army would call: 'Towel drying for the use of,' and not 'Towel, shielding person from passers-by for.'

So I picked my way to the refreshment hut and got my toasted egg sandwich with hardly any cigarette ash in it at all and a cup of tea made with health-giving condensed milk and one of the naked men who had come in from the pool said: 'It's a bit bleak today but it's terrific fun when the sun shines.'

I thought of taking off one of my shoes as a gesture, to show him that I was on his side, spiritually, but another look at the waitress's knickers and remembering what the receptionist had said deterred me. I left.

When I got home to my wife, who had watched me practise all week for this event, she said: 'How did you get on?' I told her that conditions were unconducive to nudism.

'You mean you didn't take your clothes off?'

'No.'

'Did you have to pay?'

'14s. 6d.'

'Was there anyone else there?'

'Four men.'

'So it cost you 3s. 7½d. per naked man?'

I must admit, put that way it didn't sound like much of an outing.

* * *

All through the night
Sunday Telegraph, **31 May 1964**

THERE ARE PEOPLE who insist that a visitor wishing to see London should be shown an East End chemist's shop or a bowling alley in Camberwell rather than Buckingham Palace and the Houses of Parliament. That's the *real* London, they say. 'Pulsating' is another word they like to use.

Some weeks ago I encountered a man who inquired after my night-life (I think he would have spelt it nite life). I told him that it was satisfactory. I had visited Annabel's Club, been stuck in the lift going to the Ad Lib and availed myself of the 15/6 special all-night menu at the Barrie Room in Kensington.

He was unimpressed. Have you been to an all-night launderette? I haven't even been to an all-day launderette, I said; I am just not a launderette man.

But it rankled, and at 3.15am last Thursday I tied last Wednesday morning's shirt, socks and handkerchief into last Monday's bath towel and drove off in search of erudition.

The lady who had answered the telephone number listed under 'Launderette Owners Ltd., National Association of' said that she was still waiting for details of all-night launderettes to come through.

Hasn't a single one come through?, I asked. I found your number in an October 1962 directory and this is late May 1964.

She went away, came back and gave me an address in Clifton Road, Maida Vale, another in Craven Road, Paddington, and two in Essex Road, N1. Two launderettes open all night in one road? She assured me that this was so.

Thus I made for the socially desirable hinterland of King's Cross, turned left at the Angel, and reached Essex Road at about 3.30. At Number 139 was an all-night launderette: 'The Quick Clean Self-Service Laundry. Welcome.'

There were washing machines with slots for florins; drying machines with slots for sixpences; notices, instructions and an empty cigarette packet on the floor. No people.

An all-night launderette is not substantially different from an all-night weighing machine or an all-night pin-table, in fact one has the feeling that the open 24 hours washing phenomenon is due to a proprietor's unwillingness to go and lock up his place after the late evening business. I went out. THANK YOU. PLEASE CALL AGAIN read a notice on the inside of the front door.

Down the road, at No. 352, I came across Launderama, let us bring Spring into your home, open 24 hours. Launderama was absurdly similar to the Quick Clean Self-Service Laundry Welcome but for the fact that it had an ice-cream wrapper on the floor. I went in, kicked the ice-cream paper out of the empty establishment and left.

At King's Cross a fire engine passed me, then another. In the distance I heard the clanging of many bells. Remembering my professional vows I turned and followed. Up Caledonian Road we went, down a side street, down another. At length we stopped. I gave the five fire engines a minute or two to get organized; then, clutching notebook and pencil, I moved towards the mass of helmeted humanity assembled on the pavement. There was absolutely no sign of a fire. 'Tosh said he smelt something over there,' said a fireman with a Six Counties accent. I left.

At 4.20 I reached the launderette in Clifton Road; it was closed. A few minutes later I had found the place in Craven Road, Paddington. It was bright and new, with 25 McClory washing machines on the side walls, six driers gaping open-mouthed from the rear of the establishment and instead of a chair in front of each machine, a handsome banquette with a centre partition. It was not only open, it was fully occupied. That is to say on each side of the banquette two old men were lying at full stretch, fast asleep.

They were not, I regret to say, a launderette owner's dream customers, and unlike me none of them had on or about his person a bundle of washing. On the other hand, it was a fairly considerable achievement to have got them into a launderette at all – what you might call a first step in the right direction.

* * *

The day I tried to prove a point on Brighton Beach
Sun, **1 September 1967**

IF FORCED TO pick out the high point of the day I think I would plump for 1 o'clock when two police sergeants barred my way on Shoreham Harbour and the fair-haired one said:

'I have reason to believe that you are concerned with the traffic of illegal immigrants. I shall say no more but would ask you to accompany me to the police station.'

From the onlooker's point of view 12 noon, when the dinghy capsized and deposited my four Pakistani friends and me into the swirling waters off Brighton, must have been well up in the ratings.

But let me start at the beginning.

Last week at Sandwich, on the Kent coast, eight Pakistanis were landed in the early morning mist – and due to the fortuitous presence of an elderly gentleman who was taking his dog for a pre-breakfast walk the police were alerted and the immigrants detained.

I felt at the time that if the people behind the immigration racket had picked a more British time of day – like elevenses – they could have made the landing on a crowded holiday resort beach without anyone taking a blind bit of notice.

Or could they?

There seemed to me to be only one good way of finding out – by trying to bring in some Pakistanis, who would, of course, be perfectly legal residents. So I telephoned my local Labour Exchange and indented for four Pakistanis.

'What work had you in mind?', asked the official.

I explained that it was to be light work – not unlike modelling.

The Labour Exchange man said that late afternoon was a bad time for recruiting Pakistanis but gave me an address in Bayswater where he felt I would be likely to succeed.

I asked for names.

He said: 'Ullah – they are all called Ullah … that is to say we call them all Ullah.'

The house in Bayswater was indeed heavily populated with Ullahs, none of whom were prepared to undertake a day's light employment, not unlike modelling.

I telephoned the Pakistan High Commissioner's student hostel and was rewarded with four volunteers.

They were 'most particularly agreeable to a day's employment of a nature akin to modelling and would absolutely without fail bring their passports and be awaiting me.'

So yesterday morning we went by train to Brighton and took a taxi to a boatyard in Shoreham, seven miles down the coast.

I explained to the local boatman that I would like to go three miles out to sea then sail onto Brighton beach and make a landing close to the West Pier.

He thought the waves were a bit high for landings but if the West-South-West wind turned a few degrees to the North it might be done.

After half an hour of battling against the eight-foot waves we turned sharp left and took a line on the new tower of the Metropole Hotel on the Brighton promenade.

At 11.50, a couple of hundred yards from shore, engines were reversed, the dinghy launched, my four Pakistanis called up from the hold and distributed two in front of me, two behind me in the cockleshell. The boatman said 'Good luck.' I nodded gravely.

I engaged the oars in the rowlocks and pulled tentatively for the beach. It must be admitted that the journey was hazardous; the dinghy rode somewhere between a third of an inch and half an inch above the water and when, after ten minutes of my navigation, the breakwater was reached, we veered fractionally from a straight path, took a wave side-on, capsized and swam out from under the upturned boat.

I had realized that there might be problems to landing anonymous citizens of Pakistan on a Sussex beach – but I'm not at all sure that I had given thought to the problem in hand.

However, we picked from the surf four pairs of shoes that had been removed for wading ashore, sat on the beach to dry them and replace them, got a friendly lifeguard to help us right the boat and I shook hands with my friends, apologized to them for their inconvenience and pointed out the direction of the railway station.

My mission had been accomplished; I had proved my point: you can land four Pakistanis on Brighton beach at midday in full view of the holidaymakers, two of whom even helped me – the arch and only villain – to get the dinghy back into the sea.

There is a sequel.

As the Pakistanis reached the road they were promptly arrested by six policemen who took along my shore-based assistant and the *Sun* photographer for good measure.

The lifeguard, it transpired, had rung the Brighton police to report 'an unnatural occurrence', to be told that they had already received four 999 calls on the same matter.

When I disembarked at Shoreham an hour later it was my turn. A warning word, a restraining arm, a quick drive to the police station and a kindly inspector bade me sit down and explain.

I sat, squelched a few pints of sea water onto the floorboards and said: 'You see I have this theory: I felt that if the eight Pakistanis had only landed at some civilized hour like noon they could have come onto Brighton beach instead of sampling the rigours of Sandwich in the early morning.'

The inspector asked whether I still believed this. I had to admit that I did not – though if the weather had been fine and we had not capsized and they had made a quick getaway …

At length I made a statement and the inspector said that in due course I would probably be charged.

I told him that I was likely to die of pneumonia long before that and he was really very concerned.

On reflection everyone but I seems to have come out of this exercise very well.

The public raced to telephones and dialled the police like responsible citizens.

The police acted promptly, firmly and fairly.

And the Pakistanis, who were given dry clothes by the police department, have promised not to sue me.

4
FREUD'S
FOOD AND DRINK

'The ideal summer drink, like the ideal summer girl, should be long and cool and half full of gin.'

As Emma Freud says of her father in her Foreword to this book, 'If words were his kitchen, then food was indeed his favourite ingredient. It became the constant theme in virtually everything he did.' Clement Freud's huge experience in culinary matters, from his time as a young commis chef at London's Dorchester Hotel onwards, was distilled into the book Freud on Food, *first published in 1978; into cookery series on television; and into hundreds of pieces of journalism, of which the following pages represented a very small portion.*

Mulling it over
Time and Tide, 4 January 1962

THE ADVENT OF television brought about a radical change in our eating habits; fried nasties called TV snacks took the place of such carefully matured delicacies as Philadelphia Hotpot. Pre-cooked hamburgerettes attained the popularity vote over portmanteau steak (a thick wad of tender sirloin, stuffed with peppered oysters, sewn up, and carefully fried in butter).

Some evenings ago I chastised my daughter for wasting a whole evening watching ITV. After a decorous pause for tears she retorted that I had wasted a similar period of time contemplating the log fire. This, although I had some difficulty in explaining it to my child, is a ridiculous argument. My evening was spent nobly, altruistically, unselfishly; hers basely, derivatively, commercially. She drank an unspeakable bottle of mud-coloured fizz, I mulled from time to time a pint of burgundy with a red hot poker: cinnamon stick, sugar lump and cloves sewn into a muslin bag dangled in the wine and were withdrawn.

Why, there was no comparison.

On reflection, what I really tried to convey to my daughter was that a log fire is not only attractive and instructive to watch but that it is altogether a more complete, a more composite companion than an idiot-box for a cold evening.

Take one log fire on any winter's night; add to it man's natural reluctance to move from the chair in front of the hearth. To make this a success, a certain amount of preparation or a willing slave is needed.

For wine, use up the cheap bottles of red that we will charitably suppose you were given for Christmas. No one actually buys cheap wine (I quote my wine merchant). Draw the cork before you move it to the heat, or it will decork itself. Sweeten or not as you desire.

No matter what you do, for some strange reason nasty wine is more drinkable hot than cold.

For the menu, start with corn on the cob, obtainable frozen, in packets. Skewer this, and roast it until the kernels are just beginning to colour. Then brush generously with butter.

Next a quiet white marshmallow, toasted at the end of a fork. A crumpet lightly spread with anchovy butter for a fish course. A few chestnuts, roasted in the embers – as an aperitif for the main course of prunes, properly soaked in water, then tightly wrapped in streaky bacon and skewered alternately with pieces of brown bread to take up the melting bacon fat.

Another marshmallow, a pink one, and as the comforting words of the epilogue fade into the middle distance from the next room, some more burgundy.

Then, as it is unlikely you've taken much exercise during the evening, a glass of what my youngest son calls Uncle Seltzer.

* * *

Nibble on a goldfish while you're waiting
Town, **April 1964**

SOME WEEKS AGO I went to an hotel in the New Forest which had been warmly recommended to me by its proprietor (one should also beware of tips from racehorse owners).

I entered the deserted dining room at 8.30 on a Thursday evening (one really should try to avoid dining rooms that are empty at 8.30 on Thursday evenings), was greeted with relief by the restaurant manager (a bad sign this: a good *maître d'hôtel* of an empty restaurant gives you a cold look and asks whether you have booked a table) and eventually I was given a menu. I ordered turtle soup, pâté and a fried sole.

Twenty-five minutes later I left, soupless.

The manager ran after me and proclaimed that I couldn't leave.

I had ordered dinner, on which the chef (he should of course have said chefs – even if he only employed his grandmother) was now working.

I pointed out to him that I had been waiting for fractionally under half an hour for a plate of turtle soup. There appeared to me to be but two alternative explanations for the delay. Either they were making the soup from scratch … in which case, as a turtle requires to be soaked for twenty-four hours, I was unprepared to wait. Or they were opening a tin … in which case I was unwilling to remain in a catering establishment that took more than twenty-five minutes to find an opener and heat the contents.

It is not often that one has as unanswerable an argument for departing from a place, but that evening, until I found myself at the back of a queue outside a Southampton fish-and-chip shop, I glowed warmly with the righteousness of my action.

The problem of making restaurants more efficient than they appear to want to be is an interesting one. One can buy service – by promising to be an extravagant customer. 'A large dry martini while I think about the menu and make sure that you've plenty of half-bottles of Krug on ice.' (If this has the desired effect one can always opt out of the champagne by insisting on a year they haven't got – like 1958.)

You can cheat your way to good service. This is best done by telephoning the place and telling them that you are considering a dinner party on a Monday in August, at about 6.30pm. Would they be able to accommodate twenty-eight people? They will, to put it mildly, be enthusiastic. You then say that you'd like to sample the food; would they have a table for two in about half an hour?

And you can shame them into it. A friend of mine, having waited a quarter of an hour for a menu at Shepherd's Hotel in Cairo, walked over to the fish tanks by the window, picked up a goldfish and, watched closely by the entire clientele, walked back to his table, split a roll and slipped in the fish. Before he could take his second bite he was surrounded by a crowd of respectfully attentive waiters.

Doubtless there are those whose temerity, honesty or decency will cause them to reject this sort of advice. I am afraid that for them there is only limited hope – though they could try the psychological approach. Waiters are impressed by manifestations of unworldliness; the one thing they really hate is the sneaking suspicion that you might be no better than they are. Consequently it is not a bad idea to order fresh raspberries in April – and look bewildered when they explain about raspberry seasons. Sentences like 'Cyprus? ... that's near Nice, isn't it?' are worth their weight in gold.

Asking for a hard chair when you've been given a soft one, or one without arms in place of the one you have, has also been known to impress restaurant staff out of all proportion to your resultant discomfort.

The wine waiter is probably the greatest enemy of the tentative diner. A waiter after all has the opportunity of getting at your food before it reaches you, so that his advice could be competent. The wine waiter, restricted to being made to taste wine that is corked, or forced to rely on the sedimentary puddles left in the heels of other people's bottles, becomes jaundiced before his time. His advice, like your stockbroker's, should be taken with deep suspicion. If you must consult him, restrict him to recommending, say – the driest Moselle under 30s., the best Côtes du Rhône at less than £2. And if he comes with the wine list open at the champagne page, look at it very carefully for a long time before you hand it back to him with the words: 'Thank you very much but I don't seem to see anything here that goes with braised tripe.'

That should make it game all – after which, provided you keep your distance, there is no reason why you should not become the most tremendous friends.

* * *

Drinking in the shade
Town, July 1964

THE COMPILERS OF my encyclopaedia, in a rare spurt of optimism, define drink as 'liquid taken by the mouth to maintain or re-establish normal proportions of water in the organism' ... and on my twenty-first birthday a girl to whom I offered a glass of champagne said: 'No thank you, I am not thirsty.'

The rest of us drink for enjoyment – or possibly expediency (the quickest way out of Manchester is by a bottle of cooking brandy). When the weather is cold, we take to drinks that are warm; tea they say is incomparable. Old sweats, middle-aged policemen, young taxi-drivers and my third child maintain that it is the ideal drink on a summer's day – I salute them rather half-heartedly, because liquor is not only quicker, it enhances your public image; and when the weather is warm, the drinks, in my opinion, should be cold.

It has been said that the ideal summer drink, like the ideal summer girl, should be long and cool and half full of gin. If you are no more ambitious than this, rub the rim of a tall glass with lemon, turn it upside down and steep it in caster sugar, and then to a double measure of gin add a dash of apricot brandy, a bottle of lemonade, some lumps of ice and a strip of cucumber peel. To receive the best effects, repeat dose frequently.

But this is basic stuff, and somewhere between an imaginative TOM COLLINS (the poor relation Tom Collins is gin, lemon, sugar and soda) and a confection fashioned from fresh white peaches, sugared and brandied, liquidized, then trebled in volume with good champagne before it is decorated with wild strawberries, lurks the ideal potion for your palate and your pocket.

We will start at the financially shallow end.

WATER is a drink of which I have no first-hand experience.

LEMONADE is wholesome and non-habit-forming.

LAGER, ranging from a non-alcoholic variety brewed by

105

Carlsberg to a superlative one called Löwenbräu, imported by J.C. MacLauchlin of Denmark Hill, is an acceptable warm-weather drink. Mixed with lime juice cordial, it is not as unpleasant as one might suppose.

CIDER AND WINE blend into an insipid cup for which melting ice does very little, but which becomes acceptable when added to a double brandy. This goes for most drinks.

Golden, milkless INDIAN TEA, gently sweetened, iced, flavoured with lemon juice and Jamaica rum, is handy for with-it aunts.

But if the sun shines, there is enough noise and you have a sufficiency of people, give them what you will of SPANISH BURGUNDY and HOME-MADE GINGER BEER; and remember that a thimbleful of gin poured on top of each glass is worth three times that amount put in the bottom of the jug – especially if you approach the guests after their first sip and ask if the mixture is strong enough.

Better drinks, such as are suitable for better guests, tend to be more expensive. Try to get value for money. Never buy ready-mixed drinks, and beware of names – a Collins, a Sour and a Fizz are all just spirit, lemon, ice and soda, with or without sugar. It is only the price that tends to make one think that there must be more to it than that.

Whatever your choice, let it be served in a noble glass jug containing sufficient ice to frost the outside; let the liquid be spirit-based, liqueur-flavoured, sweetened with a natural syrup, elongated with mineral water and decorated with fruit. Time alone, or rather time and a strong head, will guide you to translate this into predetermined quantities of named ingredients. Here, for my money, is a selection of drinks on which you might spend yours:

CHAMPAGNE COCKTAIL. In Birmingham a Dutch barman with a phoney Canadian accent told me that he always served Tio Pepe sherry, angostura and diabetics' tonic water as champagne cocktail to people who were smaller or drunker than he. A more authentic version consists of well-iced champagne (non-vintage, no better than that) poured onto a lump of sugar containing a drop of bitters and a tablespoon of brandy. Decorate with a half-slice each of orange and lemon.

Iced Alsatian wine ... GEWURZTRAMINER is a good choice ... decorated with Muscat grapes.

A BRONX ... one part of gin, one of mixed (half-French and half-Italian) vermouth and one part of fresh orange juice, strained through crushed ice. This is an ideal, if rather expensive, opening drink for a party.

Otherwise, if the idea of lambless, alcoholic mint sauce appeals to you, muck about with Bourbon, mint leaves, sugar, ice and soda. The result is called a MINT JULEP. Rum, Tia Maria, grenadine, soda-water and fresh lime has been called PLANTER'S PUNCH. Good bartenders refer to whisky, curaçao, soda and bitters as an OLD FASHIONED, but don't let yourself be fooled too readily. Remember the barman in Birmingham.

Whiskey – with an 'e' – is any whiskey that is not Scotch whisky. Until quite recently whisky was an allocation, you were lucky to get it at all – so you drank what was given to you. This is an appalling thing to happen to any commodity and did nothing for whisky; fortunately, it is a thing of the past.

Fortnums now sell ISLAY MIST, a 100% proof single malt, while LAPHROAIG 75% proof malt is obtainable more generally. Neither is cheap, both should be tried without delay. But these are predominantly short, sharp, cold-weather drinks; it is the lighter, blended whiskies, like J AND B RARE and CUTTY SARK, that sell like mad in America and are finding addicts even over here, which provide as pleasant a double measure upon which to pour a bottle of cold soda-water ... don't be fooled by the noise of a soda-siphon.

Americans also have a thing about cream in their drinks. As obnoxious an example as any is one called a BRANDY ALEXANDER. Equal parts of cognac, crème de cacao and cream are poured into a cocktail shaker, activated furiously, strained and, if you must, drunk.

I prefer a BLACK VELVET, that unexpectedly delicious marriage of champagne and stout. One is served iced, the other at room temperature; one is old and effervescent, the other new and heavy; one is rich, the other poor. But get a bottle of champagne and three halves of Guinness, pour them together into a jug and you have a dozen glasses of a delectable, health-giving, fattening, drunk-making, socially impeccable drink at 2s. 6d. a glass ... and no, it's not the same if you use Babycham.

What a strange thing it is that we, who enjoy less summer than most people, spend so much time and thought on warm-weather drinks, while under the blazing sun of North Africa they all sit and drink infusions of mint ... *and* insist they only drink it for their virility.

* * *

In the early 1960s Freud undertook the 'Mr Smith Investigations' series for Queen *magazine – 'wherein I set out to prove that if your name was Smith, and you looked pretty much like everyone else, you were made to suffer for your anonymity.' He started by going to lunch at various top London hotels, then moved on to art dealers (of which one out of five recognized a drawing he showed them to be a genuine Renoir), detective agencies, followed by health resorts, clairvoyants, theatres, and – a trade particularly close to his heart – wine merchants ...*

A Wine Merchant for Mr Smith
Queen, 30 October 1962

USE OF THE word 'off-licence' is now restricted to socially undesirable drawing rooms; 'wine shop' is a bit pretentious but all right. The little men around the corner, who were once content to recommend the red wine or pronounce the white bordeaux as good value, feel today that they have to get in on the act. Though their sun continues to rise and set around a pint of the best bitter they now talk of troisième cru cooking sherry and remember Cyril Ray nightly in their prayers.

In and around St James's, on the other hand, a wine merchant remains what he has always been ... a merchant of wine. His firm might have merged – or taken over another – for the greater glory of the shareholders; but they were founded some centuries ago, the man behind the counter was of an only slightly later vintage, and knowledgeable advice fairly flows for those who consult them about laying down a pipe of madeira or acquiring a double dozen Imperial pints of champagne.

The pre-war clientele of these firms consisted of predictable upper-class males (who had accounts which they paid after they paid the other tradesmen, before they paid their tailors). But exclusiveness of this sort is a fast vanishing commodity. How then have these merchants fared? How does their advertised high standard of tactfully delivered, knowledgeable advice on the subject of viniculture stand up to the demands of the ever-increasing mob of classless imbibers?

I dressed in an off-fawn mackintosh – buttoned so that one side hung several inches below the other, a stained 1930s pork-pie hat and a pair of National Health glasses prescribed for a man with a major disorder in his right eye. Thus attired I called at the West End offices of a number of eclectic vintners, as one who had invited three others to dine with him, knew nothing of wine and wanted guidance as to what he should purchase to make a dinner a success ... on a budget of £5. The menu with which I wished to regale my guests was soup, tunny fish and salad cream, roast chicken, fruit salad and cheese.

CHRISTOPHER'S 94 Jermyn Street, W1

Arrival: On the right side of Jermyn Street one goes through a handsome door into a warm, softly carpeted, handsomely furnished, panelled room. A man behind the desk broke off his conversation with another as I arrived and motioned me to sit opposite him at a desk.

I told him of my predicament. He was sympathetic, advised me most courteously and took in the menu which I recited, with fortitude. He asked me whether I wanted the wine to take with me. I said Yes. That, he said, would curtail my choice as he had only limited stocks in Jermyn Street. I said that I would be guided entirely by him. He asked me whether I would excuse him for a moment, left to offer a man who was sitting on a sofa a sherry ... poured it for him and then rejoined me.

He thought I should have a hock with my soup and fish ... suggested Mettenheimer Goldberg Scheurebe Spätlese ... how did I feel about that? He showed it me on the wine list. I told him it sounded nice. Next he felt we should have two bottles of claret – that would be two glasses each – followed by a bottle of port. He was afraid they only had wood port at Jermyn Street. I told him I was content so long as it did not come to more than £5. He assured me that it would be less, excused himself to answer the telephone, told his caller that he was currently busy and then worked on the figures and told me my wines came to 61s. He asked if he might have my name and address so that that he could send me future wine lists. I gave him my name – Grant Smith – and he asked whether I was related to Ian Grant-Smith. This was extraordinarily civil as it was highly unlikely from my appearance that I could be related to anyone.

The Wines: He left to fetch my purchases which were placed, unwrapped, in two carrier bags: one Ostreicher Doosberg Scheurebe (he was afraid that they were out of stock of the other wine he had suggested) 1961, at 14s. 6d. Two bottles of château-bottled Le Virou 1955 (with badly defaced labels, for which he apologized), at 13s. 6d. a bottle; they were 14s. on the wine list.

Payment: I gave him a £5 note and he took this to a toy cashbox containing £4 in notes, two shillings in silver and copper. It was a struggle, but we finally managed my change and he bade me goodbye most civilly. My visit had lasted eleven minutes.

GRANT'S OF ST JAMES'S 31 Bury Street, SW1

Arrival: I walked through the door beside their vinous shop window to find myself in a small office, richly carpeted, the walls hung with paintings. I told the man about my dinner party; when I got to the tunny fish course he pointed out that he was an art dealer (it was my damned glasses). I would be looking for the wine merchant next door. I thanked him and he guided me out of the door. At Grant's I was told that my sort of order would be executed by their branch office at Number 21 Jermyn Street. Number 21 was a Victoria Wine Company shop (actually it was rather like the art dealer's office, only there were a few bottles lying in a bin); a girl looked me over suspiciously, listened to my story, and told me that she would fetch the manager. There were a number of chairs; she did not ask me to sit down.

Advice: The manager was a pleasantly businesslike man. He listened to my menu and told me that I should have Puligny Montrachet, changed his mind and said the Meursault would be nicer and wondered, would I like a second bottle of that – or something else with the chicken? I said something else. He said claret and with the sweet you should have a Château d'Yquem. Each of these bottles he took from the very small selection available in the bin, told me to chill the white wine slightly – for about an hour – and serve the red at room temperature, drawing the cork about an hour before the meal. There were, he said, about six glasses in each bottle. He then wrapped the bottles and distributed them among two carrier bags, one marked Grant's of St James's, the other, Victoria Wine Company.

The Wine: One estate-bottled Meursault Blagny 1959, at £1 7s. 6d. One château-bottled Lascombes 1959, at £1 1s. 6d. One château-bottled d'Yquem 1950, at £1 17s. 3d.

Payment: He had a good, efficient till and gave me 14s. change from my £5 note.

BERRY BROTHERS AND RUDD 2 St James's Street, SW1

Arrival: The shop is large, handsomely panelled. A young man gave an elder a rueful look when I came through the door, and then approached me and asked if he might help.

Advice: I spun my tale. He had some difficulty in hiding his amusement and then suggested that two bottles was the right amount for four people. Yes, he said, you had better have two bottles of white burgundy which was best for fish and chicken. He put down the price of a bottle – 26s. – on a piece of paper, doubled it with difficulty, and then said I ought to have a dessert wine; a 1948 Château d'Yquem – you really couldn't do much better than that.

The Wines: Two estate-bottled Chassagne-Montrachet 1959, at 26s. One bottle of Château d'Yquem 1948, at 38s.

Payment: Repeating that I really couldn't do much better than I had done, he added up his sum and said that I owed him £5 10s. I gave him £6. He went to the till-roll, entered 'Gent 5-10-0' and gave me 10s. change.

The wine, each bottle individually wrapped, he placed in a plain brown-paper carrier bag. I waited on the pavement for two minutes in case he realized that he had overcharged me £1 and came out to look for me. He stayed in the shop. My visit had lasted seven minutes.

SACCONE AND SPEED 32 Sackville Street, W1

Arrival: A female receptionist asked me my business, left me standing by her desk and went to fetch someone. I transacted my entire business in the hall.

Advice: The man who came to see me listened to my story sympathetically, and consulted a wine list which also gave advice as to which wines went with what food. He asked me whether my chicken would be roast. The man said I should have Chablis with the fish, followed by two bottles of Burgundy. He asked whether I thought port or Sauternes with the sweet? He personally preferred port. I assured him through my glasses which were beginning to give me a headache that I would be guided by his expertise. He then went to fetch the wines, pointed out to me which bottles were for which course and waving in the general direction of the red wines, he said: 'Burgundy is usually quite nice.'

The Wines: One London-bottled Bâtard Montrachet 1959, at 10s. 6d. Two London-bottled Les Bonnes Mares 1952, at 18s. 6d. One bottle Pride of Portugal Tawny Port (with a torn label, for which he apologized) at £1 2s.

Payment: I received an invoice marked 'Cash Sales' and got my change from £5 quickly and accurately. The wines, unwrapped, were put into two brown and red Saccone and Speed carrier bags. It had taken nine minutes to transact my business.

JUSTERINI AND BROOKS 153 New Bond Street, W1
Arrival: One walks into a fairly large room sporting a long counter, which accommodated three men; one, wearing a Guards' tie, attended to me civilly.

Advice: He heard my story and listened to the menu. He suggested Pouilly Fuissé, then on reflection thought that Chablis was that much less dry. A bottle gives seven glasses, he said, so if I bought two bottles that would give us four glasses each. I asked whether this was within my budget of £5; above all, I didn't want to be thought mean. At this he said he had some very special French-bottled Montrachet at 27s. which he could recommend. He told a man to go down and get me two bottles and went to attend to the bill.

The Wines: Two estate-bottled 1961 Chassagne Montrachet, at 27s.

Payment: I received a bill, gave up £3 and was told that they did not have 6s. in silver, could I help? I gave the man two half-crowns which entirely flummoxed him and it took him some minutes to give me the correct change. The two bottles were individually wrapped, one further protected by corrugated paper, both placed in a red and white J&B carrier bag. The sale had taken six minutes.

CONCLUSION

Advice: When a man as impecunious as I appeared to be takes his money to a wine merchant, it would be wrong to expect a merchant to point out that £5 is a wholly unnecessary sum to spend on four people's wines; this would not only be disloyal to his employer but might well appear to be patronizing Mr Smith.

On the other hand, I feel that in view of Smith's statement that he knew nothing about wines, it was wrong to offer him a few superior vintages of French bottled wines, rather than advise him to impress his guests with vast quantities of liqueur or offer him something as immediately ostentatious as champagne. Apart from this, I feel that Christopher's choice was easily the most desirable as well as being the best value: four bottles of good wine; an unadvertised 1s. off for two defaced labels, and nearly £2 change from a fiver.

Justerini and Brooks with their recommendation of two bottles of white Burgundy – however suitable the wine might have been as an accompaniment to the meal – did me the poorest service; half a bottle per head to last through what was obviously going to be a long and tedious five-course meal is pretty unlikely to impress anyone.

To recommend Château d'Yquem to go with fruit salad – as did both Berry Brothers and Grant's – seems bad advice. The wine is so cloyingly sweet that a small port-glassful, heavily iced, is about as much as the average man can take. I realize that the high price of d'Yquem helped to bring the total up but I should like to have felt that there were better reasons for recommending it.

For the rest, there was the failure of all but Grant's to advise me on the correct temperature at which the wine should be served, no one told me how to pronounce the wines they recommended (an essential this for any inexperienced host) and there was not a man who asked whether I had a corkscrew.

Treatment: Only at Christopher's and at Berry's did I feel that I was receiving more attention than I would get from a reasonably civil fishmonger. Both firms offered me a chair and, had I looked more appetizing, would doubtless have offered me a drink. But at Berry Brothers I was made to feel an ill-dressed oddity, while at Christopher's I was treated like a gentleman by a gentleman. Saccone and Speed were impersonally all right, though by comparison the warm welcome and courteous attention accorded a man who came in behind me – after he said he wished to export wine to Ecuador – made me feel pretty unwanted. Grant's under their pseudonym of Victoria Wine were all that you would expect from the best type of little-man-around-the-corner.

Payment: It seems quite remarkable to me that any wine merchant of repute who is prepared to sell wine to all-comers should keep insufficient ready cash to change a £5 note. Only Grant's and Justerini's appeared to have any practice at handling money.

Neither Christopher's nor Saccone and Speed could have changed a half-crown, while Berry Brothers owe me £1. They will find the 'Gent £5 10s. 0d.' entry on their till roll for 3 January, immediately after one in the name of Phillips.

* * *

Eating on the run
Daily Telegraph Magazine, 22 October 1971

IF A MAN drives from A to B (the achievement of which appears to be one of the principal functions of a motor car) and A is some distance removed from B, the chances are that the motorist will require sustenance.

Regrettably, when it comes to motorized catering, cars *just* miss out: the water in the radiator is insufficiently pure for drinking; the oil in the sump neither hot nor bland enough for deep frying; the petroleum in the tank contains insufficient alcohol to give a chap a kick. This is a sorry state of affairs and one that causes writers to pick up their pens annually around the time of the Motor Show and advocate car picnics.

I should like to make it quite clear that with very few exceptions a picnic in a car is a plumb bad idea. When a man has been driving for a long time in the same cramped position, what he needs is a change of surroundings and the chance to shout back at new people.

There are actually two proper reasons why one eats in the car – and I am discounting such quirks of fate as the seat belt inextricably caught up in your fly buttons: one is pressure of time; the other pressure of money.

Here is some golden advice.

EQUIPMENT. Basically the equipment you have dictates the whole concept of your picnic. Aluminium foil is probably the most important single item. Hardy plastic bags come next. If you have plastic or Tupperware bowls with close-fitting lids then you can have a feast instead of a snack. If you have – or can induce someone to give you – a pair of Thermos jugs, you need not be ashamed to give a lift to a really discriminating gastronome.

Finally, if you have a wicker basket, you are made ... though, frankly the chances of someone being poor, busy and coming by a lot of expensive impedimenta are remote.

DRINK. The disadvantages of fizzy drinks on picnics have been wildly exaggerated. I grant you that in the case of high gravity bottled beer loose in the boot of your car on a summer's day, the amount left in the bottle is likely to compare unfavourably with that which shot out when you removed the crown cork. Remembering that it is inadvisable to give a driving man vast quantities of alcohol, put lagers, pale ales, ciders and cans of soft drinks into a polythene bag containing ice cubes. The colder the cans are before you put them into the bag, the longer will your ice cubes remain intact. I am a fan of fruit drinks such as they sell at the German Food Centre in Knightsbridge, apple juice, morello cherry juice, passion fruit cordial.

Finally, on the subject of drink do not underestimate the thirst-quenching qualities of tea and coffee.

FOOD. If you have fresh, thin-cut bread, butter it generously with decent butter, give this a thin application of English mustard and then carve slices of York ham with a knife that has been given a quick wipe across a clove of garlic ... all you then need is a couple of sprigs of fresh watercress and a sprinkling of Maldon salt to obtain what I consider to be a very acceptable sandwich.

Somehow sandwiches are considered *passé* ... mainly I suppose because of the abundance of those made with stale thick-cut bread, margarine, grated ripe cheese and raw tomatoes ... though grated raw cheese and ripe tomatoes do little to make the confection more beautiful.

My car picnic menu, eked out by Smith Kendon's Blackheart Cherry Flavour Tablets, Cadbury's Burnt Almonds, Trebor Mints and Fry's Milky Bars, consists of:

FIRST COURSE. Radishes – wrapped in foil, salt apart. Meat balls in a closed Tupperware container. (Take 1lb of minced beef. One beaten egg. One tablespoon grated onion. Ten peppercorns rough crushed. Salt and one-eighth pint soda water. Mix well and divide into 24 pieces. Roll each in flour and bake on a greased oven sheet for 20 minutes in Mark 5 (375° F oven).)

SECOND COURSE. Rice and prawn salad. Pilaff rice ... one cup cooked in two and a half cups of stock. Six ounces of peeled frozen prawns – tinned ones tend to have very little taste – tossed in sizzling butter seasoned with pepper and lemon juice. Two tablespoons Hellmann's mayonnaise.

Put the drained rice, prawns plus liquid in pan, and mayonnaise into a bowl. Blend and carry in a closed container.

MAIN DISH. Breaded lamb cutlets ... small cutlets, brushed with liquid mustard, then floured, dipped in beaten seasoned egg and dried in toasted breadcrumbs. Fry these in a mixture of half oil, half butter for three to five minutes on each side. Leave to cool on a rack and wrap very loosely in foil. Bantam eggs and small good tomatoes are ideal picnic fare in spite of the fact that everyone else takes them on picnics. If you like tomato chutney it is probably the best single all-purpose relish for the main dish.

PUDDING. Car picnics need not actually be four-course affairs ... but there happens to be in Marylebone High Street, London, a patisserie called Sagnes, where you can buy, among other delicacies, a Mont Blanc ... this being a crushed meringue in a stiff cardboard case, topped with a mousse of sweet chestnuts mounted with whipped cream.

If Marylebone High Street is on your way, and you have time and some money, do try some before a journey – after which you will probably not need to take the other things that I have suggested.

* * *

Frozen assets
Boulevard, **Spring 1987**

WHEN I WAS at my first boarding-school I saw a short film (our local cinema in Totnes was heavily into short films) in which by way of plot a man telephoned his wife and said 'I'm bringing home some chaps for dinner. There'll be five of us. We'll be an hour.'

In the fifteen minutes of celluloid that ensued, the wife threw together a three-course meal consisting of things that fortuitously happened to be around: a cold roast chicken, lurking in the fridge, was translated into a bowl of chicken mayonnaise, via the addition of sliced apples, grapefruit segments and cold turnip. She beautified a tin of soup with cream and sherry and ended the meal making a fool out of a jar of gooseberries: or it may have been the other way round.

We food writers use the scenario of the unexpected guest as part of our overall message that cooking is easy and fun, and not necessarily expensive – especially if you do it the way we tell you. Nevertheless today's man is unlikely to phone his wife, telling her about 'five of us for dinner, in an hour', mainly because this could be grounds for divorce, also because he may reasonably expect that his wife will want to get herself ready – and you can't prepare food *and* self in sixty minutes.

Unexpected meals at home these days tend to be the result not of sudden whim, but of people being unable to get a table at the restaurant of their choice. Then you might say, 'Come on folks, we'll go home and knock something together. Won't we, dear?' – and there are many prudent people who stock up the freezer for just such an emergency.

And of course there is also the shame factor – people who purchase frozen comestibles for the express purpose of hiding their inability to cook.

However, to return to a pet convention – cooking *is* easy, so do ensure, before you defrost and titillate and decant and remove all signs of packaging (finding 'sell by' labels in the lasagna presents a difficult social problem for the guests), that it might not have been quicker to have cooked it from scratch.

We cooks hope, rather as the frozen food manufacturers fear, that we shall see the return of the day when you will decide to go it alone: actually buy a packet of pasta and make your own sauce, topping it with cheese that you have personally grated ... all at about 45 per cent of the price that you pay for *Spaghetti Bolognese con formaggio*.

I have always felt that pizzas and ice-cream, those staples of the supermarket freezer shelves, should never be eaten neat. Personalize the pizza by adding a little more cheese; a fillet or two of anchovy; bake it on an oven-sheet rubbed with a clove of garlic (crush the garlic on a crust of bread and use that to wipe the metal, otherwise you'll smell like a Marseillaise bus for the rest of the day) or draw the initials of your guests on the pizza with tomato puree from a tube, using the nozzle as a pen.

If you have enough time before serving the ice-cream, allow it to soften, blend grated lemon rind and lemon juice into it (this gives the ice-cream a semblance of being freshly made) and return it to the freezer. If time is short, make a sauce by putting apricot jam and a glug of liqueur into a saucepan and pouring the hot sauce over the cold slab. My favourite simple sauce is made by dissolving a Mars Bar cut into slices in a pan containing a few tablespoons of milk and a knob of butter. The heat must be low and you have to keep stirring ... for the whole two minutes it takes to transform itself.

If you are entertaining guests, the more packaged the food, the more it must look as if you've taken trouble, because somehow guests resent the fact that the host hasn't put himself or herself out in the preparation of a meal.

Apart from plenty of drink – which is a great cure-all – linen napkins, nice china and cutlery, hot bread, a slab of butter into which you have forked some chopped parsley and a little lemon juice, a pot of Dijon mustard and a bowl of radishes all seem to be accepted as signs that deep down you care. A battery of chutneys and pickles and poppadums and a sauceboat of horseradish cream are a message that you won't mind the guests tinkering with their food.

The first course is crucial: get it wrong and the whole meal is an uphill struggle, but if it succeeds they will forgive you for all that ensues. Keep pâté in the fridge – on balance the ones from Belgium are best – or smoked mackerel fillets, which also come swathed with peppercorns and are excellent, or taramasalata which is cheaper and goes further than smoked cod's roe on which it is based. You can also buy some good soups in polythene bags which on the whole outperform tinned soups; in these, as in many other foods, a late dash of cream enhances and enriches and personalizes the dish … and halves of lemon, sewn into muslin, which you can buy in many shops (and could even make yourself) are an asset.

The caterer's cry of 'Confuse them with quantity' is only part of it. Supermarket shelves bulge with good products and it's a question of trying them, deciding what is adaptable and serving with a flourish that enables the convenience cook to gloat beside a gourmet rival.

Some helpful suggestions for beautifying what comes out of the packet:

Nothing tastes good if it has stayed in the oven too long or has been allowed to get too hot. Fresh cream is a great and enhancing cooler of dishes.

Fresh lemon juice and freshly chopped herbs enhance almost every savoury dish – as does the judicious use of alcohol. Use port and sherry neat, i.e. pour it straight into the soup or stew. However, always boil ordinary wine to reduce the volume and concentrate the taste, then add it to the dish and let it add its flavour in the oven.

If you use spirits in cooking, heat the brandy or vodka or liqueur in a pan, tilt it towards the flame to set it alight and pour it over the dish at the last moment. Don't be shy about this. A flambé hamburger is a terrific conversation stopper, and no one is going to be able to say, 'I had that for lunch'.

An important point to consider for re-hashers of other people's foods is whether or not to have a deep-fat frier. In favour of one is the speed with which you can produce dishes; the counter-arguments involve flammability and smell; although thermostatically controlled, non-smelling friers are beginning to infiltrate the market. If you think you can cope and your partner gets some training with the fire extinguisher, the culinary world opens up substantially; scampi, breaded breast of chicken, goujons of fish, chips in dozens of shapes and sizes – all available frozen and with only the fumes of the oil between you and total contentment.

My favourite quick surprise dish is triangles of Brie or Camembert, floured, egged and breadcrumbed, then fried in deep fat until the outside is crisp and golden, by which time the inside is soft and creamy. They must be well drained and are traditionally served with gooseberry preserve. These are now available in packets – look for them in the Waitrose cheese section – which is marvellous because they are difficult to make and unless the breading is immaculately done, cheese will spill out of the gaps in the coating and ruin the fat.

Perhaps the most special aspect of packaged frozen food is that one operator can produce a marvellously varied menu. Duck from Cherry Valley; vegetables from Froqual; Bubble and Squeak from Avana, via Marks and Spencer; Salmon and Asparagus en croûte from Sainsbury. Pizza by this firm, ice-cream by that … it's like having a brigade of chefs in your kitchen without anyone shouting at you in a foreign language or drinking you out of house and home.

* * *

The gastro-judiciary
Le Nez Rouge Wine Club, **Autumn 1987**

FOR MEN OF the law, the ultimate goal is to become a judge. For us who eat ... and are seen to eat, and recognized as eaters, the stamp of approval comes when we are asked to join a panel and recommend a gastronomic award.

No longer do you eat for yourself, you eat for others, and against some. You cease merely to be a judge of food but become an assessor of every aspect of the operation: how they take table bookings; the accuracy and speed of arrival of the bill; the cleanliness of the establishment; quality of cutlery and linen; security of the cloakroom; range of wines ... and only then do you turn your attention to the algebra of the fare on offer.

My first appointment to the gastro-judiciary was on Jersey in the 1960s. I was one of four judges invited to decide the identity of the best local establishment, was given a shortlist of six and a letter from the Head of Tourism explaining that 'bearer is a judge and must not be charged for food and drink, nor assaulted for failing to leave a gratuity.' We judges were to be anonymous.

So I arrived alone, unheralded, in a Tourist Board car with a vellum folder instructing me how and what to assess. 'Outward appearance of premises, condition of brickwork (if applicable) and cleanliness of the windows MARK out of 10.'

They pretended not to notice me climbing up the ivy by the entrance porch.

When it came to food, we were to judge on five counts: eye appeal, correct temperature, 'quality of ingredients', value for money and taste.

The highlight of my week came when I ordered a steak au poivre, and the chef sent out an immaculate piece of rump, sizzling hot, stunningly presented with soufflé potatoes and wild mushrooms, at a special knock-down price. Sadly the chef had spiked the meat with cloves instead of peppercorns ... and Steak *au cloux de giroffles* not only sounds awful but tastes foul.

In accordance with the rules of the contest I had to award the place 80 out of 100, way above the restaurant where I ate a sensational steak, kidney and oyster pudding at a realistic price, looking no better than such good dishes usually look, containing tinned oysters – which were fine, damn it, I was paid to notice – so had to deduct some points. With 20 out of 20 for taste it still came second to the cloven meat.

I have been involved in a fair amount of judging since those heady days. Cook of the Year; Restaurant of the Month; Breakfast of the Century ... done 'em all. I now have my own criteria which I superimpose upon the directives provided by whoever employs me:

I disqualify any establishment whose staff wear Dr Scholl sandals, ignore cleanliness unless the dirt actually gets up and hits me in the face, take little notice of décor and much of ambience and pay scant attention to waiters' recommendations – unless it is NOT to choose something (in which case why is it on the menu; for whom is it waiting?). I get apprehensive about places where there is no sane relationship between the size of the establishment and the number of main dishes on the menu: a choice of twelve entrées where there is room for only forty customers spells doom. Also if you want to sit at a particular table, I like a restaurant that says 'yes', unless there is a reason for saying 'no'.

The usual rationale for not letting customers sit where they want to sit is that they should not have it all their own way, lest they're going to be difficult to control. This cuts no ice with me. I WANT to be difficult to control; heavens, if I intended to be easy, I'd have dinner at home.

* * *

File on tea
Infusion, **Summer 1989**

I WAS SIXTEEN when my father was appointed chief fire watcher for Maresfield Gardens, North West London, where we then lived; perhaps 'appointed' is an overstatement. My father was an architect, which is not a very terrific profession to pursue during a war, and his study walls, which used to be replete with drawings and plans, building schedules and artists' impressions of houses, were bare. He was a sitting duck when they needed someone to organize the duty roster and he took on the job with enthusiasm: the old and the very young, the sick, the lame and the infirm, also the occasional worker in an essential industry provided the manpower for the tin hut on the roof of our house, selected by virtue of being slightly higher than the neighbouring roofs.

When the sirens sounded, whosoever's name was on the list raced around to No. 2, grabbed the hard hat with ARP stencilled on the front, galloped up the stairs and peered down from the window of the observation post; and if a fire was started by a falling bomb – we had a direct line to the Fire Station – we cranked a handle and shouted our message, 'Looks like a medium-sized one halfway up Fitzjohn's Avenue' or whatever; then back to our watch. As the son of the organizer and resident of the house with the high roof, I did my nightly stints and helped out when I saw that a tallish, plumpish, black-haired nurse called Miss Flanagan was on duty.

Miss Flanagan was all that I yearned for: she was a woman. I would bring her a cup of tea and sit next to her on the bench in the hut, quite close, in case she was frightened. Miss Flanagan was about twice my size and bit her fingernails and used much Nivea Creme and until I left the perils of war-torn London for the security of Army life in the greenery of County Tyrone, I brought her cups of tea and sat very, very close to her. For many years thereafter, whenever I had a cup of tea, which was often, I started to think about the comforts of Miss Flanagan and our bravery on that wartime roof.

If tea is important now, it should be remembered that during the war it seemed absolutely essential. It was rationed, therefore one used what there was to the full. Special coupons were given to fire watchers and air raid wardens and when I came home on leave, one got special 'leave coupons' which made one the most welcome guest. 'Come to dinner and bring your coupons', people said and you arrived with the ration card containing a tea stamp and a sugar stamp and everyone beamed with contentment. While the country was grievously short of tea, the Freuds were actually all right. My parents had a house in a Suffolk coastal village and my father regularly strolled along the beach to see what had been deposited by the waves. As more and more ships were wrecked, so did the beach tell the tale. Among the flotsam and jetsam there was always driftwood, often clothing, occasionally bodies and, on one occasion, from a mined Japanese freighter, dolls two and three deep for a hundred metres of the Walberswick Sands.

And one day my father found the tea-chest. Intact. Halfway along the beach between us and Dunwich. It was tremendously heavy, by virtue of its having taken on so much water, but he got it to the house and for weeks he washed the tea and dried it, first in the sun and then after washing it again he toasted it lightly under the grill. That was the tea of my youth: slightly salted, a little burnt, rather weak from having been drowned and revived, but plenty of it. No one who came to visit left tea-less. The ration at the time was two ounces per person per week and here were riches beyond the dreams of avarice. We were the tea barons of East Suffolk.

As a caterer – which I have been, and once a caterer you always identify with the trade rather than its clientele – tea has a special place in my heart. Someone has got to man the restaurant between lunch and dinner, to take table bookings, prepare the seating plan, lay tables, and while they are there, might just as well earn their corn selling tea. In my first managerial post I was paid very little money, but high commission on new trade ... And my predecessor had not 'done' afternoon tea. I took a lesson in creative tea-making: heat the pot, add tea, then just enough boiling water to cover the leaves or tea bags by one centimetre and let it infuse for one minute, then top up with water. I produced sandwiches made by cutting crustless loaves lengthwise, thinly; buttering generously, piling on crisp slices of cucumber, chopped eggs with mayonnaise and fresh dill, cream cheese and smoked salmon ... and I found a source of quite brilliant chocolate éclairs. My lunchtime trade flagged; I took no terrific interest in dinners, but Freud's Teas were renowned in that North Devon hotel and to the fury of the resident managing director, my commission was higher than my salary; his profits slumped.

My friend Robert Morley, when served with a cup of tea and asked whether it is all right, looks his questioner in the eye and says, 'This is the best cup of tea I have ever had.' Tea just brings out the best in people. In the West Country I believe that all those farmhouses that 'do' Cream Teas belong to folk of charm and ability. I have never met an antipathetic Cream Tea-maker; it is as if the manufacture of scones, the churning of butter, the production of strawberry jam (the whole fruit must be left overnight in sugar to retain crunchiness and shape) and the assembly of clotted cream bestows upon them an extra warmth.

I find a comfort in tea that I never found in coffee ... even when I drank coffee, which I have not done for some ten years. Tea is soothing, and elegant; you go tea dancing – and would look an idiot asking someone to do a foxtrot after a cappuccino. Tea is sociable, while coffee is abrasive ... And on a cold day, there is a quite brilliant warming drink made by adding sugar and rum to a cup of black tea. In Vienna they sell it at street corners; you stamp your feet in the snow and warm your hands on the punch glass, and the world seems a more companionable place as a result.

* * *

To cook the turkey, no joke
The Field, **Christmas 1989**

EXCUSE ME; DID I hear you say 'Christmas dinner' preceded by 'What shall we have for?'? You have come to the right person. Over the years I have tried all the variations: suggested a Christmas meal built around a lamb cutlet; gave detailed information for a 'green' Christmas: Brussels sprouts were the central attractions with cunningly-shaped nut mousses to make ex-carnivores think of poultry. In a spirit of helpfulness, when *nouvelle cuisine* was *de rigueur,* I described in depth the construction of Le Boudin de Noël, a sort of albino black-pudding fashioned of white bread soaked in milk and beaten into minced turkey breast, bound in cream and set with raw egg-white, garnished with that year's herb or fashionable spice.

Today, having put behind me such childish things as runcible variations on a meal requiring tradition, I say unto you: How about a nice plump turkey, followed by Christmas pudding, preceded by whatever turns you on?

The reason for a Christmas starter is the reticence felt by many to shout 'Dinner' and pluck guests from pre-meal drinks straight into confrontation with the shining, mahogany-coloured brute, still blinking at the unaccustomed brightness of the festive board.

I think smoked salmon is a wonderful first course – especially if you buy a side and possess carving skills. Lemon halves sewn into muslin are impressive and stop the pips from coming out; black peppercorns are more aromatic than white, also milder; brown bread should be thinly sliced and generously buttered.

If you are the sort of person who wants to embarrass those who have spent the morning having facials and adjusting their shoulder-pads, you could make a marvellous double consommé: take the good broth that you produce from chicken or meat bones and pour it into a pan in which ½ pound of minced beef is turning dark brown over a hot flame. After the initial whoosh, there comes a long simmer – during which you remove the soup – whereafter, say fifteen minutes, add egg white and egg shell to the broth and pour it through a sieve lined with muslin, or an old dishcloth. This amazing, delicious, aromatic, crystal-clear consommé can be garnished with quenelles of turkey liver, which will really show them the stuff of which you are made: 6 ounces turkey liver processed with 4 fluid ounces double cream, season well, stir in a raw egg-white, blend well, rest in refrigerator and simmer marbles of the mixture in dry cider.

Enough of this culinary foreplay.

In 1964 I suggested rubbing the turkey inside and out with an oily, salty, gingery solution, wrapping it in foil and leaving it from post-midnight mass until its time arrived, in the bottom of an oven switched on to mark ½. Ovens at that low temperature were not then an exact science and though everyone marvelled at the sweet smell of roasting bird that wafted around the house from the time they awoke, many proudly undid the foil to find a carcass to which the meat had dried inexorably. So what did they do?

They looked up my telephone number in the Suffolk directory and shouted at me: from noon until about 4.45pm the Freud family took it in turns to answer and sent condolences. Slow roasting is still a tremendously efficient way of cooking a turkey and if it goes right (for heaven's sake try it with a chicken the week before) you not only have the tenderest, most melting of all birds but a pint and a half of excellent, flavoursome broth that jellies at the touch of a cool wind.

Turkey suffers from a severe design fault: the breast is fine; the legs are excellent; but the way the thing is put together, if you cook it as a joint, one or the other part will be properly cooked, the other not. As cookery writers eschew philosophy, none have written the truth, which is that, given the construction of the bird, you can either overcook the white meat, by which the time the dark will be just about all right, or cook the brown meat properly and reduce the breast to over-roasted tastelessness. Or you can remove the legs and braise them in salt and mustard and honey and Guinness and do wonderfully delicate things with the breasts – like lard them and wrap them in thin puff pastry and roast this and carve it with slices of alabaster meat interspersed with medallions of best chestnut stuffing spiked with prune and candied marrow.

There is a very cunning way of stuffing the bird – not by ignominiously sticking a quantity of pork-based forcemeat up one aperture and some more up another … but by carefully loosening the skin from the flesh, starting behind the wishbone and using your thumbs until you have a sizeable area between skin and meat all around the bird. It is actually much easier than it sounds, and you can practise on a chicken. It is this gap that should rightly receive the stuffing so that a well-carved turkey consists of slices that begin with crisp brown skin and have a half-moon of elegant stuffing surrounding the oval of tender turkey breast. Cranberry sauce is OK. It has been around since time began, and what would happen to cranberries if we did not make merry with them at Yuletide, tell me that?

The very best roast potatoes are an art form, and it is worth attending to their preparation very carefully. What is good about roast potatoes is the crispy skin … so you boil potatoes in their skins, peel them, cut them into pieces no thicker than 1 inch and when lukewarm, get a sharp fork and fluff up the outside of the potatoes all around; then roast them in a mixture of good bland oil and clarified butter, basting now and then and turning when necessary; oven should be medium hot. The result is ¼ inch of crisp exterior which you will have salted with sea salt. So excellent you wonder what all the turkey fuss is about.

There are now many good Christmas puddings on the market and making your own is more about therapy than the achievement of excellence. Even if you like some things more than others in a pudding – in my case crystallized ginger, candied fruit, and brandied sultanas – this can be introduced into a bought pudding by cutting it into slices, slipping in your favoured adjuncts and reassembling it in the bowl and the cloth, prior to steaming.

I believe that good puddings should have done to them what it states on the wrapper; whereafter you need:

Brandy or rum for flaring. Pour this into a small pan and at the last moment, when the spirit is hot but not boiling, set alight and pour over the pudding in the dark. The extinguishing of the light is for effect, also to make it harder to locate the target.

Brandy butter: everyone knows how to make this.

Cream ... which must be thick and, if possible, Cornish clotted.

Silver coins: though I have never yet heard a complaint when £50 notes are scrunched up and put into portions.

* * *

In 1990, Freud was confronted with a rare gastronomic challenge – to act as sandwich-designer for British Rail ...

Freud fills in as a breadwinner
Observer, 10 June 1990

WERE YOU TO come to Wigan, the home of the British Rail sandwich, you would see, in the Eat-Fresh factory, some 160 white-coated women, green Wellington boots hosed down with antiseptic, hair covered first with a net, then by a hat, hands clad in surgical gloves – and you would feel the cold.

The temperature is low so that the sliced loaves – malted, wholemeal, wheaten, Mighty White, oatmeal, walnut or whatever, remain fresh. It is so cold that the creamed butter is brought in, a few pounds at a time, at five-minute intervals.

InterCity has a range of nine sandwiches. It publishes a league table of sales, and every three months relegates the least popular varieties out of existence, and promotes a brace of new ones. At the end of spring, sick as parrots, large prawn and sliced turkey were relegated. Then I was appointed to design two new varieties.

The Clement Freud pair that made their debut two weeks ago are teetering at the lower end of the table with sales of 10,000 a week. (Bacon, lettuce and tomato, in comparison, sells 14,500.) But me and the lads are quietly confident we can hang on in there.

My only brief in devising the sandwiches was not to repeat what had gone before. The result is fresh salmon dressed with dill and mustard sauce on medium-thick wholemeal bread garnished with Chinese leaf (£1.85), and corned beef and tomato chutney on Mighty White bread spread with butter tinged with Dijon mustard (£1.65).

The ingredients are precise; four thin rounds of fresh tomato between the two 25-gram slices of corned beef. It looks good, though obviously mad salmon disease would be a serious blow.

What is wholly fortunate is that machine-made sandwiches still involve almost 100 per cent human input: women deal the sliced bread on to the moving band of the production line; women butter the slices, trying to remember that if you take care of the edges, the centre will look after itself.

In Wigan, as the bread moves down the line it passes the woman with the ice-cream scoop who plonks down 40 grams of egg mayonnaise; the next woman smoothes this to a depth of 1.5 centimetres; the one beyond slices hardboiled eggs and places these on the smoothed mayo; on goes the second slice via another pair of hands, whereafter modern technology takes over.

The sandwich is cut and inserted into a wedge-shaped carton, sealed, labelled and packed. Dodging in and out of the line are quality controllers and women who weigh the bread before and after buttering (4 grams a slice is the amount they work on), weigh the filling, ensure the bread has no holes.

After a production run of a thousand or so, there is a break during which the workers warm up and the sandwiches cool down. Chinese leaves – which are crisper if not greener than Iceberg. Firm red tomatoes sliced thinly, matured farmhouse Cheddar, whatever.

Like mothers-in-law, railway sandwiches were always good for a laugh; everyone knew about them. Two thick slices of white bread cursorily scraped with margarine, placed on either side of machine-cut ham or grated cheese. The heat of the train caused the bread to stiffen and curl away from the filling, enabling putative consumers to obtain a clear view of the confection on offer.

This epitomized the nation's approach to gastronomy: sustaining, quick and economical to produce, devoid of any nasty foreign things and so bad when it was made that there was little chance for it to get worse as it awaited a purchaser.

It was not always thus. In the second half of the eighteenth century, when the third Earl asked for his roast beef to be placed between pieces of bread so that he might remain at the card-table instead of wasting good gambling time in the dining-room, the Sandwich concept swept Europe. Le Sandwich was one of the early Franglais words, pre-dating Le Tea-dance, Parking and Biftek.

During the next 200 years there was a marked gentrification of sandwiches but the railway one remained true to itself, crouching unloved on glass shelves of display cabinets.

The invention of clingfilm, the installation of refrigerated shelves in buffets, the enhanced expectations of the public, all mean that sandwiches have straightened out. They are now made in hygienic factories to the specifications of designers under the supervision of environmental health officers, displaying sell-by labels that confine their shelf life to a single day.

InterCity sandwiches are made in the afternoon, taken by refrigerated van and train to the twenty-three InterCity depots from which they are distributed to 450 buffet cars for sale the following day. Thirty hours after their creation – by which time they might have travelled up to 1,000 miles – they are jettisoned, replaced on the morrow by their freshly-made successors. Next time you hear a comedian mention the railway sandwich, applause – rather than laughter – would be a suitable reaction.

* * *

The clever sausage
Sunday Mirror Magazine, 4 November 1990

IF A NATION gets the sausages it deserves, I wonder what we did wrong. In Germany – the Number One sausage-eating country in the world – they have *bierwurst* and *bratwurst*; *teewurst* and *leberwurst*; *metwurst*, *rotwurst* and *blutwurst*.

The French have *saucissons de Toulouse* which are flavoursome and large, and *saucisses de Frankfurt* which are quite different and delicious and small; there are *saucisses de campagne* which contain lean pork and fat bacon and those of Perigord, altogether finer and perfumed with truffles.

In Italy, where sausages were once so popular they were banned by law, you get mortadellas and salamis and great garlicky boiling sausages that are simmered with chickens, tongues and sides of beef to make Bollito Misto – the ultimate hot-pot.

We have the banger. To be accurate we have many bangers – some with more salt than others; others with less pepper than some. There are bangers that contain hardly any additives and those that contain many, but they are of the same family. When it comes to a culinary heritage, that handed down in respect of the British sausage can be written on the back of a postage stamp.

The sausage began as a device for using up the blood and odd bits of pig after the hams and bacon-sides had been taken. Assorted scraps were mixed with saltpetre, spices and herbs, then enclosed in cleaned gut, dried, smoked and hung in a cool dark place where they were left to mature.

In Britain we adapted the recipes: we made 'sausage meat' of minced pork, breadcrumbs and seasoning and, when times were hard, the meat/bread proportions changed to reflect the cost of these ingredients. By the end of the last war, you were lucky to get a sausage containing 50 per cent pork, of which 40 per cent was fat. There are new laws, whereby a sausage must have a minimum meat content ... but they don't specify what counts as meat.

The good thing about home-made sausages, people were prone to say, is they may not be very nice but you do know what is in them. Sadly there are still some pretty awful sausages on the market; more sadly, there are people who love them, wouldn't change them for anything, so they go on being produced. The fact is that no one has ever yearned for better food than they have already experienced.

MAKING SAUSAGES

A food processor is very much more efficient for the manufacture of sausage meat than a mincer, though if you keep the machine on for too long you break down the meat to a pap, when you really need a firm mixture.

Really good sausage meat can be made of the following really good ingredients:

1lb lean pork
½lb rindless smoked streaky bacon
5oz hard pork fat
4oz soft white breadcrumbs
1 rounded tsp Dijon mustard
1 flat tsp rubbed sage
salt and pepper to taste

Process the meats and fat. Add all the other ingredients to the meats and fat and stir well. Let this mature for a short while. Take a rounded dessert spoon of this mixture and fry it gently in a greased pan for a couple of minutes on each side.

Taste it. If it is good, feel proud; if it is too sloppy add more breadcrumbs or an egg yolk; if it is too firm, dilute with water, beer or grated apple.

Remember, it is *your* sausage meat so add what you will of herbs and spices that are to your liking. Mace is excellent. Some people like vanilla. Others prefer garlic.

COOKING SAUSAGES

The best lazy way is to put the sausages into an ovenproof dish on a medium/low setting. A much better way is to fry them in a pan, sizzling them on a medium setting to get a little colour and then on low to cook them properly. There really is nothing clever about underdone sausage.

If you want an extra 'bite', paint the sausages with mustard, then roll them in flour and fry as above.

It is quite rewarding to add a spoonful of delicious blackcurrant jelly to the pan for the final few minutes of their frying time.

* * *

Funeral fare
Town, **September 1963**

THE OLD SAW of *de mortuis nil nisi bonum* does not, as such, extend to speaking no evil of the funeral feast. Nevertheless it takes a pretty good man to go up to the widow and complain about the quality of her seedcake. The passing of a loved one – or death as I like to call it – has long been the cause for a gathering, a sort of anti-party. The slowness of printers coupled with the speed of decomposition of the human body prevents the bereaved from issuing standard invitations: 'request the pleasure of your company at Golders Green and afterwards at 51c Eaton Square.'

Yet it is generally understood that one goes back afterwards, if only to celebrate the fact that one is still alive. Even if he wasn't that well insured, damn it all, you had a drink with him when he got married and at the Christening and the Confirmation and now you pick up a gloomy glass; for some absolutely unaccountable reason it's port.

They've thought about this carefully. Champagne they decided was too frivolous. Wine might be misunderstood. Beer is mean, spirits are dangerous and by the corpse you've left behind in NW11 it's a glass of tawny or ruby port … or nothing.

Now I am not advocating a four-piece band whooping it up at a five-course high tea laid out around the vacated deathbed. I simply feel that if people are invited – or attend – a gathering occasioned by the departure of you, or yours, a sip of communion wine and an old sausage roll served in a black napkin is just not good enough.

The man who lays down a pipe of port for his son's coming of age might really reserve a double dozen for his mourners-to-be.

Any decent life assurance company will let you split up your policy so that 98 per cent goes to the widow and 2 per cent to the caterer. It is only lack of public demand that prevents undertakers from catering for the reception of the funeral guests, as well as that of the corpse. Personally, I should like to die quietly; having gone I can think of nothing more galling to my departed spirit than to witness – however ethereally – a third-rate beano to mark the occasion of my demise. Surely, rather as a statue is made to remind us of the physical attraction of our dead, so should a funeral feast recall the gastronomic desirability of the subject (or is it object?) of our mourning.

For me, then, let there be black velvet, abundantly served in large wine glasses. (I have always held that shallow champagne saucers were invented by charlatans for the use of such models as have never faced a camera.) The glasses can be half filled with Guinness at room temperature as the guests leave the crematorium and topped with rather over-iced non-vintage champagne as the black cars draw up outside the door.

The size of the glass prevents constant replenishment, often mistaken for greed on the part of the mourner, and keeps down to a minimum the undesirable noise of the champagne cork, celebrating its liberty. I should like the food to be serious.

Caviare is black; and mushrooms, picked in a field, chopped and cooked for five minutes in butter with the accompaniment of a small grated onion per four ounces, with the late addition of a tablespoon each of grated cheese and double cream and a pinch of paprika, will do nothing to detract from the solemnity.

Both of these confections can be served on toast. On the other hand toast, unless very freshly made, is an unsatisfactory backing, drying or becoming sodden with the juice of its load in all too short a time.

If the cook insists on going to the funeral and is forced to prepare the food an hour or two before its consumption, tell her to try fried bread. She should give it five seconds on each side in a shallow pan of very hot olive oil, drain well, allow to cool and then insulate with a thin covering of butter. Tell her.

5
FREUD
AT THE SPORTS

'Perhaps one day Arkle will write something nice
about me: no telling what that horse might do in
retirement.'

Clement Freud's career as a journalist began in 1954 with coverage of a football match at Portsmouth, and throughout his life sport vied with food as his principal topic. The two often came together in a characteristically Freudian way – as when in 2007 he suggested that the British Horseracing Authority should appoint an official racecourse hamburger taster: 'There would be two divisions: fresh and frozen. The inspector, unless already significantly overweight, would become very fat, and would have to take into account the asking price; freshness, warmth and desirability of the bun; time-lag between cooking and selling; provision and quality of tomato ketchup, brown sauce and mustard (Heinz, HP and Dijon are best), as well as the availability and efficiency of napkins' – and before they knew it, his Racing Post *readers were being treated to his recipe for the ideal hamburger.*

As with Freud on food, Freud on sport could fill several volumes. The articles here are simply a taster menu.

Press box imprint
Observer, 1 May 1960

ANOTHER FOOTBALL SEASON is over and until next August I shall miss the press boxes up and down the country, from Newcastle where you sit in a glass-built afterthought on the top of a stand better suited to assessing players' dandruff than football technique, to Yeovil where I was placed on a small wooden bench in the front of the stand, and the word 'Press' chalked on its seat travelled all the way back to London on mine.

During the last season I have been locked into most First Division grounds in England, for by the time that I finish phoning through my match report, I am invariably the only person left in the place; there was one exception: Chelsea, where greyhound racing takes over on Saturday evenings and I was able to have a bet on a dog called Chinar Wagtail while finishing my copy. I shall miss the friendly man who dispenses whisky at Leicester's Filbert Street – not the one who bars my entry into the tea-room at West Bromwich before the match ('At half-time and after the match, them's my orders'), nor the one responsible for never getting me a seat in the press box at West Ham ("The *Observer*, what's that, a local rag?').

I shall think nostalgically of the Arsenal box where the front row receives the raindrops from the roof and is only to be entertained in fine weather; of a Midland club where a wildly inaccurate closed-circuit broadcast to hospitals is made from the press stand by local benefactors throughout the game, and a pleasant woman dispenses barley sugar to visiting journalists by way of compensation. The efficiency and hospitality of Manchester United, the discrimination at Nottingham Forest ('I'm so sorry, I thought you were Mr Hackett, you'll have to go into that little room over there').

Saturday mornings at Paddington, Euston or King's Cross, wondering who else is going to be on the train. British Railways restaurant cars ... and the consoling thought that if, as the result of a meal, anything happens to you, the entire Tottenham Hotspur team at the next tables will have it happen to them, too. And then your colleagues, those dear, kindly, hard-bitten, sober men, who seldom seem to watch the game at crucial moments, such as when a goal is scored; and keep a mystic minute-by-minute record of the match ('I make that goal 23 minutes ... I make it more like 28 ... 26 ... 25 ...') and then those who burst into the press box trying to glean players' Christian names: 'Higgs took a corner' is only four words towards the 300 words required, while 'Peter George Henry Higgs took a corner' contributes seven towards that total.

After the match, in the press room, it is, for me, almost impossible not to listen to the others' reports being phoned through. As I write: 'Matthews's form must make him at the age of forty-three a serious contender for ...', I hear a man shouting into a black plastic mouthpiece: 'Is the old maestro done question-mark, I say No full-point, does the old maestro let up question-mark, I say not on your nelly full-point.'

I remember that this is a man whose reports every Sunday are read by the numbers who read mine in two months and I recall my sub-editor, that hatchet-faced guardian of propriety who on four occasions this year, when a match of mine had produced no score after forty-five minutes, has changed my 'At half-time the game's virginity was still intact' to 'There was no score at half-time.'

* * *

Next man in ... Clement Freud
Daily Herald, 19 May 1964

WE NEEDED 71 to win, and I was the last of the recognized batsmen. As I came down the steps of the pavilion there was a fair volume of applause from the optimists in the large Bank Holiday crowd, and an elderly gentleman wearing the red and gold MCC tie said: 'Good luck, sir.'

I'll do my damnedest, I said, opening the white gate. I made for the vacant wicket, the one at the sight-screen end, a walk of about 95 yards.

Now one hears a lot about the demoralizing effect this walk has on cricketers but I have never found it an ordeal; I rather enjoy it.

I try to get used to the light in the middle, get an idea of the speed of the outfield, think about my first ball and become strangely, almost menacingly calm.

Bailey met me twenty yards from the table.

I can't hold out much longer, he said; I was a fool to put myself in so high up the order but it's been good to know that you were still to come.

I smiled. There's nothing the matter with your batting, I said, if you could only remember one thing.

What's that?

Concentrate, Trevor, concentrate.

It's easy for you, said Bailey …

People say Trueman is fast, but I find it easier when a man comes off the pitch a bit quickly; I find I don't have to hit the ball so hard. I steered the first ball along the ground between third and fourth slip for an easy couple.

Trueman stroked his mane of black hair, polished the ball furiously on his trousers and trudged back to his mark. I knew the signs; this was gong to be the bouncer.

As he tore up to the wicket I stood my ground and rose to my full height. It was the bouncer; I cracked it for a six over where square cover would have been: 63 to get and now Trueman was angry.

His next was the in-swinger, on a length. I tickled it down to the boundary past where fine leg would have been. The approval of the Bank Holiday crowd was intense. But through it all I could hear one insistent voice saying Tea, tea, tea, tea …

I said What?

Tea. Come on, said my wife. Get up. It's Whit Sunday, the sun's shining and the children want to be driven down to the beach before you go off to your cricket match.

Of course; it was the game against Eyke and Rendlesham.

I sipped my tea, got up, and decided not to shave. I then went down to the kitchen, blancoed my tennis shoes, found a near-white shirt – the sort of thing the advertisers use before they show you one that has been washed in New Whiz – and wrapped these, a pair of light blue socks and my batting glove in the lightest grey flannels I had.

I essayed a few late cuts with the frying pan.

Eyke and Rendlesham were 20 for 8. My team were jubilant. I steadied them; over-enthusiasm gets you nowhere; Kippax and Hooker had once put on 307 runs for the last wicket. Eyke's number nine hit a four, then another.

We got their number 10 lbw (our umpire), their last man slashed eight off two balls then hit across a full toss that just took off the leg bail.

We needed 39 to win and I was down to bat number five.

I called around me a few willing young men and asked them to bowl to me as practice. While 39 was not an insuperable total, one should never underestimate the opposition and this was my first game of the season.

Freud, hit wicket, bowled Peach, looks terrible, even if it's only in the *Halesworth Times*.

Their captain decided on a piece of psychological warfare. Tea, he said.

I am not one to be sidetracked; I tightened the straps on my pads, practised a few late cuts in the air and waited for the feasting to end.

At ten minutes past five, Eyke and Rendlesham took the field and we sent in our opening pair: their bodies bloated with the juice of Indian tea bags, their spirits dulled with fish-paste sandwiches.

Dennis, a foreman carpenter, missed a straight full toss.

Christopher, a trouser-cutter from Southwold, disentangled himself from his recently acquired lady button-holer who works in the same firm, marched to the wicket and returned a few moments later to the embraces of his bride-to-be, lbw (their umpire).

There is some doubt about how seriously Christopher now takes his cricket and at a recent meeting of the selection committee a proposal to suspend courting players was only narrowly defeated – two against one, I think the voting was.

Nevertheless 39 was not beyond our talents. Young Harry, an engineer who is Dennis's nephew, and Don, an Irishman who has come to work on the nuclear power station at Sizewell, hit off the runs and as the seven non-combatants said to one another on the way home – in the pub at Snape actually – it's good to be on the winning side.

I mean, young Harry, who scored 28, must have played with that much greater confidence knowing that I was due in at No. 5, and as my wife so rightly pointed out when I got home at 11.15, I *had* had that good innings earlier in the day.

* * *

I'll leave the Duchess to 'Enery tonight
Sun, 6 May 1966

FROM GHOSTIES AND ghoulies and long-leggety beasties and things that go bump in the night, the good Lord deliver us ...

Henry Cooper does not actually go bump in the night, but as part of his training schedule for his world title fight with Cassius Clay, at Highbury on 21 May, he gets up at four every morning and jogs around the hills and dales of south-east London.

His trainer Mr Danny Holland, also known as the bookmakers' friend, pedals by his side on a mini-bike.

At luncheon on Tuesday I asked Mr Cooper why he trained at this comparatively unfashionable time of day. He said: 'The air is good and there is no one about and when I get back I can have two or three hours' sleep before breakfast.'

It seemed an excellent reason, and as I had nothing marked in my diary for 4am yesterday, I decided to go and see whether this sort of training might not be exceedingly beneficial.

Accordingly I set my alarm clock for 3.15 (Cooper is woken at 3.50), got out of bed, waited until my legs became part of my body and sneaked out of the house. (Cooper spends the six weeks before a fight away from his family. My wife and I sleep in a double bed.)

As I pointed my car in the direction of the Duchess of Edinburgh public house, which is the centre of our contender's operations, it was still very dark. At New Cross I remembered about the good fresh air and opened the car window. I coughed all the way to Blackheath but began to feel better as I turned off the Rochester Road.

At 3.45 the car radio finally picked up a programme, *Workers' Playtime* in Bulgarian, and at 4.00 I arrived at the appointed place.

Cooper stood outside the saloon-bar entrance, dressed in a blue track suit and woolly cap. I was wearing medium-grey trousers and a jersey.

He said: 'You're here, then.' I thought about this for a moment and agreed.

At 4.01 we set off. Cooper trotting fast, arms held very high, legs moving easily; Danny Holland quietly pedalling his mini-bike. A police car trailing us because at that time of day there is not much else police cars can do.

Unlike the majority of long-distance runners, I excel in the first fifty yards, and it was in that time that I thought I had better get in my interview.

I said: 'How are you?'

Henry said: 'Fine.'

Danny said: 'Don't talk, you'll need your breath.'

So we jogged on silently through the good air of deserted Upper Walmsley Lane. I should have said that for sheer quality ozone, the Catskill Mountains have the edge on this part of London, but then at that time of the morning it is hard to be sure.

We came down a hill at great speed, Cooper fractionally in the lead. I drew level on the flat and as the road rose towards the Weald of Kent Cooper got away.

The sergeant in the police car kindly said he would give me a lift, by which means I covered the last three-quarters of the course.

Cooper's daily training runs are over a distance of about four miles, take 35–40 minutes. He ran well, perspired freely, breathed deeply and evenly; he walked up his third hill, galloped up the last, and at 4.25 he was back outside the Duchess of Edinburgh.

He said: 'It's all go,' grinned and did a little shadow boxing. Danny Holland got off his bike and said: 'We usually do another mile but for your sake we took the short route.'

As my legs had once more regained their independence from my body, I stood Frankenstein-like, panting, holding on to the police car and said nothing.

So Henry said: 'I am off round the back to do some exercises.' He refused my offer of a pull at my hip-flask and said goodbye; 'Nice of you to come.'

Jack Solomons once said to me: 'If world championships were handed out for decency and sheer niceness Henry wouldn't even have to go into the ring.'

As it is, Mr Cooper will be pounding the early morning watch of Shooters Hill for the next two weeks.

As for me, I have promised my wife to stay in bed.

* * *

Fans give me the pip
Sun, **10 February 1967**

OFFICIAL REPORTS STATE that more than a thousand tomatoes were thrown on to the pitch during the Naples–Burnley Inter-Cities Fairs Cup-tie on Wednesday night.

The final figure was presumably not released until some time after the match because at the whistle the ground was covered in a light red mantle of skin and pips and the tellers had considerable trouble reconstituting the ketchup.

On the face of it a 'grand' of tomatoes may not sound excessive for a crowd of 60,000. If you take the average weight of the Italian fruit to be seven ounces, it works out at a bare .116 of an ounce per spectator.

On the other hand, whichever way you look at it, one thousand tomatoes is a great deal of tomatoes, and as it is unlikely that every member of the crowd hurled a tiny red sliver, one must suppose that a couple of hundred Neapolitans came armed with a kilo each.

Even though the ways of foreigners are strange, I seriously doubt whether ten-score Italianos would take a bag of tomatoes to a football match other than to hurl them on to the pitch.

And if I am right, then the brutality on the field of play had nothing to do with this cascade of what the Latins call 'golden apples'.

As Caesar put it so picturesquely: 'They came, they saw, and having brought a bag of tomatoes for the specific purpose, they let fly ...'

I trust you will not feel that in pointing an accusing finger across the Arno I am glossing over the behaviour of British crowds.

Not only do I deplore the stupidities of our more militant football supporters, I am constantly amazed and saddened at their lack of originality, which is as if they had taken courses in demolition for backward children.

The offences have about them an inevitable ring: on the trains, break lights, slash seats, smash windows, wreck lavatories.

In this country, justly proud of its legions of skilled tradesmen, I don't know of a single supporters' club or splinter group who employ a plumber to dismantle lavatory pans or a joiner who could effectively strip the panelling, let alone an electrician to plunge the entire train into darkness, immobilize the heating and wire the carriage handles to dole out lethal, high-voltage shocks.

And the railways, who could fit carriage-locking devices which clicked into operation if anyone tampered with the light bulbs; who could cash in on the trend and issue limited-wreckage tickets entitling holders to any given combination of windows, seat cushions and improper uses of the alarm cord … the railways sit back, think and come up with the startlingly ineffective plan of limiting the supporters to so many per train.

When football fans get into the grounds, it is the same old story: throw toilet rolls, boo goal-kicks, run on to the pitch, jeer players and officials.

When did we last have a couple of hundred people faint in unison behind the goal as the penalty is awarded?

And what is wrong with an amplified recording of the National Anthem as the opposing winger races in to shoot?

If he does not stop and stand to attention, you can issue a writ for treason.

The powers of the land do little to help matters. If they catch an offender they haul him before a beak who fines him £6 17s. 9d. … which leaves the poor fellow with insufficient money to do anything but go to a football match, run on to the pitch and butt the referee in the behind.

It is clearly pointless to plead for better behaviour – but please, could people try to be a little more original?

If you must throw something, an avocado pear puts your case so very much more eloquently than a tomato.

I will give a prize of £5 for the most original form of protest.

A similar sum shall go to the sender of what I consider to be the best plan for combating crowd violence.

Please mark your envelopes PROTEST or COMBAT so that I know in which categories to judge your suggestions. Closing date Valentine's Day. Results next Friday.

* * *

Clement Freud's lifelong passion for horse racing inevitably led him to try his hand as a jockey, an intermittent career which began at Naas, Co. Kildare, in 1967 ...

The day I join the (lukewarm) tea set
Sun, 13 November 1967

ACCORDING TO ALL the omens, my race on Saturday boded little good. Photographer George Phillips and I met at 7.30, drove to Naas and walked the course, which is recognized in racing circles as 'a good thing to do'.

We found the track to be an undulating circuit of about a mile and five furlongs. The two mile one furlong start is six furlongs below the finishing post, runners having to negotiate a sharp uphill bend, gallop past the stands and move off left and downhill into the country.

A number of things augured ill. I collapsed twice during the thirteen-furlong walk and ran out on the third bend to find myself on the hurdles course. I pulled up with a painful stitch in my side. Also, we were followed by a large number of slow-moving birds which Phillips said were vultures.

The ground was very soft, there was a light drizzle and visibility was poor. I asked our photographer how this would affect pictures. He was non-committal, said he would have no difficulty in picking out the red cross on the ambulance van. We left in silence.

Back to Dublin for the morning papers. Saxon King, whose previous outing was in March when he came seventeenth of nineteen in yielding going, was quoted at around 10-1. A columnist mentioned that he was to be ridden by 'the well-known English gourmet'.

'Will you win?', asked the hotel porter.

'Absolutely bound to,' said I, which is the surefire way of putting people off having a bet.

The Nordic sauna bath on a Saturday morning is a haven of polite chit-chat, flavoured with overnight Guinness fumes. Into this well-bred atmosphere of decadence came I, to weigh myself with the option of partaking of their services.

Weight: 11st 10lb. I took up the option, sweated off 3½ lb in 90 minutes and left for my hotel. Throat parched, legs weak.

Looking up at the sombre sky, I promised to reform and go to Sunday school if six inches of rain waterlogged Naas before the 4 o'clock.

The rain stopped.

We drove to the course. I entered through the owners', trainers' and jockeys' gate and made for the weighing room. Helpful acquaintances procured for me one Michael – profession: jockey's valet.

I had supposed that such a man irons one's breeches, gives that last immaculate shine to the boots, eases a chap into his racing silks, hovers and asks whether 'that will be all, sir?' I was wrong.

A jockey's valet is a high-powered second-hand clothes man. He has a caseful of whips, a trunkful of boots, a sack of useful colours that look near enough to the real thing, and he carries enough saddlery to fit out the Household Cavalry.

He already 'did' most of the other jockeys and said he would gladly 'do' me when the time came.

There is one thing about participating in a race which I found totally unexpected … It is the cheapest way of having an afternoon out.

I went to Naas with four good things marked on my racecard and in the course of three hours of going in and out of the weighing room, watching the starts, worrying about tactics and paying an unnatural number of visits to the gents, I found myself with insufficient time to back any of the four horses – which were unplaced.

After the fifth race (my ride was in the seventh), I took the dressing room peg between Johnny Roe and Ernie Johnson, hung up my suit and put on my apparel: Michael's nylon tights, Ian Balding's breeches, Nobby Howard's boots, Con O'Keefe's colours. Only the butterflies in my stomach were my own.

The jockeys from the sixth race came in, a steward said: 'Three minutes, Mr Freud,' Michael gave me a whip and passed me a saddle, a pad, a martingale and my number cloth.

Clutching my gear, I sat on the scales. Weight: exactly 12st.

As I walked into the parade ring it occurred to me that I had not yet seen my mount. I looked round. Saxon King was a small-framed bay, about 16 hands, walking quietly and confidently in the late autumn sunshine.

A bell rang, 'Jockeys get mounted'. I had never had much faith in getting as far as this. I stood near the horse, a hand gripped my calf, I landed in the saddle and found my irons – eventually.

Toby Balding, who had generously given up his Saturday to fly to Ireland and give me moral support, led me out on to the course and took me over to the far rails.

Saxon King, entirely bored with our precautions to prevent him running away with me, gave Toby an understanding nod. I said 'all right' and we were off.

We hack-cantered past the stands and seven furlongs down to the start. In spite of Jimmy Lindley's advice, I'm afraid I probably looked more like a policeman, less 'pretty', but Saxon King behaved in the most exemplary fashion, let himself be steered like a moped and pulled up like a bath chair.

The start, they said, is the hard part. We walked round and round, our names were called and, with memories of Berkshire schooldays among the rhododendron bushes, I said 'Here, sir' when the starter got to mine.

He said: 'Put your tails against that rail and walk in slowly.' We moved forward, jockeying for positions. Twenty yards from the start, the tapes went up.

I broke about tenth, took the inside, got bumped back and bored my way through to take second place in the straight.

Crouching low, holding Saxon King's head, I galloped grimly and eased out to come past the leading horse. I expected a muttered threat and a whip aimed at my face. I received a friendly grin from Mr J.R. Cox, who said: 'Are you enjoying it now, Mr Freud?'

So that is how it is during a race. I heard the public address system giving the order – Saxon King by a length from Make Money.

Coming past the stands, turning into the country where I had walked so laboriously eight hours ago, I sat head down, feet down, hands down, hearing behind me the thud of hooves.

An unparalleled feeling of elation came over me and remained with me as Saxon King and I were overtaken by sixteen horses; the feeling returned more acutely as we made a last effort and beat one in the final furlong to finish sixteenth.

In the enclosure, I dismounted and Toby said: 'Take off his saddle and weigh in.'

'I can't,' I said. 'I am too weak.' Someone took off the saddle and I gripped it, walking on gelatine legs into the weighing room.

'Photo finish for places,' said a man, 'everyone weigh in.'

'Everyone' turned out not to include contestants for sixteenth place and I went back to my piece of bench in the dressing room.

Michael passed me a cup of tea. This was brackish, lukewarm and sugared; I don't take sugar. I can honestly say that that cup of tea was the best drink I have ever had.

* * *

Late in 1968 the retirement of a racehorse so distinguished that Freud had 'interviewed' him years earlier triggered one of his most wistful pieces:

Arkle the Wonder Horse will race no more
Sun, 9 October 1968

SO ARKLE, THE best-known Guinness-swiller of them all, will race no more. Personally I am glad, for it would have been ignominious at his age and eminence to have attempted to retread the golden road to Cheltenham.

I did not enjoy the sight of Sir Stanley Matthews spindling his aged frame along the wing at Stoke.

I was embarrassed at Sonny Liston's overweight displays in Stockholm.

It is a cause for rejoicing that where the human desire for gold and recognition tends to eschew the boundaries of prudence, horse sense prevailed.

Arkle will remain in our memories as a brave and brilliant steeplechaser who quit at the top.

Nevertheless, from this day on National Hunt racing will be the poorer – for Arkle was one of the few four-legged 'characters' to have graced our courses.

Of all the successful Thoroughbreds he was the least machine-like. He jumped brilliantly but intelligently and with enjoyment. His courage was indomitable, so that neither going nor distance seemed to alter the standard of his performance.

And he played unashamedly to his audience, keeping spectaculars for the stand customers and achieving good workmanlike jumps at the country fences.

Arkle never gave up. He ran to win and he seemed to know that Pat Taaffe was on his back, the Duchess of Westminster, Tom and Betty Dreaper were in the stands, and we the public were supporting him even at prohibitive odds-on prices. Arkle asked no more.

Few of us who backed him became rich, because he was always the short-priced good thing we knew him to be – but in all his steeplechasing days no one spoke of him unkindly or without admiration.

For this equine knight in a shining brown coat the competitive life is over, and while we shall miss his prowess and his humour I'm glad that his most humane of owners has taken this decision and saved him from possible humiliation.

Now he deserves all the good Irish clover hay that he will get, and if in years to come I see him again in the green fields of Co. Kildare,

I shall bring him a Guinness and remind him of the day we met when we were both starting in our chosen careers.

Perhaps one day Arkle will write something nice about me: no telling what that horse might do in retirement.

* * *

In October 1968 Freud covered the Olympic Games in Mexico City.

All day at the vault
Sun, **18 October 1968**

POLE VAULT DAY is when journalists tell their wives not to wait up. It starts around noon and goes on until the last man fails to jump over the bar for the third time by which hour the moon is up and the pubs are closed.

I am well aware that you at home are watching the Olympics nightly with your hot chocolate and then again with toast and marmalade in the morning. But unless television has changed radically since I left for Mexico last week you can have no idea of the sheer staying power required for this event.

When it comes to comparing medals there are always knockers who point out that a man can step up and heave a cannon ball into the back of beyond and receive the shot-put gold.

A basketball player on the other hand has to play six preliminary matches before he can play eight eliminators and qualify for the semi-final to get into the final for which, if he wins, he gets one twelfth of a medal.

The pole vault medal is one of the tougher ones. Yesterday fifteen men started limbering up and doing exploratory jumps of no more than five yards before it was for real. And then the bar was raised five centimetres at a time until there were nine competitors and the sun had gone down and Lillian Board had come second in the 400 metres final.

A Spaniard, a Russian, a German and a Frenchman failed and we were left with the 17-footers – two Germans, two Americans and a Greek.

They sat around in their track suits watching each other, seeing the bar toppled and replaced.

At 5m 40cm, we lost the Greek and one of the Americans.

A West German, an East German and Seagren of the United States all attempted 5-45.

The rules of the pole vault are that if there is a tie the winner is the one who has had fewest faults.

Thanks to Seagren having declined at 5-35 and with only one fault at 5-20 it was a question of gold for him if the two Germans joined him in being unable to push the already new world record up another five centimetres.

And so it was.

The final nine jumps took forty minutes. We discovered that Seagren is possibly the slowest stripper of a track suit of them all, while Schiprowski climbs in and out of his protective clothing like a veteran of the Folies Bergère.

The athletes jumped and cameras whirred and the bar toppled and two small American girls cheered like crazy because they realized that failures for others meant success for their heroes.

And when they had all done there came the final fanfare and the last of the day's half-dozen announcements that 'in addition to the traditional gold medal the winner has received an olive wreath by courtesy of the Greek Government.'

* * *

The box which has no magic
Sun, 21 April 1969

IT IS FIFTEEN years since I started watching sport for you, rather than for me.

In the course of this decade and a half in which I forsook Plymouth Argyle and a green-and-white scarf for going to where they told me to go with a Biro, I have seen people kick each other, hit each other and race each other in what is loosely called the four corners of the world – though many now believe the globe to be round.

During this time, I have been exceedingly conscious of competitors – not only fellow journalists, but the other media, like radio and television, which had it in their power to bring you more news more deeply, more quickly.

In Foinavon's National I stood in the press box at Aintree and was finally, with some shame, forced to ring my wife and ask her what had happened.

She asked: 'Where are you?'

I said: 'On the course, but you are in the sitting room …'

Had the World Cup final at Wembley taken place prior to the arrival of the all-seeing camera, England's third goal – the one that rebounded down from the crossbar – would have been 'definitely over the line' or 'quite certainly bounced well clear'.

Thanks to television, who had the whole thing in close-up and then replayed, we are left to writing: 'Wembley, Saturday. The all-important goal which you saw so clearly on your screens was 140 yards from where I sat … Nevertheless, I feel quite strongly …'

Last month, as a result of an injudicious piece of skiing, I broke my left ankle and have been confined to being a television viewer rather than one who dashes across the country to bring news of the goings-on at Merthyr Tydfil, Sedgefield, Dingwall and Punchestown.

Leaning back on the pillow, with leg up and pen at the ready, I have had five weeks among the ranks of armchair critics – those men and women whom I have long considered to have the best of all possible worlds.

I have watched race meetings in which I got a few well-informed phrases about each horse in the paddock, received regular betting flashes, witnessed which animal behaved and which misbehaved in the starting stalls – right up to which time I was able to ring my bookmaker and place a bet.

I saw the Boat Race from start to finish, with a first course of last year's race, a pudding of the last furlong shown all over again and also a most breathtakingly beautiful aerial shot of the two eights in the final mile.

I have heard the knowledgeable smug voice of Eddie Waring until I realized that Wigan is the capital of the world, though it is sometimes pronounced Salford.

And somehow I have not enjoyed it.

I know there are people who say that spectator sport is dead – a view that I myself have been close to airing. I know now, after my stretch of solitary, that there is no substitute for being there.

I backed Crozier quite heavily on Saturday. Had I been on the course at Newbury I would have had three minutes of reasonable cheerfulness before the photo-finish camera decided that Fortissimo had won.

As it was, I could see on the box that my choice had lost by a short head. Had I gone, I might have had a small gloat at beating the odds; telephonically, one gets starting prices.

I did not hear the good news until yesterday that the stewards, after an inquiry, had reversed the decision and made Crozier the winner and Fortissimo second.

During the 3.10 at Ayr the commentator said: 'Fearless Fred is down.' They said that about Highland Wedding at Aintree and the horse went on to win. On television I could actually see Fred and Terry Biddlecombe and my money go.

That is the trouble. You are more comfortable, but there is no magic.

And if you win, there is no real sense of achievement, like when you go to a bookmaker and he gets out his wad; or you go to the totalisator with a big winning ticket and the tote lady turns to her superior and says 'Check' or possibly 'Czech'.

Only then do you get a sense of elation, a feeling of being part of the event that no television programme, however skilfully presented, manages to induce.

I have never been one to run on to pitches or behave with anything less than maximum decorum. But I wonder whether the increase in hooliganism is not perhaps occasioned by people who have been cooped up too long in front of television sets and transistors and are celebrating with a bit of honest-to-goodness participation.

My plaster-of-paris comes off on 29 April. If you should be at Newmarket on Wednesday 30 April and come across a slightly limping, overweight, bearded man shouting home the winner of the Two Thousand Guineas, the odds are that it will be me.

You could, of course, stay at home and watch it on the box, but it won't be the same.

* * *

So who missed the big climax?
Sun, 14 July 1969

WHEN I AM old and my grandchildren come to visit me in the workhouse, one of my best stories is going to be about the Open Golf Championship won by Tony Jacklin.

'Are you sitting comfortably?', I shall say, leering at the little monsters, 'then I'll begin.'

'In those days they played the last round on a Saturday and as this was the first time for many years that a Briton was in the lead for the final eighteen holes the crowd was 10,000.'

'And you were there, grandad,' shout the little ones, having heard it all before.

'Yes, I was there. I was at your actual Royal Lytham and St Annes Golf Course – now a park for sludge-gulpers – on that proud eventful day. Not watching it on television but there, live, in person.

'I do not say that but for me the crowd would have been 9,999, but (at this point I wipe away a starting tear) I walked the course with Mr Jacklin – he was plain Mr Jacklin then – and when he reached the last green I was among the crowd.'

'Tell us what it was like,' they call.

'All right, I shall tell you. The eighteenth at Lytham was 389 yards long and around the green there was seating for 1,000. When the two players had hit their second shots the crowd surged forward so that in the centre square of fifty yards there were only the stewards and the marshals and the officials and the cameramen and a few selected journalists and the police and the police cadets and – I nearly forgot – the two golfers and their caddies.

'A 50-yard square affords 200 yards frontage and if we work on the basis of one person taking up 18 inches there were 400 people in the front row with an impeccable view, 400 in the second row with a good view and about 800 in the next two rows with a view.

'Add those watching from the clubhouse windows and the ones in the stand and nearly 3,000 people could see what was happening.'

'And where were you, grandad?', cry the chorus.

'At the back, I was. A perfect view of the boil on the neck of the man in front of me and when he moved a glimpse of a purple hat and the bottom of a toddler sitting on his father's shoulder.

'Suddenly there was a cheer and then a moan. "It's Jacklin in a bunker," came the whisper from the front. "Jacklin has fallen into a bunker," said a woman in the fifth row. "Jacklin can't get out." "Jacklin's ball is in the bunker." "Jacklin needs a wedge." "Jacklin needs a ferret." Rumour was rife.

'Behind me some men left and returned with collapsible chairs from the caterers' tent. More men left. The caterers' tent was stripped of chairs and then they got tables and stood on those.

'So there was the scene. In the stands people had waited seven hours for this magic moment. In front of them people standing on chairs and tables. Next, four rows of people standing, and in front of them fifty photographers and the people in the stands shouted "sit down" to the ones on the chairs, who shouted "shut up" back at them. Those standing shouted "sit down" to the photographers who were told to "keep quiet" by the officials who were asked to "keep still" by the golfers.

'Then a chair collapsed and there was a huge cheer and either Jacklin had putted out, or there were more New Zealanders in the crowd than I had supposed.'

'What happened then, grandad?'

'I took my chair back to the caterer's tent and a woman said it was all my fault.'

'What was your fault, grandad?'

'I don't know, but when I got home I read that Jacklin had won and England was a great nation once more.'

'It must have been lovely living in the good old days,' say the children, running off to a tooth-brushing competition.

When teeth brushing became the great spectator sport of the 21st century they redesigned bathrooms.

I wonder why the Ancient and Royal people never thought of that with golf courses.

* * *

A week of waiting for P-Q4
Financial Times, 8 July 1972

TO ATTEMPT TO be rational about an event as sensationally irrational as the world chess championship of 1972 is no easy matter. The fact is that for five long days officials, players, observers and prospective cash customers have been so bemused by the human tantrums and quirks of fate surrounding the match – or, to be strictly accurate, non-match – that the basic truth escapes them: a brace of players are about to compete for a prestigious title and a lot of money.

If you consider that in the course of seven days God created the universe, it is pretty shameful that in 80 per cent of that time the World Chess Federation, though urged on by a fair section of the world, was unable to bring two men around one chess board. Yet such was the case.

A number of reasons for this are clear: (1) Men of true genius find it difficult to deal with simple things in life – like being in a given place at a particular time. (2) If you offer people too high an incentive – like the £100,000 which the winner will take from the tournament – you can wreck anything. (3) Of all the people unqualified to run an international federation, ancient Grandmasters of chess would appear to be the least qualified.

There were also contributing factors, like the presence of so large a section of media men that players and officials behaved like prima donnas instead of people. Like the niceness of the Icelandic nationals who, had they acted with the violence of their forebears, would have had the men sitting down and pushing rooks at each other last Tuesday. Neither should one forget that in July in Reykjavik the sun never sets and the resultant sleeplessness makes for frayed nerves.

Only a week ago it all seemed to be going so well: Spassky was here in his hotel suite, training for the opening game, wowing the local ladies by his modesty and good looks ... and Fischer was playing hard-to-get in the Kennedy airport terminal, a ticket for Reykjavik securely in his pocket. (Those who deplored the American's tantrums should remember that it was just this capricious behaviour which had given the chess championship its especial appeal.)

When Fischer failed to show up at the solemn opening ceremony – and for a teetotaller to shun a bunfight at which champagne is the order of the day seems rational to me – the Russians shrugged their shoulders and said, 'That Fischer!' (which probably sounds better in Russian).

When he was still absent at the time appointed for the commencement of the first game last Sunday, the Soviet delegation had two alternatives: to claim the match by default and leave, or to grin and wait for the challenger to turn up.

They sat tight, and in doing so had the prize money doubled by Mr James Slater. To put it another way, their forebearance was rewarded by an extra £18,000 if their man lost, £30,000 if he won. They showed no gratitude, and on reflection – by the very nature of things – Mr Jim Slater is unlikely ever to be voted Soviet Man of the Year ... but when Fischer turned up they threatened to walk out.

The reasons, or rather the timing, of the intended walkout were obscure and irrational, having about them the insane logic of a man waiting for a delayed train to come into the station before complaining to the railways board that it is too late. 'Why did you not complain earlier?', we asked the Russians over and over again. 'How can we complain that he is late when we don't know when he will come?', they replied.

The Icelandic press, which had started by deploring Fischer's discourtesy, moved through aggravation to puzzled bemusement. The mood of the people moved similarly. 'It's crazy ... funny crazy,' said my taxi driver on Wednesday, adding on the following morning that it was 'pretty damn silly funny crazy.'

We all knew that while the Russians remained in Reykjavik there was every likelihood that the game would take place; and when their chess federation called a conference, only the pessimists and sensationalists expected details of their flight plans to Moscow.

This conference, intended to be grimly serious, was saved by the good humour of Grandmaster Geller – Spassky's second – whose expansive smiles did much to tone down the harsh words spoken by his interpreter. They wanted their pound of flesh, in the form of apologies and reassurances as to future behaviour ... and by the time they had finished the entire audience was prepared to give their blood; the Russians would have had to do no more than bring buckets and syringes.

With everyone rushing forward to write words like 'deeply conscious of the discourtesy and distress caused to the citizens of the USSR,' the last obstacle appeared to have been removed – yet there was more to come.

Spassky, previously so eager to grab the Queen's pawn and thrust it forward, was now reported to be 'temperamentally unprepared to play in the immediate future.' Once more we gathered to await a statement and this time we waited four hours to hear the time and place for the draw for colours. As the hands of the clock moved on inexorably it seemed ever more unlikely that our vigil was to be terminated with a simple phrase like '8 o'clock at the Exhibition Hall': but so it was.

The Exhibition Hall has not previously figured in the saga of the chess tournament, principally because exclusive photographic rights at the building were sold to Mr Chester Fox ... and with four dozen assorted cameramen gathered here to click lenses, it seemed unfair to hold meetings where they were unable to operate.

By 7.30pm it seemed as if the world had gathered outside the hall. Each arriving car, taxi and motorcycle combination was carefully scrutinized lest it contained champion or challenger. A carpet had been placed on the front steps and the two Icelandic stores in the lobby of the hall filled with airport-shop gifts and locally carved nasties were manned by eager women.

Spassky arrived at 7.54, his car swooping past the cameras to deposit him at a side door through which he raced into the building to be swallowed in a basement strongroom; and Fischer, making it at 8.01, came in by the back entrance and equally disappeared from sight. 'Is it war or chess?', a child asked his mother. A good question. We filed into the hall.

The journalists were lightly dressed for the warm Icelandic evening; photographers sat heavily overcoated with ominous bulges at the pockets, which people more suspicious than I might have thought to be forbidden cameras. The atmosphere was like that in a church, before a shotgun wedding.

At six minutes past eight a man appeared on the stage, an electronic sign requested SOGN, then SILENCE, and the official said: 'I am sorry, there will be a short delay.'

Short delays being a common feature of world chess championships, we leaned back to finish our pocket editions of *War and Peace*, raising our eyes now and then to note Mr Fox's lighting men crawl across the stage, take meter readings and line up camera angles.

At 8.32 SOGN-SILENCE flashed again, another man came on to the stage and we were informed that both players had arrived, the short delay being occasioned solely by 'preliminary discussions to the ceremony of drawing lots'.

On the stage behind the chess table there was a drape on which was painted a black knight, a few squares from a chess board, the legend *gens una sumus* ... the whole decorated by a drawing of what appeared to be a huge devious sardine-can opener.

The diligent reader may have noticed that in the course of the week we of the press have had only the odd fleeting glimpse of the players, while many of the citizens of Reykjavik no longer believe in their existence. Suddenly, at 8.46, they appeared on the stage, and to our amazement they were nice ordinary pleasant-looking soberly-dressed young men.

We had expected Fischer to come loping out of a corner on all fours, frothing at the mouth, bandages hiding the wounds from which surgeons had extracted his horns. He turned out to be a lean, gangling, engaging man wearing an uncontroversial green suit and matching tie.

Spassky, in flannels and sports jacket, gave a faintly self-conscious grin and without further preamble they sat in their respective chairs, testing them for comfort and height; the Russian leaning back to lend credence to his nickname Lazy Boris; the American straining forward as befits one who has dedicated his life to becoming the greatest uptightest practitioner of chess the world has known.

There does not seem a lot that can now go wrong. The hotel lobbies are as deserted as was Hamelin after the Pied Piper had gone, and if anyone wished to hold a press conference they would be hard pushed to find an audience.

The salmon fishing season is in full swing; a day's trout fishing licence costs 50p and trout are plentiful; until next Tuesday evening the chances of sensational news from the Icelandic capital seem mercifully remote.

* * *

Race against time for forty golden years
The Times, 28 October 1994

IT TOOK ME some years to take Roy of the Rovers seriously. When I first encountered him, Roy Race had joined the new school in Melchester, where his footballing ability soon gained him a place in the under-15s; his rival, Bert Beston, gave him and his pal, Blackie Gray, a hard time, but the pals won through; can't keep good men down.

Roy Race's end-of-term report praises his mathematics, 'especially algebra and trigonometry which he has shown an encouraging liking for'; in English language, he 'demonstrated the ability to eloquently transcribe his thoughts into poetry'. (Of form teacher Mr O'Shaughnessy, who splits infinitives and ends phrases with prepositions, we properly hear no more.)

The Tiger, price 3d, appeared every Tuesday and led with Roy of the Rovers. In issue No. 1, 11 September 1954, the local cup-tie stands at 0-0 (no record of the score at half-time) and, with his pals of the Milston Youth Club FC played to a standstill, Roy Race is the one man in the team who is tireless and on his toes. Could he score one before the final whistle? Silly question, really, and, unknown to

Roy, the game was being watched by a first division talent scout, Alf Leeds, who was in charge of the famous Melchester Rovers A team.

In December of that year, Roy and Blackie were playing in the A team and Roy quickly notched his first senior goal from a perfectly weighted pass by Blackie.

'Those two lads are working wonders ... it won't be long before they are both in Rovers' first team,' a man in the crowd thinks. He thought right. Melchester broke the bank to sign Arty Hedlow, for £10,000. Ben Galloway, the manager, said of his new signing: 'Playing alongside an international of Hedlow's character, young Roy will blossom into a player with a great future.'

Hedlow turned out to be an arrogant swine and was struck down by a mystery knee injury. He was out for the season. Melchester were knocked out of the sixth round of the FA Cup by 'lowly Storford United' (how lowly Storford got into the sixth round is not explained) and the slump continued with a 3-0 home defeat by Charnley Athletic.

In August 1956, Mr Galloway signed Pierre Dupont of Rochemont, the crack French side. Dupont put *le chat* amongst *les pigeons* at Melchester and Sam Higby, threatened by the Frenchman's presence, 'ensures that he will miss the start of the game.'

What persuaded me to read Roy as diligently as I read the Four Marys in *Bunty* was the arrival of Jumbo Trudgeon ... a man in whom I could believe, or, as form-teacher O'Shaughnessy would have said, 'a man I can believe in.'

The year was 1964. Rovers had had a fair time of it: League champions in 1957–8, 1959–60, 1962–3 and FA Cup winners twice in that time before taking the European Cup in 1963–4. Jumbo joined the Rovers in September and I can do no more than quote the Sandford match report:

'Key to Rovers' continuing confidence and success is new signing, at inside left, Lord D'arcy Plantagenet Trudgeon-Marclay, better known in the circles of royalty and society as "Jumbo" Trudgeon.

He has agreed to join Rovers on a no-pay, no-contract deal. A multi-millionaire landowner, Trudgeon has no need for seeking a living from football. He has quickly proved that he will not be a fish out of water; his second-half hat-trick against Sandford bodes many great things for the future.'

Now we were getting close to real football ... and in *Bunty* they countered with a character called the Honourable Harriet, who played hockey and was served Earl Grey tea and cucumber sandwiches on Meissen by her butler on the touchline at half-time.

Jumbo came when the team were in need of strengthening, for, on the pre-season tour of South America, Rovers had been kidnapped by local brigands, marched through the rain forests and made to play against a team of rebels; after reluctantly agreeing, they played 'and the final scoreline of 17-2 showed their undoubted superiority.'

Despite this ordeal, they managed to escape on horseback and arrive in Malagos City minutes before the kick-off, having had no sleep for 48 hours. Yet Rovers won. Roy Race, in the final seconds, scored with a scissors kick, and you can see the full back saying: '*Caramba*, it is there. Goal.'

After the first twenty years of fine fantasy, it then got a bit close to what went on elsewhere in the game; Roy is shot and they sign Sir Alf Ramsey as caretaker manager; they engage a man called 'superbrat'; Geoffrey Boycott is appointed chairman of Melchester; Roy marries; Roy has twins; they sign Emlyn Hughes and Bob Wilson; eight team members are killed by a terrorist bomb; an all-seat stadium is built; Roy sets new goal-scoring record, notching up his 436th goal.

And then Roy resigns as manager on Sky TV, Flash Gordin becomes manager, Roy is reinstated, crashes his helicopter, has his left foot amputated, becomes manager of AC Monza, his son Rocky becomes Roy of the Rovers mark II and throughout all those years nobody says 'damn' or 'bum', sniffs coke or goes bald; and

Melchester Rovers keep playing in red and yellow, which must infuriate their merchandizing department.

* * *

Memorable day when the boot was on the other foot
The Times, 5 December 1994

ONE OF THE dangers of writing about a specialist subject is that it causes unsuspecting citizens to confuse criticism with achievement … which is why, in December 1965, I played football for University College, London fourth XI on pitch No. 5 at Shenley, in Hertfordshire.

I had been guest speaker at the university's sports club dinner the previous evening: a chance remark, a jug of wine … and there I was the following afternoon wearing a blue shirt and my hosts' boots, which were soft, shallow and tongueless, leaving much of the heavy work to my socks – which were Plymouth Argyle coloured.

'We've put you on the left wing,' said the captain, swallowing. I explained that, from distant memories, such talent as I possessed was vested in my right foot. I was moved to the other flank.

After the kick off, which went to the left, I made my way in the direction of the opponents' goal, finding as I did so that the ground was very much bigger than it appears through the friendly windows of the press box. Eventually I got into the position demanded of the then-trendy W-plan and became involved in the action.

'Rowland,' shouted a man behind me. 'Roger,' shouted he. 'Laurence,' called another. 'To me,' I cried, received the ball firmly in my crotch and determined thereafter to take a less aggressive part in the proceedings. Though we were eleven and they ten, our numerical advantage was not to be a decisive factor.

I kept my position well. Indeed, it would have been hard to have done anything else with the breath coming out of me in short, painful gasps. My alternatives were smacking the ball with my green and white socks or maiming myself via a sharp blow with my sparsely covered toes. I used my instep until, at length, the cry 'to the right wing' was heard no more.

Nevertheless, the opposing full back, unable to believe that I was not part of some cunningly devilish plot, kept in close attendance and we became quite friendly, parting company only when the ball came our way.

After the first hour of the opening half, with progress becoming increasingly slow and painful, I remembered calling Mackay a coward, Greaves slow, Blanchflower past it ... and asked myself whether I had made sufficient allowances for the human element.

When Tambling, for instance, had failed to fasten onto a long ball, had I taken into account the strenuous upfield run he had made five minutes earlier? I headed a ball briefly and to no great effect and remembered Mel Charles ... whom I'd called unindustrious only the previous week; wondered what he might call me now.

I tackled a man, missed the ball, hacked him on the ankle and cannoned into him for good measure. A whistle blew sharply. The referee came striding towards me. In the happiest moment of the afternoon, I thought to myself: 'This is it; I am going to be sent off.'

I was not sent off.

Half-time came after two hours. I was given a segment of orange, refused it on the grounds that I was slimming (I had decided to start slimming soon after the kick-off) and spent the remainder of the afternoon running uphill.

'Right wing,' suddenly shouted a man on the touchline (to be fair, *the* man on the touchline). It was good advice; once more I had the ball and my friendly back had temporarily abandoned me. I was alone thirty yards from goal. I raced for the posts, the ball at my feet.

'Shoot,' cried the man; I shot.

With only the keeper to beat – as I remember writing on countless occasions – I sliced the ball off my sock towards the corner post. It had been – as I was fond of stating in print – a goal chance harder to miss than to take. On reflection, this was probably the most difficult thing I did that afternoon.

The only thing that cheered me, and this only retrospectively, was that I had once seen Kenneth Tynan act.

* * *

The mother of all freebies
The Times, 29 March 1996

ABOUT TWENTY YEARS ago I was one of a parliamentary delegation to Japan. When we arrived in Tokyo, a man from our Embassy briefed us: you are guests of the Nippon Government who will pay for everything – except overseas phone calls and drinks not taken with meals.

A colleague suggested we have dinner in the hotel restaurant and when the wine list was brought he said: 'Drinks with meals are on them, right?' I said yes.

He ordered a bottle of Lafite 1953. I was a newish MP, he a Conservative former minister. I was ashamed. He said I was being foolish: 'The more we cost them, the greater the respect they will have for us; you will learn.'

In the course of my five terms in Parliament (Heath, Wilson, Callaghan, Thatcher, Thatcher) no one ever offered me money to do anything dishonourable – Liberals were not considered sufficiently important to merit bribes – but I went on about a dozen 'freebies'; departed Westminster stocked with House of Commons gift-shop cufflinks and ashtrays and returned with expressions of our hosts' friendship, usually in the form of ashtrays and cufflinks. It was harmless and pointless. The reasoning was that the Togolese knew they would not be invited to visit Britain unless they invited us to come to Lomé. So we went – expenses paid except for drinks, laundry and overseas phone calls.

I still have a silvery lapel pin depicting the President of that largely forgotten country, where I hope they still cherish my cufflinks.

In Finland the House of Commons ties and scarves got us each a hunting knife, a tin of ptarmigan pâté, some cloudberry liqueur and a mounted street map of Helsinki.

They asked us to table an early day motion: that this House regrets the diminution of Scandinavian pulp imports.

Last Sunday I arrived in the United Arab Emirates as a guest of the committee of the Dubai World Cup: the richest horse race ever run, prize money $4 million.

I had been sent a Club Class ticket; on arrival there was a stretch limo to the hotel. In my room I found a letter welcoming me to the event, explaining that all phone calls, food and drink and laundry and dry cleaning were on them. Cars and buses would be available to and from racetrack and functions; enclosed was an enamelled silver badge, inscribed 'VIP Dubai World Cup', for my binoculars.

There was an invitation to dinner and a rock concert on Monday, to an *Arabian Nights* extravaganza in the desert on Tuesday, to the post-race banquet on Wednesday; and an embossed, multi-pocketed briefcase and a stunning heavy silk dishdash with embroidered skull cap and black braids in case I wanted to go native.

The next day they sent me a T-shirt, a hat, a leather cover for my passport, a handsome notebook and I nearly got a basket of fruit; that ended up in the room opposite.

With the exception of D. Skinner MP, who never goes on freebies, shuns the Commons tea room because it is subsidized and travels in standard carriages on his first-class rail pass, the *modus vivendi* of most of my political and journalistic colleagues embraces an element of prostitution. The hack whose response to the welcoming letter in Dubai was to ring his wife and ask her to Federal Express the washing, cash on delivery, was an extreme case but I have no right to criticize.

'We've already established what you are; now we're haggling about the price,' sums it up.

The first running of the Dubai World Cup was a brilliant affair and the hundreds of guests who had been so lavishly softened up were now served molluscs and crustaceans, smoked fish and baked meats, puddings and *grande marque* champagne (if one were hellbent on criticism, the caviare was not up to much).

Had it rained, had there been a false start, a stewards' inquiry resulting in disqualification, a riot, fatality, outbreak of camel disease, or beriberi, not one of us would have had the bad manners to bring such a matter to the attention of our readers. Damn it, there has to be a degree of give and take – and we had taken.

Skinner – who rather enjoys racing – would have accepted none of the proffered gifts, paid his own fares and found fault with nothing, for it was wonderfully well done and the Sheikh's thinking was probably on the lines of 'I shall organize the richest race in the world; let it be in front of the most cosseted hacks and VIPs ever assembled.'

What can one say? Long live Sheikh Mohammed. May his people prosper. I had a good time, and got my suit dry-cleaned. It was the mother of freeloads. Thank you. I still feel a bit uneasy

* * *

In August 1998 Clement Freud started writing for the Racing Post, *and was at his computer composing his weekly column for that paper when he collapsed and died on 15 April 2009. These pieces – a collection of which was published soon after his death under the title* Freud on Course – *regularly reflected his great love of jokes, and for the last two years of his life his column on Saturday mornings was the first port of call for large numbers of readers, desperate to see Freud's weekly joke.*

Horses and racing – what else would you expect?
Racing Post, 20 December 2008

THIS MAN CAME up to me at Sandown and asked whether I might consider making the odd mention of horses or racing or breeding or betting in my weekly 'joke column'. I was hurt; however, it being the season of goodwill to all men, it occurred to me that he might have a point and I will try to do better.

A mortician who liked going to evening all-weather meetings at Wolverhampton and Great Leighs was working late one night, as he prepared for cremation the body of an owner called Schwartz who had had a passion for jump racing, especially favouring Huntingdon, Fakenham and Towcester, where he had once famously landed a double at very long odds.

Looking down at the cadaver, he could not help noticing that Mr Schwartz had the most amazingly massive member, too rare a thing to push into the oven, so he cut it off, wrapped it in foil and placed it in his briefcase. When he got home, he told his wife that he had something remarkable she might enjoy having a look at, unzipped his bag, took out the huge willy and put it on the table.

'My God,' she said. 'Schwartz is dead.'

One afternoon, in a field of sugar beet at Walkington, which is just west of Beverley racecourse, the BHA official deputed to deal with the track's marketing and publicity was walking his Labrador and wondering why nothing exciting ever happened in his life other than the time an amateur jockey had weighed in 7lb light and been disqualified from fourth place. He looked up to see a hot-air balloon hovering some 10m above him.

The pilot leaned out of his basket and shouted: 'Excuse me, can you tell me where I am?'

The man below shouted back: 'You are in a hot-air balloon hovering 30 feet above this field.'

'You must work in IT,' said the balloonist. 'I do,' replied the man. 'How did you know?'

The balloonist said: 'Everything you tell me is technically correct but of not the slightest use to anyone.'

The man said: 'You must work in management.' The balloonist answered: 'Yes, how did you know?'

'You don't know where you are nor where you are going but expect me to be able to help; and you are in the same position as you were when we met but now it's my fault.'

This young man had been involved in a dead-heat on his second-ever ride: a hunter chase at Exeter over three miles on heavy going. He was dating a girl who rode out for a well-known trainer – who asked me not to mention his name lest it gave his yard a bad name, but told me he thinks he probably has the winner of the King George.

The young couple got on really well, and one day she asked him to come to her home, meet her parents over dinner, and go to bed together. He was very excited.

Being a virgin, apart from a single nocturnal grope in the stable lads' hostel at Taunton, he went to a local chemist to buy condoms and seek advice, coming away with interesting knowledge and a family pack of Durex.

On the appointed evening, his girlfriend met him at the door and took him into the dining-room where her parents were waiting. The boy kept his head bowed, asked if it would be all right if he said grace, and remained in the position of prayer for a very long time. After ten minutes, the girl whispered to him: 'I didn't know you were so religious.'

He whispered back: 'I didn't know your father was a pharmacist.'

In ancient Greece, Socrates was widely lauded for his wisdom.

One day, the great philosopher came upon an acquaintance outside the local dice parlour who ran up to him excitedly and said: 'Socrates, do you know what I just heard about one of your students?'

'Wait a moment,' Socrates replied. 'Before you tell me, I'd like you to pass a little test – the test of "three". The first test is Truth. Have you made absolutely sure that what you are about to tell me is true?'

'No,' the man said, 'actually I just heard about it.'

'All right,' said Socrates. 'So you don't really know if it's true or not. Now let's try the second test, the test of Goodness. Is what you are about to tell me about my student something good?'

'No, on the contrary ...'

'So,' Socrates said, 'you want to tell me something bad about him although you're not sure it's true?'

The man shrugged, a little embarrassed. Socrates continued: 'You may still pass though, because there is a third test – the filter of Usefulness. Is what you want to tell me about my student going to be useful to me?'

'No, not really ...'

'Well,' concluded Socrates, 'if what you want to tell me is neither True nor Good nor even Useful, why tell it to me at all?'

The man was defeated and ashamed. This is the reason Socrates was a great philosopher and held in such high esteem. It also explains why he never found out that Plato was banging his wife.

No jokes this week, though a happy Christmas to all my readers.

6
FREUD'S
SUMMER SEASON

'I ask for a Pimm. The waitress says: "Pimm's?"
I say one at a time.'

In 1996 Clement Freud wrote for The Times *a six-part series covering the major sporting events which took place in one month between 18 June and 18 July. From Royal Ascot (an occasion he loved) through the Lord's Test, Wimbledon, the Henley Royal Regatta and the British Grand Prix at Silverstone to the Open Golf (an occasion which he did not love), the summer season provided perfect ammunition for his unrivalled power of oblique observation.*

Fashion tips favourite among the Ascot clothes horses
The Times, **19 June 1996**

THEY WORK TO different criteria, those long-legged, mid-skirted, designer-hatted, kid-gloved women in swirls of silk, muslin and taffeta, from whose pastel-coloured faces comes undemanding conversation, the purpose of which is to appear involved while projecting their good side to passing cameramen. Here is a preview of Oxfam's 1998 collection.

This is the start of the season: the first day of Royal Ascot. Tell them that you have positive information of the well-being of Wall Street in the St James's Palace Stakes and they look at you in bewilderment. The fact that there is racing is accepted but not critical to the day's entertainment.

Clothes matter; companions are important; as is to whom you talk and who sees you talking to them. Designers matter: Thomasz Starzewski is the most glittering of these, therefore matters most. Hats, if at all possible, should be by Philip Treacy or Graham Smith – this season's 'in' milliners according to the social editor of *Harpers & Queen*, the 'in' social editor.

There are two Cherry Blossom shoe cleaners, one male, the other female, so that a woman may have a shine without the fear of a member of the opposite sex glancing up her thigh; something not quite right about shoe cleaners at a party such as this. Damn it, we shone our shoes before we left home and gave them an extra polish on the backs of our trousers waiting to enter the golden gates guarded by bowler-hatted attendants. Is it imagination or have their faces softened? They now look as if they did not really despise us.

A hairdresser, here to keep his eye on a couple of his clients, tells me that the women are in a quandary: Thursday, Ladies' Day, is when you must be at your best, but on Thursday the competition is seriously fierce, so one or two of them have gone for it today. You can please some of the photographers some of the time. Women shimmy out of the enclosure (no cameras allowed inside) to provide photo opportunities on the way to the paddock and back. Ideally, companions should be unobtrusively morning-suited and be recognized ... but not famous, else the companion might hog the picture.

The place radiates perfection: the lawns are as smooth and as green as a snooker table; the salmon is fresh, the champagne cold, the sandwiches generously filled; and this year they expect a quarter of a million racegoers. I am proud to be four of them, for I go each day. Most of us will lose our money and run up substantial dry-cleaning bills and be forced to have our top hats re-brushed ... and consider it all a small price to pay.

Her Majesty and the horse-drawn coaches containing family and friends reach the mile post soon after 2pm and you can hear the ooh-aaahhh as racegoers see first Her Majesty and the Queen Mother.

'Would you call that magenta?', asks a woman with a notepad. Not me.

A colleague offers me 25-1 against the second coach overtaking the one in the lead. I decline, possibly the only correct decision I made all afternoon. For the first race, the prophets of doom, they who said: 'No one will come, not when England are playing Holland at Wembley before we can get home to our television sets,' were forced to swallow their words. The racecourse had looked about only half full yet, when the horses appeared, the terraces were a dense forest of black and grey toppers rising like fungi from the ocean of millinery.

Favourites tend not to win at Royal Ascot. Last year Nicolotte took the first race at 16-1 and here in the 2.30 was Charnwood Forest at odds-on. We looked for something to beat it, we who knew a thing or two. Charnwood Forest won. As it was going to be one of those days, we backed the next favourite, found there were joint favourites, backed them both. Neither finished in the first three. Nobody looked sad or dejected, the way they do when they lose at real race meetings.

Time for a glass of champagne; time for a plate of lobster. 'What do you mean, can we afford it?', asked a woman in a hat that made it impossible for her to see, never mind eat, a crustacean. 'You've just lost Olivia's dress allowance for the year.'

In the building that houses private boxes, 260 of them, each bulging with festive humanity, there is a Tote Hall. The better dressed the punter, the smaller seems to be the bet. Between races is the time for moving around: winner's enclosure to paddock to seafood bar to a call on friends in the car park who have hired a Swedish caterer to prepare open sandwiches served from the boot. The day is warm, but not unbearably so; men's stiff collars are becoming limp, women glow becomingly, an outsider wins the third race and another takes the fourth.

As Ratty nearly said: 'Believe me ... there is nothing, absolutely nothing half so much worth doing as messing about in Ascot.' Today I shall go back and put my money on Donna Viola in the Hunt Cup; you would be foolish to take my advice.

* * *

But Donna Viola finished fourth in the Royal Hunt Cup at 20-1, providing a good return for each-way backers. Two days later the second event of Freud's summer season found him closer to home.

* * *

Seasonal run finds game Bird down the pecking order
The Times, 21 June 1996

THE WEATHER WAS more Burberry than shot silk; in the hospitality boxes they put away the champagne and served turtle soup laced with Madeira. In the way of fashion, most of us wore what everyone else wears: a light suit, white shirt, MCC tie and the women dressed unprovocatively. Women at Lord's are there to be heard rather than seen. Women come along to drive their men home when the day is done. Women are not allowed to enter the pavilion.

As part of 'The Season', the Lord's Test is a minor event. At Ascot there is a race every thirty-five minutes and you can pace yourself: socialize, stop and bet and watch, then carry on with the initial activity. The folk who go to cricket either take in every detail and discourage conversation or go for diverse reasons: political preferment, knees-up in the Tavern bar or the discreet lure of corporate hospitality.

Pity about the weather. Unlike race meetings that get abandoned, invitation cards for lunch at Lord's include the words: 'In the event of rain, luncheon and tea will be served.'

There was no rain, just slight problems with the light, which delayed the start, but, at half-past eleven, the teams came out and, as this was umpire Bird's last Test match, the players made a guard of honour and Bird passed through it waving to the crowd with one hand, using the other to mop his eyes with a white handkerchief.

In the box of the chairman of the Test and County Cricket Board we were served coffee by a Portuguese waiter; cunning move that – had he been a native of Britain he might have been tempted to ignore us and watch the action on the field of play ... though not sorely tempted.

Before luncheon, there is much intermingling of guests among the boxes; the Lords Parkinson and Archer were in that of the president. Sir Garfield Sobers in one two boxes along. Lord Rix held court in the passage outside. Much of the talk is about times long ago, also 'Whatever happened to so and so?' and 'I didn't see you at Walter's funeral' and 'Is that Charles's new wife?'

There is a buzz. 'It is the colonel,' and people come and shake the colonel's hand: the president, the chairman, the chairman of the selectors. A waitress asks whether I would like a drink. Of course I would like a drink. As no one else is drinking, I say no. Then I see a man with a walrus moustache and an I Zingari tie, sipping from a glass that might contain Wincarnis or elderberry wine, possibly port.

I ask for a Pimm.

The waitress says: 'Pimm's?'

I say one at a time.

There is a loud appeal after the fifth ball of the innings. Umpire Bird, whose day this was meant to be, puts up his finger and Atherton walks.

'Fancy Dickie giving out skipper in first over,' a Marlburian says.

'It would have been because his leg was in front of his wicket,' his wife says.

After half an hour, England have scored four runs. 'What do you think?', I asked the chairman.

'We could do with more runs.' We get more runs, though not too many. At lunch we are nicely into double figures and the Indian sitting next to me asks whether I think we are not having beef because of BSE or because of his country's religious principles. I say, 'Some of each'.

We eat pork. There is a vegetarian option. Then mango bavarois served with a compote of berries. Mangoes at Lord's, clearly to make the Indians feel good; then cheese which has the opposite effect.

At my table, a Wykehamist is talking about postwar Somerset captains. We serve each other names like ping-pong balls and return them with *élan*. Mitchell-Innes, Meyer, Brocklehurst, Tremlett, Atkinson, Stephenson …

Stewart is clean bowled. As he walks back to the pavilion, the Marlburian said: 'Bird could have called a no-ball.' It might be Bird's game but it does not appear to be England's. Hussain is out, then Hick, then Irani. A man is introduced to me as secretary of the Italian Cricket Association. Soon to receive official recognition.

The Portuguese waiter starts to serve afternoon tea; whatever happens on the pitch, none of us in the boxes will come to much harm.

* * *

Lobster eaten, net-cord judges beaten
The Times, **25 June 1996**

WHEN PEOPLE ASKED me what I would do – 'you know, when you pack it in' – I used to tell them that I fancied becoming a tennis net-cord judge. For this high office you require neither sight nor hearing; just sufficient feeling in one digit to notice a tremor. Then do you shout 'let'. It is all an elderly chap wants, a central position and the opportunity to be heard every now and again.

What was a serious blow, this Wimbledon, is that my chosen calling is no more. Like the dodo, net-cord judges are extinct. High tech has taken over. A magic eye, laser beam, aluminium chip – I know not what, but, in some dank, dark basement where no mention of the men shall be heard, they sit considering a Luddite rising. It will not come.

The sun shone on the opening day of Wimbledon 1996, as neatly organized a military operation as one could encounter. Queue here for strawberries, there for Pimm's; the new No. 1 Court which looks like a Roman arena will, in God's good time – probably next year – seat 11,000 people; *son et lumière* tells how it will be and there are architects' plans and a full complement of television screens showing graphs and statistics.

Sampras is on Centre Court; Becker on No. 1. A queue of groupies sit outside a door from which, rumour has it, Agassi will appear when the match on No. 2 Court ends.

I lunch in the Wingfield restaurant; lobster, almost certainly killed in accordance with RSPCA recommendations. Then black and white chocolate mousse, which I eat looking at the purple and green theme of the All England Club, compared to which the MCC is dangerously liberal.

Look where you will at Wimbledon and something is going on. The smell of hot-dogs, which are called Dutchees, permeates the air; there is the opportunity to buy sweets, described as bonbons.

An announcement asking people interested in questioning Mr Radulescu to go to the interview suite comes over the public address system. I buy an ice-cream. Three naval cadets, wearing hats respectively inscribed *HMS* this, that and the other, go briskly about their business.

On No. 14 Court, they are cheering Jeremy Bates. I ask a girl to tell me why.

Well, she says, he has lost 6-2, 6-3, 6-4, so he was getting better all the time and 'he gave us a lovely wave as he left the court.' Five girls, each carrying a card bearing a letter to complete the word 'Bates', trail off, their duty done.

On the adjacent court, two Amazons are playing long rallies. The marker board identifies them as Miss Makarova and Miss Studenikova; I ask a security man which is which. He asks me whether it matters.

He says: 'Have you seen Sampras?'

I tell him that I saw him last year, and that Becker is going to win Wimbledon; the man who works for Radio Ward, a hospitals broadcasting service, who looks as if he knows what it is about, told me.

A cushion shop sells its wares at £5; not only do you get a soft seat but a couple of inches of extra elevation. At the back of Centre Court is a notice stating: 'Some seats are behind pillars and these are reduced in price.'

In the press room, which is long and thin and has windows overlooking many courts, an engineer is repairing the Coca-Cola dispenser. Nothing serious. At the desk in front of me, a Japanese journalist chokes on a salt and vinegar crisp; nothing serious there, either.

Chang loses. In his recorded television interview, a hack asks: 'Where did it go wrong?' Chang is a deeply religious man; he tells the journalist more politely than I would have done. Time for tea.

On my way to the strawberry room, I pass a door marked International Commentary Position and assume one: bend forward, hands cupped to my mouth, left foot raised. A naval cadet wearing an *HMS Nelson* hat asks whether I am feeling all right. During tea, possibly because I was wearing my MCC tie, a man comes to inquire what is happening at Lord's. I tell him that I now think we are not going to lose.

He asks: 'Who is we?' Back to the action.

They do not dress very well at Wimbledon, except for those in the royal box, and the members of the All England Club. These men wear nicely pressed trousers, handsome blazers, purple and green ties and are of an age, of a size, all with heads of hair: the sort of people who, when I was an MP, steadily displayed posters bearing the name of my opponent in their windows.

* * *

Young blades' fowl deed
gives rowers food for thought
The Times, 4 July 1996

HAD MY HAIR been long, my coat ribboned, collar winged, cravat pink, trousers white, boots made of buckskin, with a boater upon my head, buttonhole in my lapel, striped umbrella in my hand – no one would have given me a second glance.

As it was, hatless, wearing dark trousers and a mackintosh jacket, they looked at me with interest: one of an uncommon species seldom encountered at Henley, but they have better things to do than discuss strangers. There was the luncheon marquee, the tea tent, and the club tents; the Pimm's enclosure, a blue-and-white tented village where strawberries were *de rigueur* and the conversations centred on 'What have you done since last year?'

Henley man – also Henley woman, who is part proud mum, part acquisitive sister, and occasionally uncomplaining wife of plumed ex-rower – have a rotten time of it for 361 days a year. This is their time; no self-respecting people-watcher should miss the Royal Regatta.

Sadly, the heavens served up a day to challenge the sartorially ambitious. An overcast sky sent down rain that dimmed the gloss of the finery, made limp the starch, and reduced boaters to become vessels best suited to the Irish delicacy 'soup-in-a-basket'.

At the end of the lawns which provide opportunity for the peacock strut and the compulsory conversation opener, 'How has it been?', punctuated by short silences to show respect for those fallen off the perch since last year, is a river. The river. Rowing boats pass by at five-minute intervals; announcements interrupt the well-bred buzz to inform us of who is who, rowing on which bank, for which trophy, at which point in the race they find themselves; also the number of strokes per minute and how far ahead of one is the other.

The rowing is crucial to some, significant to many and irrelevant to about half the spectators.

The elders of the kirk, bedecked with panama hats and clinking metal badges as they go hither and thence, have done a difficult job with skill born of experience; the worse the reason for attendance, the further from the action are you placed.

Thus, the Stewards' Enclosure is filled with knowledgeable folk who can tell navy blue and white from garter blue and white, call, 'Row hard, Ridley' at the correct time, and are, therefore, placed a hundred yards from the finish. For this privilege they must wear jackets and ties, may not bring in glasses or hampers and are discouraged from breaking wind.

Half a furlong on the wrong side is the Members': wear what you will, slosh around pints of ale, shout. Further down are hospitality areas for corporate entertainers – many of whom manage to walk in unaided, though few emerge of their own accord.

The problems of rowing as a spectator sport are considerable. Rewards come from honest endeavour and fitness and balance and strength.

Cricketers manifest charisma by huge scores, taking many wickets, reverse sweeps, lightning stumpings, googlies and chinamen, remarkable catches in the covers.

Rowers row: that is the extent of it. In, out; backwards, forwards; speed it up, slow it down, watch the boat behind, or if in arrears notice by the size of the puddles in the water how far behind you are.

Unless they win several Olympic gold medals or write film scripts about the University Race, rowers' names are not known; they fail to be selected for *Question of Sport*, let alone *This Is Your Life*.

But appearance at Henley does guarantee them a lifetime of Royal Regattas where they can dress up and reminisce and tell all over again of how it was when they experienced their finest hour. Henley, just so long as you are a Henley person, is the best fun there is.

I thought carefully about the advisability of beginning, or ending, my article with the event I am about to relate. I also considered using the incident for a separate front-page piece, headlined King Kills Duck … decided this was not the way we do things in broadsheet newspapers.

The time was 3.45pm. King's School, Canterbury, were rowing against Canford in the Princess Elizabeth Cup. Canford were a canvas up at the quarter-mile, striking 34 to KSC's 36. The lead stretched to half a length, diminished at the three-quarter-mile post when they came into sight of us in the Stewards' Enclosure.

In front of them, a family of ducks swam contentedly on the Buckinghamshire side of the river, and as the people around me shouted, 'Row for home, Kings', one of their men – it would be invidious, tabloid-like, to name the culprit – decapitated the duck swimming in fourth position.

It could be a watershed. Next year, rowing may well be recognized as the cruel sport it is, picketed by RSPCA militants. This could bring new blood into the event which may not be altogether unwelcome; alternatively there could be roast duck for lunch tomorrow in the Leander Club tent.

* * *

Pit stops dedicated to provide refuelling for the inner man
The Times, 15 July 1996

VIETNAM VETERANS WOULD have felt at home; the sky was occupied by an unending parade of helicopters, entry to where you wanted to go was blocked by fences topped with barbed wire and weary, ill-dressed people shuffled along bearing heavy polystyrene boxes. Ever and anon furtive men sidled up to ask: 'Who wants a ticket?' Which probably meant something more sinister.

Security is absolute: hung around my neck is a complicated plastic postcard-sized identity document intended to enable holders to enter the assembly area. A footbridge across the track to the paddock is like an obstacle on an assault course: negotiate a passage between posts, mount the steep staircase, crawl beneath the tarpaulin, race along a narrow straight before commencing the descent. Then, when you think you have arrived, comes the ultimate electronic entry procedure to the inner sanctum. This requires a sweep of your card which causes a camera to show the enemy that you are who you are, also how you are and more.

My card is rejected. I take another sweep, wait and I am told to try another machine. One of the security men says Fiat's Signor Agnelli spent fifteen minutes getting his card accepted. I sweep the other machine, wait: a light flashes recognition and punches up my blood type, hat size, fat-to-muscle ratio. I am in. (Agnelli once told me: in any successful company there must be an uneven number of directors and three is too many.)

Behind the pits is a street of huge trailers in some of which the teams live and work and eat and are massaged; others are hospitality vans with tables and chairs and fruit and coffee in which folk with my sort of high documentation can obtain sustenance. It is probably cheaper to feed anyone who comes along than put into place a screening system for guests. Comrade Oliver Holt of this newspaper says Ford's is best. I take a glass of fresh orange juice and a Danish pastry from the Sauber facility, a slice of bread and some Dolcelatte from Ferrari and join my colleague for a modest fried egg and bacon.

I am wearing the wrong clothes: no one mistakes me for a racing driver because my name is not embroidered on my shirt and I wear no badges on my sleeves or cap; my shoes are black leather instead of white canvas. Nevertheless a kindly man invites me into the pits and introduces me to both Ukyo Katayama and Mika Salo, whose Mild Seven badges have been unstitched to make way for the altogether more acceptable Tyrrell label.

The Tyrrell drivers are starting from positions 12 and 14 on the grid – disappointing. Salo is hugely talented, considered to have a bright future. We talk of Helsinki and the affection accorded all who carry white crash helmets with their names printed thereon. Salo says he gets a lot of affection even without that aid.

Katayama goes off to have a massage. The Tyrrell man explains that it is the team's ambition this year to outperform the second division outfits (he does not call them 'second division'): Ligier, Arrows, Sauber, Jordan and Minardi. I wish him well. This is a team after my own heart and I would become a Tyrrell fan if supporting Plymouth Argyle did not take up so much of my time.

Lunch is sensational. Perhaps that should be lunch are sensational. McLaren's trailer has a man with a face like Alain Prost and the body of a flat-race jockey standing at the door.

It is Prost. He is consultant to McLaren-Mercedes and I ask him about the relative merits of the two potato salads: one dressed with dill vinaigrette, the other covered in mayonnaise. The ex-champion has no views so I try some of each with a bottle of Bavarian beer and adjourn to ice-cream in the Williams trailer, coffee with Footwork, a bag of Walkers barbecue crisps in the press enclosure.

There is a regrettable lack of bimbos at the grand prix. Apparently teams discovered that it was, how shall we put this, more cost-effective to distribute tickets to sponsors than give them to underclad girls who always ended up in the mechanics' arms.

As we approach the off there is an upsurge in activity: television teams, officials, stewards and engineers race along the pit lane with the impedimenta of Formula One cars: gas cylinders, bottle openers, widgets, spare cufflinks.

The drivers do their positioning lap, line up, start.

Oh, the times I have sat in front of my television watching it all, then watching it again in slow motion. Now it is the real thing. I am there, standing 100 metres from Hill on pole in his Williams. The red lights go out and in the course of two seconds I have swivelled 180 degrees and seen, well, twenty cars coming at me and racing out of sight, then 80-odd seconds later coming back and affording us spectators rather less time to notice anything – except the extraordinary noise that sounds like the passing of a zillion angry bees.

* * *

Welcoming the 19th hole with Open arms
The Times, 19 July 1996

I WOULD LIKE to recommend Ansdell and Fairhaven station. It is an uncomplicated railway terminal boasting but a single platform at which the train stops on its way south to where Albert was eaten by the lion; a quarter of an hour later the three-carriage diesel returns from whence it came – Preston.

The northeastern exit of Ansdell and Fairhaven station is an excellent place to be, especially if you have goodish eyesight or own binoculars. It is adjacent to the 8th green and overlooks the short 9th of Royal Lytham and St Annes. A man could stand there and get a pretty adequate idea of what goes on without the hassle of buying tickets, displaying badges and waiting for people empowered to control the ebb and flow of humanity to direct them hither and hence. It was from this vantage point that I observed three men I did not know hit balls I could not see to a green that was just out of vision … but by the applause accorded one player, the ooohs that met the others and the body language of all participants I followed proceedings with considerable enjoyment in the company of folk who were making a day of it there.

'Should work harder. Freud favours the easy way,' schoolmaster Rotherham wrote in my report many years ago. Recalling this harsh assessment of my industry, I summoned the energy to make my way along neat suburban roads to the clubhouse and media centre. Once arrived, I followed the Open Championship as the organizers intended. Once again I have failed sartorially. My trousers were long when the fashion is to wear shorts, my shirt was a primary colour, long-sleeved and tailored while all around wore T-shirts in pastel shades, and I had neither panama hat nor spiked shoes.

There are a number of ways of watching championship golf:

You can occupy a seat in a stand surrounding a particular green and become hugely knowledgeable on, say, the short 5th. Take it as your subject on *Mastermind*, read about who did what, when, at that location in the eight previous Lytham Opens. It is a minimalist pursuit, the half-acre in your field of vision confines pleasure, though in the distance is the scoreboard which tells you of players' progress around the course.

Or you can select a threesome and follow them on their four-and-a-half hour peregrination, learn their strengths and weaknesses and admire the officials who hold up 'Quiet' and 'Stand still' signs. I expect they go home and tell their families they are 'running the Open'.

Refreshment points are dotted around the course: very ordinary cold fizzy drinks. Obvious food from the consumption of which people dissuade you. Egg and sausage sandwiches, really thin white wine, heavy hog-roast baps unsuited to temperatures in the eighties.

At around noon I disengaged myself from the marching crowd, many of whom wore Senior Citizen labels in their lapels; this is downright cruel, as if you could not tell by looking at us.

I sit down overlooking the 18th green, sit next to a man with so immaculately creased red trousers that he hovers to preserve their sharpness. The 18th is 414 yards. In the distance you see three huddles of player-and-caddie lining up second shots and three balls land on the green: plop, plop, plop; we applaud, applaud, applaud.

The players approach the green, Faldo, Zoeller, Allenby, and putt to obtain respectively birdie, bogey, par. Fifteen minutes later Faldo appears in the media centre for his interview. 'Talk us through the highs and lows of your round', his inquisitor said.

'The first I pulled a three-iron, had a good save on three flying a five-iron; six I came up short, good pitch; good save on 13, holed from 15 feet and birdied the last; pleased to have played the last nine in three under.' Faldo speaks in a monotone, told a questioner that teeing off at 7.30am presented no problem; he got up at 5am. Another got the message that it was great to have so many people supporting him, shouting happy birthday. There was no smile.

As a performance it was entirely dull and patronizing to boot. Faldo manifests neither fluency nor warmth; district surveyors' reports at housing committee meetings are more fun to witness. Were he less than staggeringly brilliant, he would have few fans.

Of course, it is not over until the fat lady sings and she has yet to approach the piano. By Sunday evening, when the winner walks up the final fairway to the whispers of 'He's the man', some 200,000 spectators will have been to Royal Lytham. With the exception of those getting paralytic in the sponsors' tents, watching the event on television, I envy them hardly at all.

7
FREUD'S
FUN AND GAMES

'All went well until we reached 2,000ft when there was a sharp noise, a yellow lever sprang from its housing and we realized that our time had come, thought about all those years, some of which had been good.'

Between 1993 and 1995 Clement Freud wrote a regular series in The Times *which chronicled the quirky goings-on of some of the less trodden sporting byways.*

Cast adrift in the skies above Hampshire
The Times, **30 July 1993**

AT FIRST SIGHT, it looked like an exceptionally successful Liberal election meeting: more than 200 well-behaved people in a large hall listening attentively to a commonplace speaker. On closer examination, the audience was a bit young and masculine for a political assemblage and on the platform, instead of pictures of our Paddy, was an aerial map of Basingstoke – looking no prettier than it does from the ground.

The word 'task' was heavily in the air, followed by place names: Fovant, Salisbury, Wylye, Cricklade, and our guide explained that task means route. This was a briefing session for the day's heat of the National Gliding Championships.

We had been invited to attend a day at the championships and be taken up by an instructor in order to get the feel of gliding. As ever uncertain about how to dress, we decided on dark trousers, a silk shirt (weight is important and we already weigh nearly 100kg, which is over 15st in old money) and a blazer. Jeans, jersey and a document case would have made us indistinguishable from contestants.

GEC Marconi are the sponsors – provide hospitality, donate prizes, fly their flag above the marquee at Lasham Gliding Society HQ, where it takes place. We had not previously glid, admired the assembled ranks of sleek six-metre sail-craft with wing spans of 15 metres and a width not many inches greater than ours.

Gliders come complete with trailers – long white coffins on wheels that look as if they might house a beached whale or huge Cumberland sausage; they cost upwards of £20,000 and have dials that show air-speed, altitude, direction, speed and degree of climb and descent; also a switch marked Boom. Mic. Soc, which could mean anything, but clearly contributes to the high cost of purchase.

Now you would suppose that if one managed to get the thing into the air – by catapult or tow-rope behind a small aircraft – one would sit back and be immensely chuffed, until one came down again; especially chuffed if one came down in one piece. Not a bit of it: they race. The championship involves fifty gliders that are projected into the air, hover above the starting line, then set out on their 'tasks' which is a triangular 100-mile trip on each of nine days, weather permitting. Pilots' times are verified by aerial photographs of start, target areas and finishing lines – taken and developed by the aviators – the winner being a mixture of the Red Baron and Karsh of Ottawa.

As the contestants dispersed to have coffee, examine maps and consult meteorological gurus, we received advice on the mechanics of gliding: thermal gusts of air provide lift; gliders are steadily flying in a downhill attitude, even as thermals raise their height.

The instructor said we would soon pick it up, and strapped us into the front seat, using hardy-looking straps with heavy-duty buckles to secure shoulders, waist and both legs. A lever protruded from between our legs; the instructor took up his position in the back, a tow-rope was attached to the lower front of the glider and as a light plane in front of us moved off, we followed – at speed – achieving an altitude of 30ft by the time the plane left the ground.

All went well until we reached 2,000ft when there was a sharp noise, a yellow lever sprang from its housing and we realized that our time had come, thought about all those years, some of which had been good.

'Now we are flying on our own,' said the instructor, the noise having been the detachment of the tow-rope. Our airspeed dial showed 50 knots, the headwind was about 25; this meant we were doing the aerial equivalent of kerb-crawling, which is apparently not a crime above Basingstoke. The lever between our legs gave some heavy twitches and we turned, the glider by 90 degrees, its passengers by only about 45. Thereafter we glid over the green fields and uplands of Hampshire, thinking about those who maintain that

Britain is becoming a concrete jungle, wishing they were with us to appreciate the error of their contentions. It was quiet; had it not been for the wind, it would have been eerily so.

Thermals lifted us to 2,500ft, we turned, increased airspeed, had a look at a village called Bradley, over-flew the airfield, held off from the strip which had been chosen for landing and touched down smoothly, stopped. We had not thought this through. There was no 'follow me' truck to guide us to the airport building; we got out and after a while some helpful people came to push the glider to a convenient resting place. Soon after that some fifty Standard class gliders embarked on their 'task'. We had a glass of whisky, will look for the result of the championship in Sunday's paper and will not be nearly as angry next time we are held up behind a long white trailer in a country lane.

* * *

Squidgers, squops and the flip side of success
The Times, 29 October 1993

THE 39TH CHALLENGE for the world tiddly-winks title takes place this evening in a private room at St Cross College, Oxford. The champion, an Englishman from Hendon, won the title in Boston, Massachusetts, in September 1992, has comfortably defended it twice and is favourite to retain it. This week, I invited him to dinner.

The world champion arrived carrying a roll of white industrial super-felt and a cigar box containing his equipment. He is slight, studious, bespectacled, looks like a ringer for the man on the No. 13 omnibus; turned out to be the man on the No. 13 omnibus.

Mr Geoffrey Myers, for it is he, is twenty-five years old, has a first-class degree in economics from Cambridge, a masters from Oxford, and works as a senior economic assistant at the Office of Fair Trading.

He drank a glass of Sancerre, sweated a bit, posed for the photographer with practised ease while using a two-inch squidger to flick winks into the small red plastic pot with deadly accuracy.

Success at tiddly-winks, he explained, is a mixture of skill, tactics and strategy. The championship tonight is contested over seven games, each consisting of twenty minutes foreplay, whereafter red, green, blue and yellow have five rounds at the pot apiece. Dinner will be served after two games and play resumes at 8pm. The result should be available to a waiting world by ten o'clock.

What will there be for dinner? He shrugs his shoulders. There is no traditional tiddly-winks food. Real ale is the popular drink.

In Britain, the game at the highest level is played only at Oxford, Cambridge and St Andrews, seems to appeal to scientists rather than students of the arts, is shunned by women, has not yet attracted black or oriental support.

I ask how long it takes to achieve genuine proficiency.

Myers said it took him about two years to get to championship standard, then another two years before he started to win. His great moment came in Massachusetts when he took the title by 25 points to 24, his opponent having had a pot to win ... which he missed.

How was the atmosphere? Myers said it was electric.

How big the crowd? Myers said it was in the high single figures, though tonight there is every likelihood of this being exceeded.

The real problem, he opined as he ate poached salmon with mousseline sauce, is that the crowd needs a certain level of knowledge to understand the game. For the opening phase it will see the players position themselves advantageously, rarely achieving a pot-out, but building piles as high as ten winks, deploying intricate positional strategies, thinking three or four moves ahead. They deliberate on the hardware as golfers do ... though in tiddly-winks there is no limit to the number of utensils you may carry.

The world champion has eight different squidgers with which to propel the winks: a two-inch squidger with a sharp, firm edge for potting – though if it is very close to the pot and the wink is small (they come in two sizes for no particular reason other than to make it more difficult), he would deploy the one-inch flexible squidger. There is a squidger for a low squop (squop is when a wink covers another and holds it captive until it, in turn, is squopped and released), and one for 'uncultured shots', like breaking up a sizeable pile. 'You play to your advantage, that is what the skill of the game is about,' Myers explained.

I had rather intended to challenge the world champion, had considered the consequences of my victory: the glory, the plaque on my house, the fans waiting outside for autographs.

We did not play. I watched Myers squidge a wink from under the lip of the concave cup high into the air and straight into the receptacle; then squidge another fifteen inches along the felt to land squarely on an opponent and realized that my playing the world champion at tiddly-winks would be as close a contest as my challenging Pete Sampras at tennis.

Also, he admitted that in the thirteen months since winning the world championship, he has yet to be mobbed at all, which gave me even less incentive.

Myers ate blackcurrant jelly and cream, drank both white and red wine, took his coffee black without sugar – though today he will eschew caffeine in order to ensure a steady hand.

After a while he rolled up his felt, kindly offered to leave me a box of winks and squidgers.

'We are aware that tiddly-winks, at the moment, is only a minority sport,' the publicity officer of the society had written, 'but we are anxious to see the game increase in stature.'

Their motto is: *Hic squop ibi squop ubique squop squop.*

If the Savoy Theatre is reluctant to provide the venue for the next championship contest, perhaps old McDonalds will.

* * *

Touché – as we say in East Anglia
The Times, 29 April 1994

SOME YEARS AGO, I talked to a doctor about memory loss: could the fact that I used to remember more telephone numbers than I do now, and was able to name – but can no longer – the Plymouth Argyle teams since 1938, be the result of natural winding down of a senior brain … or something more serious? I mean, was it the disease whose name steadily escapes me?

Alzheimer's?

Yes, that's the one.

He asked whether I ever went into the kitchen and when I got there, forgot what it was I had gone to do.

Yes.

Well, he said, most of us do it, a manifestation of temporary forgetfulness. Alzheimer's is when you go to the kitchen, look at a kettle and can't remember what it is for.

The news caused me to cheer up a bit, go to the kitchen, switch on the kettle and then wonder to what use to put the boiling water to make something with which to celebrate that I knew I did not have whatsit.

Last Sunday, I was introduced to Gionayi Szalay … and I thought of the kettle. Szalay is tallish, youngish, thinnish, was dressed in a padded white fencing suit which is wired to a central control; a beekeeper's helmet covers her face and head: a woman, presumably a woman, in a uniform I could not penetrate concealing a name I could not pronounce.

Before I could say, 'Take me to your leader', Szalay was speaking in Hungarian to the folks back home on a Euro link. She might have said I am champion for the third time in four years. Hungarian is not one of my languages.

It happened in Ipswich on Sunday at lunchtime when it would have been my normal custom to weigh up the respective merits of horseradish cream and mustard as accompaniment to roasted sirloin of beef. Instead, I sat among a tight three-figure crowd of competitors, coaches, lovers and friends watching the final of the women's épée championships.

Over the previous days, the eighty-six contestants had been whittled down to eight and the twenty GBR fencers had been eliminated; our Carol Greenwood did best, but not well enough.

There had been the quarter-finals and the semis during which Katya Nass – the name means wet in German – had fought Hormay of Hungary and fellow countrywoman Funkenhause, despatched them both, was now ready to compete for the Ipswich Cup.

I wanted her to win. I could pronounce her name. Life is hard enough without having to remember Gionayi Szalay.

At the time I usually decide to keep the blackcurrant jelly and cream for supper and eat Mr Green's matured cheddar from Chewton Mendip with walnut bread, battle commenced.

Women's fencing takes place on a piste which is 40 metres long and the wires from the contestants' suits and épées register on the scoreboard first by lighting up the colour of the one who has been hit, then translating it into points.

If the hits are simultaneous, both colours glow and the president holds up one finger of each outstretched hand – reminiscent of the late King George VI entering into the spirit of singing, 'Underneath the spreading chestnut tree'.

The president (referees are known as president, useful fact for general knowledge quizzes) stands in front of the contestants to shout '*allez*'; just why the Dutch lady should shout in French to a German fighting a Hungarian in England is not instantly comprehensible. It most probably has to do with tradition. Until 1893, the épée was a weapon to be reckoned with: a sharp point at the end of a metal lance meant that there was no argument on whether or not a hit had registered – the blood was there for all to see.

Master Baudry invented the *pointe d'arrêt* in order that the weapon could just pierce the fine cord of the jacket without necessarily impaling a vital organ – considerable sophistication before the invention of the electric épée shortly after the last war.

In olden days, duelling as a spectator sport never caught on – because of the remoteness of the location, unsociability of the hour and briefness of the combat.

Fencing on a Sunday lunchtime on the outskirts of Ipswich does at least go on for a while. The fights last for nine minutes – three by three-minute rounds or fifteen hits, whichever comes first. If there's a tie, they go on for one minute, whereafter, if scores are still even, the bout goes to the one with the higher international rating: the good old Tory system of giving to those who have.

And where there were seconds and doctors and lawyers and paramedics with leeches, there are now many men and women who are knowledgeable about the rules, expert on the subject of combat and experienced in all precedents. They occupy small tables marked Leon Paul which is to fencing as Slazenger is to tennis. The president would turn to these people in case of dispute.

Fencing is hugely skilful, requiring stamina, balance, the ability to move backwards and sideways as well as to lunge and thrust forward.

Nass attacked. Nass shouted when she scored a hit rather as a stuck pig squeals and Szalay (I practise saying, 'May I call you Gionayi?') scored as she defended, hit as she went back from the German's onslaught, took the final 15-10.

It was all over at around the time I usually get mint tea and the rest of my family drink their coffee.

* * *

Targeting medieval skills in Housman Country
The Times, 17 June 1994

THE TROUBLE ABOUT archery used to be that the wholly satisfying thud of swift arrow hitting soft object was followed by the agonized screams of object's demise.

This has ceased to be a problem. With few exceptions, 'object' is now inanimate: a mounted target with a gold centre, ringed in turn by red, blue, black and white – and the only after-noise of the agreeable thud is the archer's grunt of satisfaction or disgust as he assesses the point of his arrow's impact.

Agincourt was archery's finest hour; the invention of muskets did about as much for the craft as did the Boston Strangler for door-to-door salesmen.

Today, despite Henry VIII's unrevoked law that on highdays and holidays men aged between twenty-one and forty must practise archery in market places, it is not a sport across which you come without due diligence and careful research.

Having observed in a sporting publication that the UK Masters Tournament was to take place at the National Sports Centre in Lilleshall last weekend, I made my way north. The centre is situated in Shropshire, doubtless to deter the oft-repeated accusation that everything worthwhile in this country is located in the South East. The siting is certainly a radical departure from accepted opinion, being not only inaccessible but not in Lilleshall, either.

Nevertheless, four miles or so from that village, at the end of a very long drive affected by a severe curse of sleeping policemen, I reached a manor house with the requisite nomenclature.

'Archery,' said a woman behind a reception desk such as you find at the Grosvenor House antique dealers fair, 'is by the pavilion.'

There followed a half-mile walk between rhododendron bushes of quality, in the course of which I encountered athletes of most ages and sexes, and signposts as varied as Tennis Courts and Test Beds. Passing a gatehouse and making my way through an aperture intended for slimmer men than I, a field replete with targets and canvas wigwams and a cream-coloured Portaloo was spread before me.

Let me try to explain the sport:

Archers, wearing padded waistcoats to cushion their shoulders, carry state-of-the-art high-tech bows fashioned of magnesium alloy risers with limbs of laminated glass-fibre. A quiver is slung about their midriffs and this is filled with personalized arrows made of carbon-wrapped aluminium.

There is a waiting line and a shooting line; contestants, at the whistle, move from one to the other and then have four minutes in which to dispatch six arrows at the targets ... which are 90, 70, 50 and 30 metres distant.

At the end of the allotted shooting time, archers and officials move forward to inspect the targets, agree the scores, remove the arrows and return to the waiting line ... and so it goes on.

The competition consists of 144 arrows, three dozen fired at each of the four distances. This is known as a Fita, from the initials of the Federation International Tir a L'arc (a pressure group founded after the battle of Crecy).

A perfect score would be 1,440; the world record stands at 1,352. Koreans, Americans and Russians are the finest exponents of archery; Hoyt/Easton, of Utah, Yamaha, of Japan, and Stylist, of Farnborough, the most prestigious suppliers of equipment, and it would cost around £500 for accoutrement, though the expenditure of £1,000 on a bow, £20 each for arrows, is not unusual.

Our No. 1 man, significantly superior to his fellow archers and taller, also, is Stephen Hellard. Simon Terry, of Lincoln, another fine exponent of our team, won bronze at the Olympics in both Seoul and Barcelona.

I ask about the future.

The breaking up of the Soviet Union into half a dozen countries that will each field talented teams will be unhelpful to our cause.

Archery is a minority sport. I was the only journalist, indeed the only spectator, but it is all geared up for breakthrough into the big-time. There is provision for dope tests; a rulebook with a chapter on etiquette ('the good archer does not talk to another competitor who obviously prefers to be silent') is available.

The National Indoor Arena in Birmingham has been selected for the European championships next March and a 70 square metre screen will be installed to bring immediacy to the huge audiences both there and via some yet-to-be-given-a-licence television channel.

As I left that green field in Housman country to get a taxi to a bus to a station to an InterCity train, dedicated archers were 'tuning' their equipment, matching arrows of varying degrees of rigidity to bows of differing weights ... some with built-in pulleys and automatic triggers.

Had these been available to the Red Indians, America would not carry the political clout of San Marino.

* * *

Rolling up for a bracing day out at the seaside
The Times, 8 July 1994

IT IS NOT romantic. On either side of the railway lie great fields of wheat and cabbage ... and the land is as flat as the Cambridgeshire fen where I always kept two telephone directories in the boot of my car, so that when I stopped I could stand on them and get a view.

And it is not central. Skegness is an hour and a half from Grantham, which is not itself very close to anywhere. The bullet train stops at Rauceby and Heckington, Boston and Wainfleet, where Bateman's award-winning ales are brewed. At the edge of town, a sign states 'Home of Fravigar sweets' and the station has a statue of The Jolly Fisherman.

He is to Skeggy what Santa is to Lapland: the reason people go there, though originally they went because of John Hassall's turn-of-the-century London and North Eastern Railway poster, Skegness Is So Bracing.

Bracing remains an excellent word to describe an agreeable seaside resort that the sun seems to bypass, which has a beach that only just qualifies under the Trade Descriptions Act, whose pier lost its end in the storms of 1987.

The population of Skegness is 14,000 in winter, over 100,000 during the summer when the Midlands Chizzits come to town. (The name derives from the visitors' appearances in local shops where they ask: 'How much is it?')

It is heavily time-warped to the extent that I had a great desire to approach people and tell them news which may not yet have filtered through – like 'the Waleses' marriage is iffy'.

What is uplifting about Skegness, apart from its honesty, lack of pretentiousness, overt hospitality and good inexpensive fish-and-chip shops, is that something goes on all the time. This week it is bowls at the Suncastle on the front; next week it is bowls also. The English Bowling Association (EBA) July tournament attracts 350 contestants. There are 24 rinks, 48 players per session and the winner of the men's singles receives £120 and ... a statue of The Jolly.

Money, the players will tell you, is unimportant. 'A few years ago, the tournament winner coolly walked out of Ladbrokes with £800 in cash. Later that afternoon, when they gave him the porcelain figurine of The Jolly, he broke down and cried.'

EBA rules state that 'players shall be dressed in white above the belt and grey below', and they are. Everything is absolutely right. The greens are perfect; the deportment of the players faultless. Bowls is a serious game and they play it with proper seriousness, giving every aspect of the action the most careful attention.

Dennis Kimberley lives in Warsop, in Nottinghamshire. He has been coming to Skegness at least twice a year for thirty years to compete in the July and September tournaments; last year he won the singles for the first time. The Jolly figurine, he explains, is at home 'on show, has pride of place like, among the trophies; the wife looks after it.'

Kimberley plays with bowls made from Tyrolite, a compound that is heavier than the Hensolite used by many of the players. He is seventy, retired as a materials officer from Welbeck Colliery 13 years ago; he used to lodge in boarding houses but now stays in his touring caravan parked nearby. He and his wife have breakfast 'in', eat 'out' at dinner time and have tea 'like salmon or cod with salad' back in the caravan.

We talk in the equipment room of the Suncastle, which is run by East Lindsey district council, whose chairman will award the trophies this afternoon at 5 o'clock.

For £1.20 you can hire shoes (bowlers' footwear must be smooth and have no heels), woods (these are genuine lignum vitae wooden woods at least forty years old and maintained with care and love) and use of a rink for one hour. The door opens and The Jolly makes an appearance; he is employed by the council, dressed as a fisherman with a large plastic head topped by a sou'wester, and he moves slowly, shakes hands, nods a welcome, traditionally does not speak. Like Santa, it is the outfit rather than the personality which has security of tenure.

As metropolitan functions employ strippers, kissogram girls or after-dinner speakers, a successful Skegness do gets an appearance from The Jolly.

I note that more bowlers adopt the 'fixed' style, in which the leading foot remains in situ and the bowl is given impetus by the arm movement, than the 'athletic' style, in which the body is bent. The quality of play is high and, as the players draw and rest and wick and block and trail and fire, their wives and their friends and the tournament officials around the green watch with knowledgeable interest. As suggested in the EBA rule book's chapter on etiquette, only appreciation is voiced. 'Good shot' and 'well bowled' are the buzz-words.

Opening rounds of the tournament are decided on twenty-one shots, semi-finals and final on eighteen ends. An umpire with a black box of measuring equipment hovers.

The lounge is large and comfortable and there is quiche, chips and salad for £1.95; burger, chips and beans for £1.50. In the background, somebody is playing 'Do You Know the Way to San Jose?'; I eat a really good brown bread egg sandwich and go to see what other oldies are in stock on the jukebox ... and find that the music is live.

* * *

Floating voters wage a clean campaign
The Times, 12 August 1994

ON FISTRAL BEACH, west of Newquay, this week, you will see a large off-white trade marquee. Inside, there is considerable action as buyers are sought for leisure clothing, sandals, sunglasses, backpacks, surfboards and wet suits made of flexible Yamamoto rubber, reinforced with titanium to provide minimum weight/ maximum heat-retention.

There is also a stand displaying the logo Surfers Against Sewage.

I ask who is FOR sewage.

An earnest woman fixes me with an ancient-mariner look and explains that SAS is a non-profit-making, apolitical organization campaigning for the cessation of marine sewage.

I join. It is not the first non-profit-making, apolitical, anti-crap group aboard which I have climbed. They give me a pamphlet. I learn that SAS's finest hour was in the spring of 1991 when a coachload of Cornish grockles donned rubber suits and lobbied Parliament, sadly getting mixed up with an anti-poll tax pressure group.

The reason for all this activity at Newquay is the Headworx Pro Surf championship, carrying prize-money of $60,000 (£40,000).

Lest there be those ignorant of surfing, possibly unable to tell a 'natural' stance from one that is 'goofy', a thin double overhead barrel wave from a reef break, nor identify tail-slides, pipelines, sunsets and floaters ... let me explain.

There exist at present, in the five continents, some 100 professional surfers. They tend to be stocky men with low centres of gravity, though now and again they will be gangly and greyhound-like.

They come from Australia, Hawaii, California, Brazil, Cornwall, South Africa, Florida, France or Tahiti and are sponsored by companies that are into surfers' lifestyles: Quiksilver, Headworx, Rip Curl, Animal, Hot Tuna, Sex-Wax, No Fear.

Rather as there is a stall selling yachting caps to holidaymakers when they alight from the Isle of Wight ferry at Cowes, so do these companies follow the pro surf contests and endeavour to make supporters and innocent passers-by look like the intrepid men on state-of-the-art ironing boards.

Nobody is sure how the sport began. A piece of driftwood on a wave, a child clinging onto this for a ride, lying on it, defying nanny and standing up … then getting purpose-built driftwood, selecting waves of quality, riding them with innovative skill.

Today's professional will have eight or nine boards and select that of a length and weight most suitable for the strength and size of the waves to be ridden.

Kelly Slater is the world's No. 1: an all-American, wholesome, Huckleberry Finn 22-year-old from Cocoa Beach, Florida. He is fearless, disciplined and his performances on tail-slides and aerials are especially admired.

Our own best hope for glory in this elite circus may be Russell Winter, London-born youngest of three sons whose parents spared neither effort nor expense in making him one of the most talented and aggressive surfers in Europe.

Judges' criteria for marking performance are based on length of ride, quality of manoeuvres and control, selection of waves. Four contestants compete simultaneously; five judges score the four superior rides in the allotted time and, as in diving, the highest and lowest marks are ignored and the mean of the three others decides the winner, and with it the value of the man's endorsement contract, the colour of the stripe on the grunge slacks and the logo on the baseball caps that will be worn from Papeete to Thurso in the year to come.

Lifestyle surfers are a big market, even if they have no ability, lie down on the boards: what pros call 'shark biscuits'.

In Australia, the continental shelf causes tubular waves that roll on without collapsing; they are best. 'In keeping with much else,' the publisher of the European surfing magazine says, 'Britain's surfing beaches are not great.' But Newquay is best and Fistral Beach the *numero uno* in Newquay.

Ten years ago our competitors were miles behind the best, but we seem to be catching up; Spencer Hargraves, a local lad, was world pro junior champion, which won him a contract with Quiksilver, the biggest surf clothing company, and is worth watching. What else was there to watch?

Well, the rain bucketing down, the sea as flat as a boarding-house duvet, a couple of hundred surfers and officials wondering what to do in Newquay, where the streets were gridlocked with cars.

The fact is that when it rains in Cornwall the thousands of campsite holidaymakers on the north coast decide to drive to Newquay – where thousands of holidaymakers think that this might be a good time to see how those poor souls on the campsites are getting on.

As a consequence I saw no surfing, met no surfers, ruined my shoes, spent an hour and a half in a traffic jam, missed my plane and had a Cornish set tea – which they serve at the Headland Hotel without plates.

* * *

Flick of a wrist starts War of the Worlds
The Times, 26 August 1994

ON THE OUTSKIRTS of Colchester, where the classy holiday trade peels off for Frinton while *hoi polloi* sing merrily in their coaches bound for Clacton-on-Sea, there are AA signs inscribed 'Ultimate Worlds'.

Lest there be those who think that this will direct folk towards Essex man's Valhalla, and wonder why the rest of the country is losing out, let me explain. 'Ultimate' is the name of a Michigan-based company that has cornered the competitive Frisbee market. 'Worlds' is short for world championships.

On the playing fields of Essex University this week, some 1,000 competitors from twenty-five countries are contesting the Ultimate and Guts competitions in open, masters, juniors and women's classes.

The ruling body is the World Flying Disc Federation of New York, motto 'The most fun wins'; the president's letter on page one of the programme begins 'Hello', and is signed 'Ultimately yours, Nob'.

Examining the men who sit and wait and watch and play Ultimate, you realize that Nob is a good, representative name. Today's Nob is a relative of the Camra man of the last decades, though fitter.

What is so brilliant about flying discs is that, with a piece of plastic that retails at £7.50 – and probably costs less than a tenth of that to produce – you have the wherewithal to play compulsive versions of American football, baseball, tennis, orienteering and even Russian roulette.

Ultimate is the most popular game. Ultimate is American football without the violence. Squads of twenty or more provide ever-changing teams of seven; they play on football pitches that have 25-metre end-zones. A point is scored if the disc is caught in the opposition's touchdown area.

The catcher of a disc may not move more than three paces. Marking is close, no contact is permitted and the good player is fast, fit, skilled and able to project the disc accurately to distances 100 yards away, throw vertically, horizontally, ambidextrously, over the spoiling defender's head, beneath his blocking arm, spinning, skimming, hovering before it descends, emulating a boomerang …

The United States are favourites. Their masters (men over thirty) demolished Japan by 21 points to one. Non-contestants (there are virtually no spectators, just people waiting to play) stand on the touchline and chant:

'What time is it?'

'Block time.'

Also: 'Get a D', and quite a lot of 'Toast them'.

On the adjoining pitch, the Italian women are playing the Swedes, who are better but not so vocal. A woman wearing a T-shirt with 'Italia' written along the sleeve is being filmed by Channel 4. 'Effessissimo,' she shouts, waving her fists and pulling her scarf over her head to denote anguish. It transpires that she is an extra from central casting; *effessissimo* is not a word in common usage. Around her, real Italians shout '*libera*', meaning that someone is unmarked.

Ultimate is a tremendous game, well worth watching: fast, continuous, honourable … there are no referees; if a catch or a throw is in dispute, it is taken again.

In the open pool, Great Britain beat New Zealand. On the touchline, much time is spent decanting cold water from a large plastic container into individual bottles, for the afternoon is hot. They shout 'GB, GB, Sean, Scott, Sasha, Wayne', then 'GB' again.

A number of marquees dispense food and drink: good beer at £1.20 a pint; fruit juice, salads, sandwiches, pasta – which is now undisputed athlete-fare – and, inevitably, there is merchandise – handsome sweatshirts and shoes and hats.

If anyone is in any doubt about anything – the history of Colchester, the nearest zoo, sticking plaster to repair a graze or the location of tonight's party – then a squad of helpful people wearing purple shirts inscribed 'We're here because we care. Yeah … right', do a tremendous job.

And then there is Guts, the other contest using the same implement. I thought Guts was an acronym: Groin Under Terrible Stress, something like that. Guts, apparently, owes its name to the quality demanded of practitioners. It is a passive form of baseball.

The teams stand 14 metres apart. The pitching side chooses its man, who then winds himself up and unleashes the Frisbee at quite staggering velocity towards the five-man team, who may wear soft, protective clothing and unpadded gloves.

The scoring zone is an area within which a receiving player, by using optimum effort, can reach an oncoming disc without moving his feet. A point is scored by the throwing team if the disc is good and none of the catching team makes a good catch.

The first throw I witnessed smashed into a man's midriff and laid him out; the second removed three fingers of the prospective catcher's left hand. It was explained to me that this was only a practice session; the real match would begin in an hour's time.

Guts has a lot going for it.

* * *

Sport and serenity, no strings attached
The Times, **14 October 1994**

GETTING THERE IS uplifting. Leave the A1 at Stilton, make for Caldicote, look for the Lutton signs and then meander through Polebrook on the Oundle road. The villages shine, like the shortlist for the 'best kept' competition; not a sweet wrapper or cola can in sight. Thatch in pristine order. Cars parked with due care and geometric understanding.

Driving from London, visibility for the first sixty miles had been minimal; every now and then one picked up a yellow light, moved slowly towards this in order to decipher the message, and found it was 'FOG'. I could have told them that; there must be a better way.

At Alconbury the autumn mists gave way to the maturing sun, just like Keats said, and outside the village of Ashton the Northants police had placed cones at the sides of the road – always a sign of a compelling happening. Then, where the official signpost stated 'Village Green' was the further information, 'World Championship'.

It was what I had come to witness. Local officials, whose big day this is, waved vehicles into fields and we parked, walked back, paid £1 per head to gain admission to the green and a further 50 pence

215

for a programme – all monies to charities that help the visually impaired.

It was like a Disney set: men and women dressed to be noticeable, some with lederhosen and feathers in their caps; others like extras from Robin Hood or itinerants supplied by rent-a-tramp. Half were men, children outnumbered women. The public address system was operated by one who sounded like a mature hippie whom nobody had told that the Sixties were over. He broadcast dispensable information – like 'will numbers 26, 28, 29, 33, 36 and 38 please register before it is too late'.

In a corner they had erected a coconut shy: seven solid coconuts wired into their holders, daring anyone to dislodge them. No chance ... until a boy of about five lobbed a wooden ball in their general direction and the overlord used pliers to permit one to fall from its housing.

A woman sold apricot shortbread: moist pieces of home-baked confectionery, six for 50 pence, which would cost at least that sum were you to make it at home.

I counted eight tombola stands displaying ordinary, medium and desirable prizes; also one Super Prize like a magnum of wine or gallon of whisky. I would like a hot dinner for every committee on which I have sat discussing the methodology of distribution: how to retain the stallholders' honour while ensuring that the best prize remains as a come-on until late into the evening.

Candyfloss was the dish of the day and filled rolls were sold beside a notice stating 'made by the blind'. I did not purchase one to discover whether this was beneficial but admired a signpost, 'Additional Women's Toilets'. There was a queue. I did not know about Northants and additional women.

'It is coming up to 10.30,' the man on the Tannoy says; it was actually 10.45. At the far end of the village green stands a pub called The Chequered Skipper, where I drank half a pint of ale, was surprised by the high asking price but remembered that it was all for charity. Moments later the barman came and told me he had made a mistake, gave me back 50p.

The Master of Ceremonies requested a minute's silence in memory of a man who died last week; we stood for a minute, it seemed the least we could do.

Both Northants ambulance and fire services were in attendance. The man from St John did not consider this a dangerous event; the fire people also maintained that it was benign and then ... it started: the championship.

All conkers and strings supplied by the Ashton Conker Club. Each competitor to take three alternate strikes until one of the conkers is shattered. Three snags lead to disqualification. The length of lace in play must be no less than eight inches a strike.

There were ten platforms, each with a presiding judge. Two hundred and fifty-six contestants would be whittled down to two finalists and then ...

There is nothing gracious about swinging a conker on an eight-inch string to strike another suspended a similar length – nor is it a wholehearted sport like flinging a welly, tossing the caber, putting the shot or punching someone on the chin.

Conkers is minimalist: a short, hard swing to achieve a tap on the opponent's chestnut. There is no pain barrier to cross, no way you can manifest contempt or hatred for the enemy.

Measure, swing, tap ... try not to look petulant, remember that hitting the other's conker may harm yours as much or more than his.

By early afternoon we had the winner. The world conker champion. Oh world.

* * *

No snow, but huskies get the drift
The Times, 9 December 1994

MY WIFE ASKED whether I had lost much money. I said no. She said: 'First time for a while that you've come back from the dogs in pocket.'

217

I explained that they had not been the usual sort of dogs, and she remarked that if there was a kind of dog I could go to without forfeiting my cash, why had it taken me so long to find out about them; also, why was I so wet?

On the far side of the Severn Bridge, you take the road north to Monmouth, and at Chepstow racecourse turn left towards Devauden. I knew it was the right road because the van in front of me bore the inscription 'Siberian Husky Team. Phone: 0501 62821'. Why people would want to telephone Siberian huskies is something of a mystery.

I had travelled west to witness the Baker's Complete Wye Valley 1994 British Husky Racing Championships, sponsored by Edward Baker Limited with special thanks to Forest Enterprises; eventually, having followed the van through the driving rain down a woodland path, we passed a banner marked 'FINISH'. A furlong on, we came to 'START'. In between was HQ: a space that served as car park, location of mobile lavatories, hamburger, sausage and tea vehicle, and a shed in which competitors were briefed and course charts pinned to a board.

Formula One, the top competition, was for teams of six dogs over a five-mile course shaped like the African continent with the start at Lagos and the finish at Lome. (Intermediate class is for four-dog teams run over a shorter distance.)

At 8.30 the chief steward silenced the hundred-odd crowd – though not their dogs, which kept up a steady chorus – welcomed us and explained that the track was in good order though wet, was 'all downhill', which was met with hollow laughter. 'While not the M1, it was flattish and the chicanes had been filled in.' I made a note of what had been used to fill in holes – bark, twigs, sawdust … I seem to recall, but the pad on which I wrote failed to withstand the elements and dissolved into bluish pap in my pocket.

Let me try to explain husky racing: the dogs are whitish in colour, Alsatianesque in breed, strong, handsome, loud. And they are harnessed to pull a sort of three-wheeled Zimmer frame which has a platform for each foot over the rear wheels. Husky racing is done against the clock; teams have three minutes between departures to get into position; are counted down, regardless of readiness, and at the word 'Go', the driver, known as the 'musher', races alongside his chariot and jumps on as it gathers speed: a start similar to that in bobsleigh racing and that ultimate of laxative events – the Cresta Run.

There is no steering. The smartest dogs are put in front and a musher explained to me that there are husky words for 'left' and 'right' and 'watch it' … which were entered in my notebook.

Team No. 1, six hardy-looking dogs wearing red booties, driven by a dark, lean gladiator from Penalt nearby, disappeared into the teeming rain at 9:00.00.

Team No. 2, sleek, tough, bootless huskies, commanded by Alex Laidlaw from Lothian in Scotland, galloped off 180 seconds later. And so it went on: eleven teams of six, each furiously yapping dog led up by a handler, attached in three pairs either side of the tow-rope. They strain against this, waiting for the release of the anchor and the command to go, disappearing into the early morning wetlands of Gwent, where they have nineteen words for rain and nobody carries a hip flask.

I wandered off to the finish – which is at the end of a one-mile uphill straight. On this punishing final stretch, mushers run beside their frames or propel them with one leg, as one propels a scooter. The dogs were black with mud and sweat; the drivers splattered with bark, twigs, sawdust etc., and as they passed the line a tarpaulined official recorded their time to a hundredth of a second.

Laidlaw won, at an average speed of 16 miles per hour over two circuits. His huskies ran barefoot and there was some talk that sodden booties at the end of an uphill squelch were less of a help than a hindrance.

A man from Thetford, who had been expected to do well, explained that Norfolk, as Noël Coward once remarked, was very flat, and his dogs were unused to the hilly terrain.

219

At the burger bar, over a bacon butty, I met a man who had travelled down from Thurso, a 14½-hour drive in his 'dedicated vehicle' – a Transit fitted with three tiers of cages. Racing huskies is his passion. It costs him £50 a week to feed the team (they eat Baker's Complete) and then there is transport and vets' fees ...

Behind us, six huskies who had just run their race were being dried off by their handlers with good-quality bath towels. I asked a girl who had transformed a mud-caked hell hound into a fluffy, silver-coloured pet whether she might care to give me similar service.

She was of the 'four legs good, two legs bad' persuasion.

* * *

Penthouse sport where professional rolls his own
The Times, 6 January 1995

THE PAMPHLET STATED: 'Men in their seventies and eighties derive enormous pleasure from playing, although their joy is as cerebral as it is physical.' As that is exactly my kind of joy, I telephoned the Harbour Club in Chelsea and asked if I might have an hour with their professional.

They said: 'It will cost £25.' And as their professional is Lachlan Deuchar, three times a contender for the world real tennis title, I considered the great value of this compared to say, twenty three-minute rounds with Evander Holyfield: more instructive and less painful also, I should imagine.

Deuchar, a London-based, fifth-generation Australian with Scots ancestry, met me at reception, escorted me to a pristine changing-room in which there was not a towel out of place, opened up a locker for my clothes and said he would come back in a few minutes.

Under the heading 'Dress', the pamphlet had proclaimed: 'Normal tennis attire is requested.'

I have ceased playing tennis, subsequently I have no normal tennis attire – a predicament I appear to share with P. Sampras, who wears khaki-coloured shorts, and A. Agassi, garbed in coats of many colours. I settled for grey slacks and a cream-coloured jersey inscribed 'The Mississippi Queen' – which I had been given on the eponymous New Orleans riverboat and seldom wear to avoid misunderstanding. (In the 1960s, Her Majesty attended a party at our embassy in Washington, a man was presented to her and she asked him what he did for a living. He said: 'I am a photographer.' She replied: 'What a coincidence, my brother-in-law is a photographer.' He replied: 'What a coincidence, my brother-in-law is a queen.')

Deuchar said: 'You have played this before?'

I agreed.

'You remember some or most of the rules?'

They will come back, I said, optimistically. Nevertheless, he gave me a synopsis of the game, featuring favoured words like 'chase', 'penthouse', 'hazard', 'tambour', 'grille' and 'dedans'. He selected a racket – these are shaped like the late Robert Maxwell's carpet slippers on sticks ... and bade me occupy the hazard while he served.

The opening stroke is not the fierce Ivanisevic drive that fizzes across taut net at 118mph, but a gentle lob onto the sloping roof of the penthouse along which it rolls, picks up speed, executes a right-hand turn when it reaches the end wall and trickles onto the concrete floor. I manage to get a racket behind it, miss the court and hit the *Times* photographer who is sheltering from play in a side gallery.

Deuchar is impressed: where I have mishit the ball turns out to be a scoring shot. The photographer is less impressed, but then he is ignorant of the rules of contest.

Things begin to come back to me: the sagging net, two feet lower in the middle than at the extremities. The fact that the bounce of the ball is uneven: Deuchar's shots make Shane Warne's deliveries predictable by comparison. The player at the service end has much going for him, not least the buttress or Mail wall in the receiver's end, which juts out at an angle of about 130° and causes balls that hit it to slither unpredictably across the court.

If you know how to score ... and there are Byzantine benefits that advance your cause, as unpredictable as the prizes in the lottery, you change ends every now and again. In our game, after a few rallies known as 'rests', it was me to serve onto the penthouse and try to get the ball to trickle down the far wall at minimal speed; as in squash, the perfect landing place is the crack where the wall meets the floor.

Thanks to the shape of the racket and the unevenness of bounce, I miss the ball as often as I hit it. (Deuchar denies 'unevenness', calls it 'variety'.)

Some time later, armed with three large soft white towels, I adjourned to the changing-room, removed my attire and was about to go to the showers when I heard two women talking animatedly in the area I was about to visit. I waited. Their conversation continued. Had I been a member of this admirable club, I would have written a note in the complaints book ... which would not have been a good idea, for when I stopped to listen, hoping to glean the time of their impending withdrawal, I realized it was a television discussion on the men's changing-room set.

Deuchar met me in the restaurant, bought me an egg benedict and told me that it was he who made the balls – an integral part of the job of a real tennis professional: a 60-gram piece of cork, often the piece of cork that has formed the base of a clapped-out ball, wrapped in strips of cotton webbing until basically round, placed on a circular piece of yellow felt and firmly hand-stitched to secure a seam.

'It is dull work; tedious and not terribly skilful, but if you don't take care you have produced a crummy ball.'

Which would be out of place at the Harbour Club ... I suggest.

He agrees. I ask how you can tell a cunningly executed top spin from the bounce of a ball that is ready for the knacker's yard.

The answer is 'experience', and when I suggest that an amateur might blame playing errors on equipment failure, he replies: 'It is incumbent upon me to ensure that that excuse is available to the clientele.' An Oz diplomat. Rare species. Man will go far.

* * *

Water sport that reaches absurd depths
The Times, 27 January 1995

IT IS LIKE this: two teams of six, one lot dressed in swimming gear with white caps – the others wear black caps – all twelve with snorkels and flippers and white gloves reinforced with bath sealant to protect the knuckles and white or black hardwood sticks that look like boomerangs which failed their inspection, stand at the pool ends waiting for an official to say 'go'.

Then they dive under the water, as do two water referees, who wear red caps and have yellow rubber washing-up gloves on their hands. If you're watching, which would be foolish for this is the ultimate in non-spectator sports, you see an occasional flipper break the surface of the water and ever and anon players come up for air before going back down again.

We are asked to believe that at the bottom of the pool is a 3lb, solid, lead puck which looks like an outsize tin of gentlemen's relish and at each end a three-metre-wide metal gully with a trough; that it is the aim of the teams to use their sticks to flick or push the puck into the opponent's trough, an event which is signalled by a raised yellow washing-up glove and acknowledged by the chief referee, who is out of the pool and rings a gong that reverberates under the water and persuades participants to come up, return to the side and wait for the command to continue.

If this is a hoax, I fell for it. The people at Guildford Leisure Centre insisted that the game is called octopush (there used to be eight in a team) and is regulated by the British Octopush Association (BOA), the controlling body of underwater hockey in the United Kingdom; that there are over 100 British teams spanning the social spectrum; and every two years a world championship. Last year this was held in Normandy and in the women's division we beat the French 1-0; got stuffed 16-0 by the South Africans. In world rankings, the United Kingdom is third behind Australia and South Africa.

A game takes thirty minutes, fifteen minutes each half with two minutes for rest and repairs. It is veritably a game of two halves, especially in pools which slope. Crystal Palace, Ealing, Manchester and Sheffield are the only four locations that have evenly bottomed pools.

Goodness, what else can one say?

The flippers worn by players are longer and more flexible than those worn by divers.

The sticks, which are whittled by players and can be of any hardwood of their choice, have a 15-degree bevel on each edge so that you can flick from the outside, scoop from the inner ... and it is a non-contact sport, not that one would notice an underwater assault until the blood rose to the top.

Touching the puck with anything but the stick wins the other side a free puck and if a foul is committed in the goal area, it is a penalty. Simple contest: two attackers against one defender. They usually score.

Teams may have four substitutes who can go in as soon as an injured or weary player comes out; subbing on the fly, this is called, and although I was unable to find a copy, there is – they insist – a quarterly magazine called *Octopush News* with a print run well into three figures.

What a lot I do not know about.

Clare Straiton is the development officer of the BOA. A sculptor of talent – I was shown her work and admired it a lot – she is a seasoned international, our foremost woman player, wears a shirt bearing the legend 'UK Barbarian Underwater Hockey Team', which is a 100 per cent conversation-provoking logo.

Should any reader have good lungs, a love of water, the ability to whittle 12-inch pieces of walnut into bespoke underwater hockey sticks (one white and one black) which fit the size of the hand … and have no need for supporters because when you are underwater you can't hear anything (there is also the considerable problem of player identification) you should consult no one else.

The address is Culver Farm, Old Compton Lane, Farnham, Surrey GU9 8EJ.

If you live within driving distance of Guildford, the Leisure Centre – clearly signposted from the A3 – is the jewel in the crown of leisure centres of the world *and* it makes money for the local authority.

Admission is 50p. Ice skating, netball, tenpin bowling, gymnasiums, pools, saunas, Jacuzzis, exercise classes, martial arts schools, squash, amusement machines and a host of other activities are good value extras. Cappuccino costs 70p, Glenfiddich single malt £1.39.

* * *

Just ducky, bobbing along on the Liffey
The Times, 28 April 1995

SO JOHN BUTLER became the world duck-racing champion for 1995. A Cambridge-based haulier who hails from Fifeshire, Butler's other passion is football; he played for and still passionately supports – the team many Radio 5 listeners believe is called Raith Rovers Nil.

A bright blustery morning on the River Liffey had levels down to 14 inches, winds gusting from the south-west to Force 6, which is not everyone's ideal water; nevertheless, Hilary Cload, from Warwick, who has been described as 'the duck racer's duck racer', achieved second place.

Sean McManmon has been waterkeeper of the critical four-mile stretch of the Liffey for upwards of sixteen years. The river rises at

Manor Kilbridge in the Wicklow Mountains and meanders its way to Dublin Bay yielding several million gallons of Guinness a day as it goes.

The great race is run in the grounds of Kildare Hotel and Country Club: from the metal bridge north of the golf course to a finishing line determined by the judges. It is an ideal location. There are swans and badgers, six pairs of otters live in the riverbank by a rape field replete with hares from whom you hear the continuing sounds of daily exertion – or it may be hare-speak for 'How was it for you?'

Downstream are salmon and brown trout waiting for the rising of mayfly drawn here by the silt. Mayfly attract fish that feed at no other time and when the lilac starts to blossom around 15 May and the flow of the river is right, this becomes a fisherman's paradise; a time when Mr Jack Charlton, who makes no secret of his priorities, ensures that Ireland's football team has a break from fixtures.

Dr Smurfit, who owns this pleasure dome, has planted 20,000 hardwood trees whose trunks are coated with a foul-tasting emulsion to deter the grey squirrels from reaching the foliage and feeding on the eggs of woodpigeon and sparrowhawk, robin and wren, teal and widgeon.

This is a bird sanctuary: melanistic and Scotch pheasant strut the grounds as if this were a giant zebra crossing; mallards come by executing the dog paddle and while weather reports make mention of morning frost and overcast skies around the British Isles the sun shines its bright approval on the contest about to be staged here.

McManmon has been with the ducks since early morning, adjusting them to cope with the conditions, drilling beneath their tail feathers and injecting water to afford the gravitas required for stability in the swirling stream; wind against current creates whirlpools when in the best of all worlds wind and current provide fast shipping lanes. After an inspection the judges decide that the championship course should be short: two chains.

Shortly before 9am a motley selection of men and women are seen to emerge from the neo-Georgian façade of the hotel. These are the contestants. If breathalysed, few would pass the test for the previous evening was spent at a trattoria in Celbridge where Barolo flowed and even more alcoholic beverages were available in generous abundance. They are surprised to see so many of their colleagues in such good shape; there is nostalgic talk of the night before – who did what, sang which, flirted with whom.

Ducks are selected and given final instructions by their owners; the countdown begins: 5,4,3,2,1: 48 ducks hit the water and the banks are alive with the sounds of encouragement.

The organization of acceptable corporate hospitality is an art form: agreeing to pick up a client's account at the Paris Ritz is beset with danger. The dispatch of fine wines and kilos of Beluga tends to be mistaken for bribery while the complimentary provision of women, boys or goats is an invitation for vilification by the tabloids.

But 'come and join us for a party' is benign. Nobody can object to that … and when Volvo Truck Finance GB invited forty of its best customers to stay at the Kildare Hotel, visit the Irish National Stud, spend an afternoon at Punchestown on Gold Cup day, have dinner and compete for the world duck-racing title on Ireland's foremost waterway, there were few who could say no.

And shame on those who think that this is a contest in which luck plays a part. I myself competed, selected bird No. 24, launched the beast into what I considered an especially favourable stretch of current. No. 24 finished last.

When the ghillie fished the winning bird from the water, John Butler, the new *numero uno*, made a modest acceptance speech, in the course of which he mentioned the close rapport achieved between man and duck. It was a day he will not forget.

* * *

Sharp-shooting spectacle draws a blank
The Times, 12 May 1995

NOBODY PROTESTED. THERE were no antis, nor did anyone carry a notice demanding the release of the Uttoxeter 200 ... the number that are shot in the name of sport in the hinterland of that Staffordshire town.

The English Open clay pigeon shooting championship started on Wednesday, ends on Sunday and, if you were intending to go to watch, I would advise you to desist. It is less exciting than witnessing the growth of a bay tree in a window box, and less rewarding, for bay leaves give a rare succulence to food while broken pieces of whatever 'clays' are made of – something hard and cheap and light and plastic – are of no use to man or beast.

About 300 shooters a day will make their way to the Doveridge Sporting Club; what they have in common is a quiet determination to do better than their fellow-shooters. They carry shotguns in canvas cases. Many are Japanese Browning 325s costing around £1,200, though a Purdy or Holland and Holland over and under at £27,000 might just give an edge. Satchels hold ammunition, which is likely to be Lyalvale, but there are those who believe that Baschieri Pellagri is not just hard to pronounce but more effective.

If you think 'clays' are all the same, let me disillusion you; they use standards and midis and minis. They also use battous – which are thinner and fly faster and are therefore harder to hit.

Clay pigeon shoots are not unlike fish and chip shops. People like to have them around but nobody wants to live nearby ... in the case of shoots, the nuisance is the noise rather than the smell.

The club is on the Marston Montgomery side of the village of Doveridge, not very far from Somersal Herbert, yet there are still people who complain about the noise, especially on Sundays, which is clay pigeon shooting day and the day that country people sit out on the lawn to sip a quiet glass of gin.

Some years ago, I visited the University of Southern California's sports department, where they analyse the configuration of champions. It is their boast that, given an athlete's height and weight and rate of heartbeat; size of feet, circumference of wrist and neck, thigh and upper arm; the distance from shoulder to fifteenth vertebrae; width of fingerspan, angle of instep, ratio of upper leg to lower leg, expansion coefficient of lungs and a host of other statistics, they will tell you whether the person's sport is basketball, boxing or butterfly stroke; pole vaulting or ping-pong; skating or sculling.

'And you can look at the Olympic march-past and tell who does what?', I asked the head of department.

He said: 'Yes ... except for shooters; shooters do not conform to any pattern other than a natural eye-hand coordination which is what makes them good at racquet sports also. The reverse does not apply.'

The winner on Sunday, he who will be richer by £750 and a gallon of Famous Grouse whisky and a gold medal and of course the honour ... will have shot more than eighty out of 100 clays during the qualifiers and finished in the top six after seventy-five birds on the final day. Then comes the shoot-off.

George Digweed, the three-time world champion, is the favourite, if that is not the wrong word for a man about whom nobody speaks with much kindness. 'Charisma bypass ... arrogant', were verdicts on offer. I rather took to him.

Digweed comes from Hastings; master butchery runs in the family. He is thirty-one, plump and dedicated to winning. 'Extremely competitive,' is how he describes himself. He does not shoot for good fellowship but to show that he is the best; if that upsets people, he loses no sleep. Something of a loner, soon to be married to a hospital secretary, he won the World Sporting Jubilee at Hodnet in 1988 (shooting, like boxing, has a number of authorities that accord championships) and is undoubtedly the biggest name in the sport.

He took the world title in Okeama, New Hampshire – clay pigeon shooting takes place in locations that require Ordnance Survey maps to find – with a record 191 out of 200.

I asked whether he will shoot in the Olympics. He hopes to be selected, but Olympic clay pigeon shooting is a different game altogether – an exercise in concentration; production-line shooting with the same targets coming at the same speed from the same traps. Sporting shooting such as this requires the ability to read targets, manifest fast reaction to one bird coming from the left and another, smaller one, going straight up into the air.

Arnold Palmer is the captain of the England team which won gold in San Antonio, Texas – five seniors and three each of veterans, women and juniors. He is a team man. As we talk, people smile at him, exchange a friendly word, wish him well and he explains about the classes in the competition – double A, which is for real, and then A, B, and C, which last category can be won with an average score of 55.

Winning class C is like being the tallest dwarf … and there are 'sandbaggers' – people who fiddle their qualifying scores so that they get into a lower class final.

With fifty traps releasing upwards of a quarter of a million clays over five days, twenty referees seems a modest figure to control the event, but as the whole battlefield is 'dry', there might have been difficulty finding volunteers.

The nearest pub is about a mile and a half away as the birds fly.

* * *

Tale of the riverbank and boats that go bump
The Times, 16 June 1995

ON 10 JUNE 1905, the Ditton Ferry overturned and three persons were drowned in the River Cam. A turn-of-the-century photograph of the ferry adorns a wall of the dining room of The Plough at Fen

Ditton, where, yesterday afternoon, I sat looking at the picture, waiting for the arrival of my spotted dick, keenly priced at £1.99, wondering whether it would arrive before the next division of the May Bumps passed by.

May Bumps is the name given a sport whose bottom line is to provide material for the chart in column eight, page 44 of *The Times*. It now takes place in June; nor do Bumps remain a necessary part of the exercise, for, when one coxed eight has made sufficient progress to reach the bows of that which set out twenty seconds earlier, a 'bump' is conceded; then, bumper and bumpee pull into the bank to leave the water clear for other, chasing boats.

When those have gone, the conquerors adorn themselves with greenery from the water's edge. Thus do they paddle to the end of the course displaying grins of achievement, while the vanquished – whose horizontal line on page 44 takes a dip to the southeast – homeward plod their weary way either in silence or to the chanting of doleful tunes from *Songs For Swinging Losers*.

The Plough at Fen Ditton, in the bar of which establishment is a holograph of a young couple in a boat captioned *Cam's Punt*, is midway up the course and recognized as a good place from which to observe.

Every forty-five minutes, a division of eighteen boats comes by and, on the far side of the water, their trainers and their supporters cycle along the towpaths shouting words of encouragement or warning.

It is a bizarre pastime. On the river, they who row can only see those who chase and have to accept the word of the one who steers about the likelihood of achieving a bump on the crew ahead; and those who chase do so looking for signs of joy in the cox's eyes.

On the towpath, the cyclists, urging their eight to achieve a bump or escape their pursuers, forget that success or failure on the water tends to involve running into the back wheels of their adversary's followers, also.

Tom Stoppard, after the first night of *Rosencrantz and Guildenstern Are Dead*, was asked by a critic: 'What is the play actually about?'

He replied: 'It is actually about to make me very rich.'

The May Bumps are actually about providing undergraduates with a non-academic theme to see them through the summer; to provide fodder to the question: 'What else did you do at Cambridge?'

The spotted dick took its time, which is a good sign, for you must never hurry the steam pudding, and I went down to the water's edge to witness the passing of the fourth division women's boats: a dozen and a half undersized future bank managers and accountants shouting: 'In, out; sit down and pull; now ... now,' and other exhortations to octets of tomorrow's lawyers, politicians, scientists and drop-outs.

On our side of the river, the lawn looks as if it had been left out all night and there is a marquee selling half-pint bottles of beer and cider at £2 a time. Foreign students, Japanese tourists with cameras, and the halt and the lame occupy the static side of the Cam, peering at boats for signs of a friend or relative.

'Cream or custard?,' asked the serving girl when I rejoined my table. I chose custard. The pudding arrived: a machine-assemblage of curranted gruel which had been frozen, microwaved into a semblance of life and dumped on to a cold soup plate containing warm custard made regardless of skill. A steam pudding requires treacle; there was no treacle. Even a poor steam pudding, if such a dish must be served, demands a gesture of sympathy or understanding from the waitress. There was none of that either.

Sitting under my lemon tree in Portugal earlier this week, I scanned a book called *Good Things From England* and took note of Scotch Woodcock from a recipe dated 1885:

'Take two slices of white bread and toast them; butter both sides and make therewith a sandwich of minced anchovy. In a dish, beat four egg yolks with half a pint of cream, add salt and cayenne pepper, and make this very hot but let it boil not. Pour the egg over the toast and serve at once.'

A recipe such as this would cause folk to think well of our gastronomy. The Plough's spotted dick, and to be honest The

Plough's Cumberland sausage (£3.99), is what will deter them from witnessing rituals such as May Bumps on overcast days unless their nearest and dearest are involved; in that case, they would be well advised to bring with them a hamper and a hip flask.

Sloe gin would be my choice for filling the latter; enough sloe gin would have made the whole outing bearable. Instead, it left me hungry and worried about how, ninety years ago to the week, three persons could have been drowned on a ferry that traverses fifty feet of shallow river in the Cambridgeshire Fens in June.

* * *

Dinner, dance and the Domino Effect
The Times, 6 October 1995

I HAD DONE my homework: looked up the whereabouts of Coldharbour Lane in the London gazetteer; verified that Wray and Nephew, sponsors of the United Kingdom Domino League, are the very same West Indies wine and spirit merchants who produce Jamaican over-proof rum known on the island as 'Be rude to your mother in-law'.

I confirmed that the game played in the league is not five-and-threes, which we play in East Anglia, but the follow-on or penny-a-spot game; that teams consist of six pairs who use 'codes' ... secret signs between players to denote who holds which stones. Dominoes without 'code' is known as 'mental', considered fit for women and children. And dominoes is a sport, not a game.

A 'bower' is one who gets rid of all his stones and wins the match. A 'block' is when no player can follow on, when the winners are the pair that hold fewest points. If there is a draw, there is no score but the next game is called a Derby and counts double. The winning team is the first to 151 points and Brixton, who hosted this encounter, head the premier league table. Sheffield United, their opponents, hold it up.

My informant who gave me directions to the venue also instructed me in Brixton-speak, and taught me 'Let me have a toke at your spliff', so that I would blend with the indigenous citizenry. Toke is like drag, only deeper; spliff is a joint and it was with some consternation that I entered the Brixton Sports and Social Club on the night of the match, went to buy a drink at the bar run by so voluminous a woman she would have lasted me all my life were I careful, to find a notice stating: No drugs. No swearing.

I asked politely for an Appleton Estate, which is white rum reminiscent of high-quality lighter fuel, and I think it would be wise to confine consumption of this potion, were you intending to do anything serious over the next few days.

The Sheffield United team had arrived by coach soon after 4pm – a 3½ hour journey for twenty players and fourteen supporters – wives, girlfriends or just people who thought Brixton greengrocers' yams might have the edge over those in the North.

They pay £10 a head, which includes travel, cups of beef soup on arrival, dinner after the game and dancing until 2am, when the licence ends.

If you think that you now have a general idea of what goes on, you are wrong. The room beyond the bar is divided by a rope and on one side are the six tables and 24 darkly intent men in suits and collars and ties (there is a dress code) who slam down their stones in the manner of Corsican peasants depositing their cards in bezique – and when a pair win they hit the table with their open palms and shout; on the far side of the dividing rope their supporters, who cannot see the stones but can read the body language, cheer and punch the air and jump up and down. Each side has a scorer who gauges the result from the identity of the noisemakers. There are team captains who monitor what goes on and exchange players who are not performing as they might, have had an Appleton too many or too few. At the far end of the room a man with a definitive scoreboard provides the running total.

The Sheffield captain is a quiet diplomat; Brixton's wears a red beret, is younger and louder. Reserve players wait by the rope or sit in the bar. I get as close as I can to watch the game, try to work out the signals, which are minimalist tic-tac – one gesture to denote the number, another the total of stones held bearing it. 'Rising' means indicating which piece you want your partner to play; twiddling your fingers means you want a double ... but the sport is about winning, about enabling you to hit the table with brio so that your supporters can shout and cheer and blow whistles and get you another drink.

Claudia makes most noise, has the shrillest whistle; she is 27, a secretary, her boyfriend runs his own computer business, plays for Sheffield and she travels to all matches. There used to be a lot of women, when Sheffield were good, but she thinks the team has gone off, needs commitment. 'I don't want to insult anyone but we need more new players.' She has a soft Yorkshire accent, has been to Jamaica on holiday, believes that what her team requires is, well, commitment. 'Like now we are nineteen points ahead but the lead is shrinking all the time which is how it goes.'

Upstairs in the dining-room and lounge that seats more than fifty people there is a kitchen where the women are cooking the dinner: curried goat, rice 'n' peas, tomatoes and lettuce. As in Jamaica, nobody seems to be working and everything gets done and smells good and is spotless.

When I come down again so many people crowd the viewing side of the rope it is impossible to get near the action. The countrymen (domino language for away team) are making more noise, slamming their palms on the table with more force; the fact that they are winning, that Brixton are losing, filters through to the fathers, mothers and grannies who are arriving for the dance with eager daughters straight from the hairdresser.

Four and a half hours after the start, it is over. Sheffield have won. Claudia's whistle shrills without pause, Delroy and Linford, Sheffield steelworkers who started as reserves but got to play, hit their table in delight, and from the kitchen above wafts the delicately pungent aroma of curried goat.

8
FREUD'S
LEARNING CURVE

'The book points out that it is important to repeat everything three times, *viz.* "Mayday, mayday, mayday." "I have been hit by lightning, I have been hit by lightning, I have been hit by lightning," making it easier for your next of kin to be given your last words.'

Clement Freud was never averse to having a go. He rode in horse races – starting at Naas in 1967 (see pages 150–53) and famously winning a match race at Haydock Park in September 1972 against his old friend Sir Hugh Fraser – and tried his hand at any number of other activities.

In 1968 and 1969 the Sunday Telegraph Magazine *had him starting from scratch as – among other pursuits – a racing driver, as a pilot, and (with a less happy outcome) on the ski slopes.*

How (for £80) I learnt to be a racing driver
Daily Telegraph Magazine, **10 May 1968**

CERTAIN THINGS REMAIN in the mind more clearly than others, like the crash helmet; it goes on your head if you pull out the straps – and comes off easily enough if you don't mind losing an ear.

I shall not forget the opening drive, with Peter Arundell sitting next to me holding a long pink 'Analysis of Faults' form, sub-divided into 'Approach to Corners', 'Cornering', 'Line' and 'General'.

There were 36 possible faults like: Excessive revs on 'blip'.

We did three circuits, and when we stopped he looked pensive and then wrote 'got a lot to learn' across the sheet. Like a dancing teacher who needs customers, he did say that I 'had a certain rhythm' and that I seemed to have sympathy with – or was it sympathy for? – the steering wheel, and steered smoothly. I thought that this might have been a compliment until I went round with him. He goes into a bend, skids and adjusts the skid, sawing at the wheel with small sharp snatches while I hung grimly and silently on to the passenger door …

There is no prototype racing driver. The man with too much devil in him dies before he makes his name and he who is too careful will stay away from the track. The Motor Racing Stables' course provides battle inoculation … and will be of the greatest help in telling talentless would-be Graham Hills to think seriously about going to the Labour Exchange.

It all starts in the time-honoured way. You pull out your cheque book and having relieved yourself of the appropriate amount of money you sign a form giving them the name, address and mileage of your next of kin. This is followed by briefing. The briefer is called Marc Anthony and you think desperately that there should be a joke there somewhere. He points out the control tower – from which a disembodied voice will eventually call your name – and explains the procedure. You will go in a two-seater with an instructor … and then if you are good enough, you go in a Formula Ford.

I am going to be good enough. Damn it, I am doing it for the *Telegraph* and if there are any doubts about my ability I shall take the matter to the Press Council or my solicitor.

This may be the time to declare my interest. I never learnt to drive, having started my motoring career in an Army three-ton truck filled with prisoners of war. 'Actually, sir,' I said to the Adjutant, 'I don't drive.' 'Serve the bastards right,' said the Adjutant.

I have driven ever since; a bit slovenly about hand signals; have an endorsement for dangerous parking with a year and a half to go before it disappears from my licence, but otherwise I drive fast and true. My mother's favourite driver if she can't get either of my brothers.

For the record I have absolutely no idea of what is under the bonnet of a car and why.

'Well now,' said Marc Anthony, 'we want you to do three laps with an instructor to see how you go into a corner and if you come out; to see what line you take. The car you can take is over there, a TVR.'

I said, 'What?'

'TVR,' said Marc Anthony, 'is the make; how could you not have heard of it? I've heard of you. Here's your helmet; mind your ears.'

Peter Arundell asked whether I was comfortable. I was not. It seemed pointless not to tell him. The helmet was tight and heavy and tall, so that I got jammed, with my helmet stuck to the roof and my seat glued to the seat. I then rounded my back and it was slightly better, but not much. Peter Arundell wrote 'complains of discomfort' on the pink form.

We drove off; it has been a very long time since I had a passenger who fancied my driving so little.

When I get to a bend I tend to steer round it. Clearly that was for the dogs. In a word, my sin was speed – an utter lack thereof. I never realized before how sluggishly I drove, and Arundell said he had no idea people could drive so slowly. I seemed to have my foot pressed hard on the accelerator but cars similar to mine passed me, going at about twice my speed.

I said I was uncomfortable and didn't like my hat and why can't I look out of the driving mirror to see what is behind me? He said I would get more comfortable by and by and he was looking out of the driving mirror to see what was behind me. 'Have faith.' I promised to try.

For further faith there was a man on the course who waved a blue flag which means 'there is someone behind you.' This is presumably in case neither of us was looking.

On reflection Peter Arundell was quite polite about my gear changes. He went out with the next pupil and I waited until there was a gaggle of us and we went to be briefed some more by Marc A. in front of a blackboard.

Freud, Wrottesley, Smith and Miss Jenkins sitting around, listening – the other three very intently. There is talk of heel and toe – one of these must be on the clutch even as the other is on the brake or the accelerator – anyway that sort of thing saves valuable seconds. 'Use the most sensitive part of your foot, roll your foot … see what I mean?' They do. I don't.

The quickest way round is to imagine you are on a tightrope … keep the balance, imagine you are on a tightrope all the time. Here is a picture of a corner, the first part; brake, then gear change, the slowest part is approaching it, about thirty yards before the corner, then make for the apex, foot down hard as you go into it, set the wheels and let the car go round. 'Look, I'll give you a tip; the apex of the corner is further round than you think.'

I decide to file this in my 'post-humorous hints' folder. 'When you get to a complex bend like Druids and Bottom it is better to make a mess of the first part, then at least you come out of it fast.'

Now about the flags: A red flag means stop. Yellow: caution, and do not overtake. Blue: there is someone behind you. Chequered:

finish, or 'your money has run out'; or possibly 'we have just been informed that your cheque has bounced.'

'You overtake on the left, always. If you are baulked by a car in front, you get a free lap ... on the house.

'Braking and changing gears must be done in the straight ... when you better 60 seconds (Denny Hulme has done it under 57) we can talk about that sort of thing again' – a fair way of saying goodbye.

Briefing is over.

We go down the steps from the briefing room, across the track to the pits. The shell-like cars are there, waiting. You get a crash helmet and goggles that mist up. The man in the pits says they clear as soon as you get going. The cars are constant, only the bodies of the drivers are different. How about you? Short in the leg? Here is another seat, still not right, here is Sid Fox's flying jacket to tuck behind your back. Be careful, it's alive, things crawl out of it.

'It is very important,' says the man, 'that you should be comfortable ... now, can you reach the pedals?'

I should have thought this came under the heading of essentials rather than comforts; anyway, I can reach the pedals.

The car has a starter. I had imagined they pushed and you crashed into seventh gear when they got you up to 35mph. I imagined wrong. You press the starter with your foot hard down on the accelerator. The engine roars fiercely, the gears are away from your left hand ... first and second up and down by your knee; third and fourth by the door; that's the lot. If there is a reverse no one bothered to tell me. You leave the pits and are told to stay behind the yellow line until the track is clear – basic motorway-joining procedure. Track clear, foot down, third gear, fourth gear and you beetle off towards Paddock, take a right-hander and it is Druids and Bottom and some bends whose names escape me but are taken in top gear and you are back in the straight making for Paddock. The whole thing lasts a surprisingly short time. Every time I got to the bottom of the track, man-with-blue-flag was waving and I would look in the mirror and he was right, there was always one, sometimes two cars waiting to go by.

Overtake on the left, Marc Anthony had said. They did.

The fifth time round he gave me the chequered flag and I drove back into the pits. Arundell said he was surprised I went so slowly; he thought deep down I was more of a whiz-kid. I said deep down there is an element of whiz-kiddery left. On the surface desire for survival is strong; it probably showed.

We talked some more and I got into his car and he drove round. If he disliked my driving, I must admit in all honesty that I hated his. He went into bends on a full throttle, skidded and sawed at the wheel and said he was going quite slowly. I said if you are going that slowly try pulling in to the pits and see what happens. He did.

More of Marc Anthony; a tour of the control tower where a man watches you and records your lap times and showed me a whiz-kid in a white car. Look at his line ... he seemed to be going round the track the long way. I was unimpressed.

'Ready for another ten laps?' I looked round the control tower. As we were alone I reckoned he could only have meant me, so I said, 'Yes, if it's part of it.'

It appeared that it was.

The first three laps were dull and then one or two bits of advice came back to me. That part about toeing and heeling. It could not have been the clutch and the brake. Must have been the brake and accelerator ... so that you rev up and brake and rev up again almost at the same time.

Arundell had said that when you got to Clearways bend you aim for the F on the FINA placard then swing in; that seemed to work pretty well. By the time I got my chequered flag it was becoming almost pleasurable.

My times, said the man when I got to the control tower, had been around 78 seconds (average 50mph) on each of my last four laps. That is about what we expect. See you next week.

I got into my car, drove along Death Hill towards London and found I was doing 85mph.

In my second week I considered myself something of a veteran. I went into the canteen where I greeted the coffee machine as an old friend; dialled 'black without', remembered just in time to put the cup under the jet, said good morning to the canteen lady who is employed to stand behind the counter and wait for the bread to arrive, and agreed to drive a mechanic down to the track. I drove with just the right blend of boredom and nonchalance – and crashed gears for the first time this decade.

'You might as well do a few laps to warm up the car,' said the man in the control tower ... and I did a few laps warming up self and car.

Then I came in and we had a talk. The instructor said, 'Make more use of the road,' and drew a picture of a corner. 'If you swing right out before you get to it you can drive faster into it and if, when you get out of the bend, you don't find yourself on the far side of the road, you know you could have gone faster.'

I got back into the car and it worked. My lap times were 67, 67, 78, 69. 'What happened on the 78 lap?', he asked. 'Metal fatigue,' I said. If he hadn't seen me spin round at Druids, there seemed little point telling him. 'Revs all right?' I had been told to use no more than 5,000 revs. I said, 'Yes, fine.' Actually I had had a devil of a job getting up to 5,000.

We went back to the canteen. I tried to pour a cup of coffee into the machine and get 6d. out but it only worked one way.

The canteen filled up and I realized that the social aspect of motor racing was as important as the driving part. They had a lot of words with which they punctuated the otherwise intelligible conversation: torque, differential and oversteer. I decided to learn the group starting with *c* and ending in *h*. Crash, clutch, crunch, crutch, clash ...

On the way home, lying back in the driving seat and doing Death Hill at 90, I thought of the instructor who had said: 'If on a bend you find you use only half of the road, it means you could have gone into it twice as fast.' That was the most useful single sentence of my racing career. Sixty-seven seconds per lap is an average speed of just over 60mph. My instructors were pleased.

The following Sunday I drove to Biggin Hill Aerodrome. Michael Dashwood is the director of the skid-control centre and the instructor is Sid Fox – whose upper and outer garment had been such a help to me in my two-week racing career.

The Skidpan is a frying-pan-shaped circuit, treated with a special non-stick solution.

'The idea of this school', he said, 'is to give you greater safety in driving. We don't show off or mess about. We cater to the lowest common denominator in drivers. Men of seventy, girls of seventeen … anyone.' I felt myself included.

He turned on a tape recorder and a comfortable pipe-smoking-type voice went into a monologue: first, accident figures; then 'What is a skid?'

'It is when force exerted overcomes the grip of the tyres. There are three types of skid. Rear, front, four-wheel. You will see all three, and learn to rectify all three. You must be on the right part of the road at the right time in the right gear.'

The tape ended with the old saw that it is better to be twenty minutes late in this world than twenty years early in the next.

The next hour and a half did more for my driving than I believed possible. I had not previously given a great deal of thought to skids, but was of the opinion that a skid was the beginning of the end – you close your eyes and commend your soul to God and when it happened it was a matter of luck whether you crossed yourself and died in a state of grace or met your end with a four letter word. Thanks to Sid Fox and a battered Anglia I learnt that the brakes are almost the last thing to use; that when you skid you declutch to stop rear wheel thrust, you steer, you accelerate and then brake. We skidded into 180 degrees and round 360 degrees. I got the Anglia off the pan into the mud and Sid Fox helped to heave it back on again.

In the end, I drove onto the pan, went into a deliberate four-wheel skid and managed to stay on the track, as often as not facing in the right direction.

In the course of that short session, I had skidded more than any driver is likely to skid in his lifetime. And retrospectively, I forgave Peter Arundell for taking me round the bends and sawing at the wheel. In fact I quite looked forward to trying it myself.

At the time of going to press I have done a further ten laps. My time is down to 63 seconds which is 70mph and I have started overtaking people. This should not happen to a dog because you get sharp stones and surprisingly substantial flies plummeting in your face and were it not for a man called Ken, who lent me a face mask, I might have given up the whole thing there and then. As it is, I continue.

It would be wrong to say that I consider myself the darling of the pits (I am very much an elder Pitt) but motor racing now makes sense. I can go into a bend and calculate the danger element. At Brands Hatch I have landmarks in trees and posters and bales of straw at which I change gear, swing out and cut in; I know where are the apexes to clip, or roughly where.

At the moment my weakness is overtaking people, also I get a sharp muscular pain in my left hand ... and my feet seem too big, or the pedals too small to turn smoothly from accelerator to brake pedal without withdrawing the leg. Peter Arundell is sceptical; Pat Brangwyn – who manages to time four cars, shout to a mechanic to prepare the Lotus Elan for a PI, call in someone for overtaking on the right and remain kind and relaxed and enthusiastic – thinks I should be ready to drive in a race on Saturday.

Freud drove in a Formula Ford event at Brands Hatch the following Saturday, and finished second.

* * *

If you can walk away from it, it's a landing
Daily Telegraph Magazine, **20 September 1968**

ANY FOOL CAN fly a plane; most people can take off without much difficulty; the snag is that hardly anyone can land.

As a result of this an ever-increasing number of flying schools are opening up, and desirous to be of their company I went to the Gregory establishment at Denham and enrolled as a pupil.

The economics of taking to the air are less frightening than I had supposed. You pay around £8 an hour for lessons – which means that £100 should be enough to give you the doubtful privilege of going up on your own. (At no addition to this modest price your instructor waits on the airfield hoping to welcome you when you come down.)

Perhaps I should point out that flying solo is not the ultimate aim; flying solo means, very simply, taking off, having a flip round the airfield upon which you keep a constant and mistrustful eye, and landing at-from-whence-you-came within ten minutes.

After that you learn navigation. This takes longer and is consequently more expensive; I mention it in case anyone might think that my eleven hours in the air achieved in two weeks of waiting for breaks in the oyster light that passes for an English summer would make me the ideal man to fly their mother in-law to Lourenco Marques. In fact, I have the utmost difficulty telling Aylesbury from Princes Risborough … and if it were not for motorways, railway lines, a compass and, mostly, my highly skilled instructor, I should be a distant duck if not a completely dead duck. But let me start at the beginning.

Gregory Air Services occupy a 90-acre field hard by Denham Golf Club, in Buckinghamshire. There is a fairly undesirable pre-fab building which estate agents might well term as *large, dtchd. bung. 9 rms. 2 wcs.*, known as the control tower; this would have surprised me less had I not recently been 'welcomed aboard' a terraced house in Kilburn by a naval officer.

It should be said at this point that I was not a representative pupil; I have never had any great desire to fly. Further, the nature of the exercise forced me to take my lessons two at a time, weather permitting, over a short span of time: I realize that the ideal method is to fly for an hour and think about it for three days. However.

It starts with a small cheque-exchanging ceremony and goes on to the classroom. A man with two bands of gold braid on his shoulder goes up to a blackboard, draws upon it a wing that looks like a head-on view of a fillet of plaice and says the air has to travel more quickly to pass over the curved side than it does to whistle past the flat side ... so the faster air above the wing gives lift. I believed him when another instructor took a thin sheet of notepaper, held it in front of him between thumbs and forefingers and blew steadily over the near edge; the far end, which had drooped down, rose up.

Now for controls: in a nutshell a plane has a rudder which sticks up at the back and is operated by foot pedals. Pressure on one or the other causes the plane to skid – or yaw as they call it – in the direction of the foot involved. There is a control column which you push forward when you want to go down and pull into your stomach when you wish to climb, while this same column can be twisted sideways, causing you to bank. The reason for the banking is ailerons – small projections tucked on to the ends of the fixed wings – which move right side up left side down and vice versa. There are also flaps which give you the required lift for take-off and drag for landing.

The instructor spoke intelligently and used an excellent wiper to clean the blackboard.

Now for the programme: my exercises would be effects of control; taxiing; straight and level flying; climbing and descending; turning; stalling; spinning. After that, circuits of the airfield until I was ready to fly solo ... say ten to fifteen hours.

He gave a final wipe to the blackboard and we went out to a small blue and white plane made by a firm called Cessna – an American organization who have the good sense to equip their machines with Rolls-Royce engines.

Our first job, explained my instructor, was to examine the machine from the outside. I immediately diagnosed two people sitting in the cockpit but was asked to ignore them; they were an instructor and pupil returned from a lesson. The things to look for were damage to the skin, breaks in the joists that hold up the wings; the propeller should not be missing; neither should any of the three wheels which, ideally, ought to have tyres pumped up and in good condition. We checked the petrol tanks in the wings which the designer has fixed in such a position that a pole-vaulter, or a man with a stepladder, would have the edge on ordinary mortals. We also carried out an oil check on the engine. There is an inspection cover held down by two Woolworth-type wing nuts which undo at the flick of an index finger but take a tediously long time to re-engage. You check the oil with a dipstick – which I understand is something mechanics in garages do to motor car engines.

The inside of the plane was comfortable, two seats, next to each other, and an instrument board which went rather further than that on my car. Among unfamiliar dials was the oil temperature gauge showing that the oil could get just hot enough to blanch chips. In the course of the first few lessons one gets a general idea of flying, though being told to bank sharply to the left and smile up at the photographer in the luggage compartment does nothing to facilitate the exercise. Flying is a question of attitudes. You climb and judge the rate of ascent by the nose attitude. You come down – nose attitude again; level out and check that you are level by the general overall attitude.

In the beginning you spend a lot of time on checks. Fuel check. Oil temperature check. Power check. Suction check. Harness check. Radio check. Rudder check. Trim check. Ailerons check. Then you shout 'yoho' in case anyone has crept under the propeller and if no one answers you start up and taxi off. You stop near the end of the runway, check some more – in case someone has snuck up and turned off the fuel, blown into the suction or fiddled with the flaps. After that you turn the plane downwind, have another quick check, put the flaps down and in the fullness of time the instructor takes off and you sit there holding your end of the dual control column, feet on the rudder, body throbbing in sympathetic vibration to his actions.

You take off on full power and when you have reached a height and an attitude you reduce to 2,300 revs. Climbing is done at 70mph, cruising at about 90; the speedometer gives the speed irrespective of windspeed so that you can fly at 80 into an 80-mile headwind, remain static over the ground and still register a respectable 80mph.

As you come in to land there is a further series of checks – for this they have the useful code word BUMPFFHH, an easy word to remember. B stands for brakes – which should be off. U is undercarriage which must be down (the fact that the plane has no retracting undercarriage does not come into it). I forget what M stands for but P is pitch, which does not apply either. F is flaps and one of the final H's is harness – in case you have undone it since you took off.

You do turns on the ailerons which give you bank and having adopted a left turn attitude you invariably end up having turned left. A compass in front of you (which has to be adjusted to agree with the other compass) helps you decide whether you have turned 90 degrees, though ideally you should fix on an object and fly towards that. Formate is another good word to use.

After a while the controls are yours. You fly around and the instructor by your side keeps a weather eye on proceedings. The wind blows you around in the rocking-horse weather and you adjust the plane's progress with ailerons and rudder. You fly uneasily around the sky wondering when you will attain air sense, rather as an agnostic sits in church waiting for God to tap him on the shoulder and show him the way.

First realizations of the benefits come after a couple of hours. On the road you are permanently ten feet away from disaster. In the air you have a couple of miles. You begin by sitting tensely, straightening out every quiver of the plane, remembering attitude, looking at the compass, fuel gauge, oil temperature, air speed indicator, altimeter, scanning the sky for other aircraft which you never see but the instructor constantly points out ... and then you begin to look down and look round with a positive feeling of pleasure and you realize that tension is no part of a pilot's attitude.

I received a number of documents like a *Pilot's Log Book*, the legend printed in gold on royal blue, and for the first three lessons I religiously entered every minute of my flying. I inspected a volume called *Flight Briefing for Pilots Volume I* which contained words like 'slipstream helix', which never did make me go on reading a book.

More exciting, I found a Board of Trade publication called *Radio-telephony Procedure*, price 3s. 6d. This contained such handy remarks as: 'The language normally used by that station may not necessarily be the language of the State in which it is located.'

It also said: 'High-pitched voices transmit better than low-pitched ones,' which I took as a straight insult. I read in this the procedure for grade A emergencies which are prefaced by the word MAYDAY from the French *m'aider*. There is also the word PAN which is less urgent meaning something like: 'I am not going to crash but doubt if I shall land.' The book points out that it is important to repeat everything three times, *viz.* 'Mayday, mayday, mayday.' 'I have been hit by lightning, I have been hit by lightning, I have been hit by lightning,' making it easier for your next of kin to be given your last words.

At first the plane's radio microphone, which you detach from a hook and use as contact with the ground, is an instrument of embarrassment. You look at the letters – G-AZPH on the panel in front of you and say: 'This is Golf Alpha Zulu Papa Hotel' ... fully expecting the people at the other end to say: 'So what?' They do not; they are permanently polite and helpful and if you get the name of your plane wrong, they get it right.

When you have shown that flying is not going to be a fleeting fancy you are advised to complete a form, have a medical and send

£2 to the Board of Trade in order to get a Student Pilot's Licence – without which you may not fly solo. As my own doctor was on holiday I went to one recommended by my secretary; he took the job very seriously and in the course of an all-out investigation went as far as scratching the soles of my feet to ensure that the big toes curled up and not down (this must be the cause of many air disasters).

There is an air of wizard prangyness about the people on the airfield. Gregory Air Services pilots come in from – and go off to – far off places like Swindon and Addis Ababa and shove their flight documents down on the desk and make jocular remarks about the journey like: 'I remembered to bring back the plane, haha', and 'Listen to this recording of someone talking to flight control Birmingham in the fog.' It all goes down very well for they are an appreciative lot. In the bar it is frowned upon to drink but OK to talk about hangovers.

In the office the ladies who man switchboards and read telex machines that belt out meteorological information are married to pilots or about to be married to pilots and wear glasses and drive cars and say 'Hello you' to people they know and 'Good afternoon' to others.

In the normal pupil's flying instruction, stalling and spinning comes after seven hours of beetling about the sky. In my case, on what I suppose could be (but should not be) called a crash course, it came after three hours, and I did not much care for it.

The point is that if an honest man with gold braid on his shoulder says to me: 'This plane will stall at forty-five miles per hour and being nose-heavy will fall, regain speed and be manoeuvrable' – I believe him utterly.

Protest as I would, he insisted on giving me a practical demonstration. 'Look. We climb, we cut power. Now watch.' The stall warning machinery produces a small scream such as you might get from a rhubarb plant cut in the prime of its life. It protests shrilly, clamouring for attention, and eventually the plane that is pointing up stops and drops and you reach out for your stomach, hoist it back and notice that as you fall forward you pick up speed. The control column is then pushed forward, as if you had meant to dive, and eased out again to level the plane.

'I see, thank you very much, very interesting. Just as you said.'

'Look,' said the instructor, 'I'll show you again. Strap yourself in tightly,' and he does it again.

'Thank you very much. Yes, I see.'

'Now you do it,' and there comes that inevitable aid to memory in the form of initials, this time HASEL that mean: have sufficient height, don't do it over a densely populated area, make sure it is not a Tuesday in Lent, etc. I climb the plane and cut power and the stalling noise comes, giving me the spine-chilling shudder that I thought I only got from police cars' gongs. Stall. Drop. Regain speed, steer. We do it again.

We land and I help myself to a draught of sheep-dip which hisses into a plastic cup when you feed 6d. into a slot and press a button marked 'Black coffee'. 'Now,' he said, 'we move on to spins.'

We climb through the cloud to reach the calm of the upper sky; above the sun, below us a mountain range of cotton wool peaks. We climb to 6,000 feet and the instructor says: 'You remember what happened when we stalled? We climbed and stopped and dropped and picked up speed and regained control.'

I remember.

'Now, for a spin, you climb and cut power and as you do so press hard down on your right rudder, like this.' This is a particularly cunning manoeuvre. As we stop, instead of falling forwards we fall sideways in a great groin-squeezing swoop. 'Press on left rudder, forward with the controls,' says the instructor, who is now sitting beneath me, and we stop going sideways and dive down and pull out when we get level. The altimeter shows 4,500 feet and I say: 'Very good, I see, thank you.'

Unable to leave a good thing alone, he does it on the other wing which causes him to sit on top of me, and then asks me to do it, one spin on each wing. When we come out of the clouds, considerably chastened, he asks me to fly the plane for an hour or two while he works out our position and in the fullness of time he says. 'Aha, there's Amersham.'

'How do you know?', I ask.

'I can tell,' he said. 'I can always tell Amersham, been over it so often.'

There is a look of expectancy on the faces of the girls behind the counter as you come back from spinning. 'All right was it?', they ask, with an evil glint on their glasses.

They do not actually tell you that you are going solo on a particular day; they make suggestive noises and wait for the moment of truth.

Approaching the moment of going solo I flew round the aerodrome in triangles instead of rectangles, which was unimpressive but I realized it was a triangle, which was reassuring.

On the third take-off we hit a hare; after the fourth circuit I came over the airfield so high that I applied full power and took off at once, having never got closer than about twenty feet to the ground.

'Good,' said the instructor. 'If it is not perfect, don't attempt to land; take off again, full power on, carburettor heater in, 10 degrees of flaps off, hold the nose down because power develops lift, and climb gently towards another circuit.' Another circuit, a decent landing. And then it happened. The instructor undid his straps, opened the door, asked whether I was sure I was all right, and got out. He stood outside the plane looking apprehensive. I asked him whether he was all right. He nodded. We were both sweating slightly. I said I was fine. He said, in that case he was all right. 'Remember,' he said, 'you've got enough petrol for two hours' (a circuit takes ten minutes).

I checked my fuel tanks and said: 'Yes, I have'.

'If you come in too high, or too fast, do another circuit.'

'Yes.'

'Be careful.'

'Yes.'

'Goodbye, goodbye. Good luck.'

'Thank you.'

I looked at my instruments, adjusted the screw on the power lever, mixture rich. Carburettor heat cold, flaps down 10 degrees for take-off. I picked up the microphone. 'Denham, Golf Kilo take-off clearance.'

'Take-off runway 05 at your discretion.'

I looked discreetly into the sky, saw nothing coming, gave some power, turned the plane towards the runway, gave full power and saw the instructor standing by the hedge, looking anxious. I aimed for the cricket pavilion, watched the accelerator, and helped the plane up at 50mph.

It swayed a bit and I looked at the vacant seat by my side for advice. It was very, very vacant, the seat belt neatly fastened over nothing. At 300 feet I took the flaps up, and went into a climbing turn.

When the gasometer came upsides my right wing I turned into the base leg, put on carburettor heat, reduced power, to 1,500, waited for the speed to drop 85 and put down flaps 20 degrees; with one hand on the power and the other on the control I banked into the final approach. 'Golf Kilo final.' 'Golf Kilo final.' Eight young RAF men from Rent-a-Cadet, whom I had never yet seen on their feet, were standing, watching the landing from outside the control tower. My instructor had disappeared, apparently behind a hedge. I came down at 70mph picking a landing place along the left hand side of the plane.

At 80mph I pointed the nose up to reduce speed, lost height, put on more power. Passing the hedge I took off power and gripped the control lever. I was still going a bit fast about 15 feet above the ground. I pressed the front pedals, the way I press the brakes on my car (I can't stop myself doing that) and started sinking down, levelling out with insufficient authority so that I hit the runway and bounced up again. Keep the nose down, straighten up; at the second bounce I held on and taxied and slowed. The cadets went back into their hut. The instructor appeared from behind the hedge. I cleaned up the aircraft, flaps up, carburettor heat off and taxied back towards the hedge. The instructor came up, opened the door and shook my hand.

'I thought you were coming in a bit too high but it was all right,' he said.

'Not, I am afraid, one of the great landings.'

'It's all right,' he said, 'if you can walk away from it, it's a landing.'

* * *

Freud slides down the slippery slope that ends in a wheelchair
Daily Telegraph Magazine, 16 May 1969

IF I HAD a scrap book the whole episode of C. Freud, skier by appointment to the *Daily Telegraph Magazine*, could be summed up in a double-page montage. The bill from the Brothers Moss for hiring ski-pants, anorak, socks and gloves; one from Jaeger for a cashmere jersey. A Swissair ticket London/Zurich and a polite letter wrapped around a box of Nestlé's chocolates welcoming me to a short overnight stay at the Schweizhof Hotel.

There is a Zurich/Davos return rail ticket, a crumpled Davos press pass entitling me to unlimited free use of ski-lifts, mountain railways, hire of skis and boots, and a tin of lip salve, essential when you get into the mountains. I have a bill for six glasses of Glühwein, which is hot and sweet and not very strong and two francs a go, but which helped my muscular pains after the first day on the idiots' hill (which I always thought was called Nursery Slopes). Also the picture of me shaking hands with my ski instructor whose name was Christian (his mother must have had a sense of humour), and an entry in my diary stating 'Titus Oates was not a bad judge' (he was the man who walked out into the snow of the South Pole to die). Then comes the bill for 75 francs to the Parsenn Ambulance service; an account for 145 francs payable to the Davos Hospital, an X-ray of my left ankle showing a first degree fracture of the malleolus and a letter from an English insurance company asking whether I was quite certain that I should be utterly unable to pursue my chosen profession for a period of six to eight weeks.

A small boy I know was asked whether he enjoyed going to school; he said yes, he liked going to school and he loved coming home from school. It just so happened that he hated school.

Well, I enjoyed going to ski. I like Swissair, I approve of trains that are clean and punctual and in Davos I stayed in one of the best-run hotels I have ever patronized – it is called The Fluela. I thought après-ski the ultimate in boring eight letter words, though in choosing Davos during the German doctors' conference fortnight it is possible that I was in the right place at the wrong time.

My excellent hotel apart, nothing that happened on what we veterans call the slopes, or *la piste*, had very much appeal.

I reached my resort at 12.48, changed into the hired ski clothes, found that the Brothers Moss had loaned me a broken trouser-zip, struggled, and was claimed by the head of the local ski school at 12.59. It was going to be that sort of holiday. He took my hand like a man who has been much complimented on the strength of his grip, looked me in the eye with a gaze worth half a hundred Christmas cards from English spinsters, said he had read my article on motor racing … was I fit? I confirmed this by trying to break his hand, gave up and withdrew my own four fingers and what was left of my thumb. As a badge of office, ski instructors wear grey jerseys with blue and yellow stripes on the upper arm. We got into his Volkswagen, he lit up four or five Swiss Gauloises and we drove off to the ski-school where I was introduced to Christian.

In a fantastically short time I was kitted out with boots and mini-skis – which are the super new way they have of teaching safe skiing. The first size of mini-ski is 65 centimetres so that there is hardly any protrusion of ski in front of and behind your foot. It has been established that this minimizes time-consuming falls. Ski boots turned out to be massive leather construction jobs that fit your foot like a vice; there is a platform up front and a wedge at the back so that the skis can bite. The boots have a ratchet tightening device and the skis have a platform, tailor-made to the boots with a locking lever at the back, in case you should think the whole thing is too easy. You get on to the ski, engage your foot and then bend down like a bunny girl trying to preserve her cleavage while you grope behind for the elusive catch. Finally you succeed and straighten up with a feeling of immense achievement to find that was only the beginning.

You now have to learn to ski.

Christian, who had put on his skis in about three seconds, asked whether I danced; I should have read the writing on the wall.

If I understood the preliminary chat correctly, the idea was not to glide downhill over the snow, which any fool can do ... but to slow your descent by turning like this: down, UP, turn, down, UP, turn.

We tried it together in front of the ski-shop. Down – bend knees and keep the weight over the rump. UP – straighten knees and as you rise turn the skis from facing forward to about 40° left and then down UP and 40° right. We walked up a small slope pigeon-toed, digging the inside edges of the skis into the snow, and then trundled down; bend knees, UP and turn; down UP and as the weight is removed you turn your skis. An hour and twenty walks and skids later Christian said that we could go up in the ski-lift and attempt the big descent.

There are two types of ski-lifts in Davos and the one we used on the first day was of the soup-plate variety. This is attached to a hard rubber thong, suspended from a conveyor belt. You stand on the launching platform, skis pointing uphill, and an attendant grabs the next soup-plate on the line, hands it to you and you quickly feed it through your legs, engage it against the cheeks of your behind and grip the steadying thong in front of you as you are pulled forward and up. Christian bent his knees slightly, leaned back and slid easily towards the top. Unused to propulsion via that part of my body, I leaned forward to get better balance, stuck out my behind and at the first sign of uneven ground felt the soup-plate scuttle through my legs and picked myself off the side of the track. It is moments such as these that bring out the quality of an instructor. Mine looked at me and said: 'What'sthematterwithyou. Pickingflowersorsomesink?'

It was a moderately amusing remark and would have been forgiven had it not been repeated every ten minutes for the next four days.

He also sang the words 'roll me over', which may well be part of a song. If this is so, he knew no other lyrics.

Taking stock, we had come halfway up the slope and had now to go down. The snow was pleasantly thick, the slope gentle and I got up as instructed, pointed my skis downhill, took the weight off the inside edges, which had a locking effect, and commenced the descent. I gathered speed. Christian beside me said: 'Now down, UP, turn … if you do it twice I buy you a glass of beer.' I did it ten times coming down the hill – never saw the colour of his money.

That afternoon we went up the ski-lift eight more times and came down a similar number of occasions. It was quite pleasurable in a muscle-searing sort of way, but I noticed that whereas Christian stood upright as he came down, I did it looking like a cross between the Hunchback of Notre Dame and Toulouse-Lautrec.

My balance was sufficient to get me down at some speed – but this is frowned upon. What is required is a fast descent involving a succession of quickly executed minor turns, each one with the weight of the body on the lower ski, facing the valley, placing your top ski just ahead of the lower one, keeping upright, skis together … 'what'sthematterwithyou … pickingflowersorsomesink? roll me over.'

At 4.30 the ski-lift stopped for the day, Christian put me on a bus back to my hotel and promised to meet me at 9.30 the following morning. Down UP turn like dancing ... you dance don't you?

I denied this.

On the next day we exchanged 65 centimetre skis for one metre skis and walked to the other ski-lift. This is similar to the soup-plate variety but involves a double-edged meathook on which two people ascend together lightly holding the centre cord as the dull blade of the yoke pushes them across the buttocks.

For the whole morning we went up in this lift and came down in a series of turns and falls and getup whatsmatterwithyous. As I react unkindly to being shouted at we had an early lunch in a restaurant overlooking the slope. I asked for a soft drink. Christian addressed the waitress in Swiss-German and procured for me a glass of thin, sharp local wine.

At 2.15 the ski-lift started up again and we did a few more descents down, UP, turn. Shoulder pointing downhill, upper ski ahead of lower ski, weight on lower ski. When one falls the tension on the ski dislodges it from the boot; this is a safety device. It also means that you have to pick up the ski, find your foot, place it in the slot and lean back and grope and try to clip the bloody thing on again. There is only one reaction from other skiers to people who fall on the slopes: laughter. Absolutely straight, unashamed look at him hahaha laughter.

We stopped at 4 o'clock. I had cramp in both legs, was beginning to hate skiing and had become acutely conscious of the people who zipped past as I lay on the snow. For the most part they were fat middle-aged nonentities who made me feel 'if that one can do it ... it just cannot be difficult.' So I would get up, try again and get the standard 'whatsmatterwithyou pickingflowersorsomesink?'

That night the photographer arrived and asked how it was going. I said slowly. He grinned. We decided it would be a mistake to get drunk, but went to a place called a Stuebli where we had sausages called Wienerli, potatoes called Roesti, and I felt sickli.

On the next day we went up into the mountains.

Davos is in a valley surrounded by unpronounceable peaks, some of which have their own railway. If you have an early breakfast you can start queuing at the station just before 9am and get to the top soon after ten. The journey takes about fifteen minutes and you are crammed into carriages full of prototype skiers: Teutonic, leather-faced, dedicated. The prototype ski is eight inches longer than its proprietor and as mini-skis are new and, like boys at boarding school, no one wants to draw attention to deviation from the norm, you have the choice of putting them on the ground and letting everyone ask 'whatthatthen?' or holding them in the crook of your arm so that they end up eight inches above your head; that way no one notices but your arms get tired.

You would think that in encouraging people to learn to ski they would have brought on to the market a few aids: some simple mechanism for keeping mini-skis together with a separate strap with which to join the ski sticks. Not a bit of it. You hold the skis curved side up, blades facing away from each other. In the other hand you have the ski sticks sharp ends down and at the station they ask for your ticket and you drop everything and grope in your pocket with a gloved hand and take off the glove and the goggles fall over your nose and you find the ticket and they nod ...

Outside the top station there is a platform on which you put on skis and the side of the mountain is yours. This was my third day, a Sunday. The local paper announced that the subject of the sermon in the evangelical church was 'Oh Lord, wherefore has thou forsaken me?' Having started the day walking like Frankenstein's monster with a hernia I had taken some pain-killing pills which the photographer said 'had a few interesting side effects'. Combined with my appetite-killing pills and my tranquillizers I was possibly the junkiest man on the slopes.

Christian got his skis on first, pushed himself away with his sticks and started off downhill on one ski ... shouting look, one leg. You do it.

The photographer follows him on two feet and I plod out and push myself forwards on the sticks and begin to shoot down the mountain. At 30mph I say down, UP, turn, and find myself racing for the railway line. Up and turn, that's better. 'You rotate,' shouts Christian who has come up behind me. 'Whatsematterwithyou? How often I tell you?' I say 'frequently' through clenched teeth. Rotating means that instead of making a delicate adjustment to your direction, you go all the way round facing uphill, with your skis spreadeagled behind you. It is reasonably effective as a means of stopping but definitely inelegant.

I do not know what the mountain looks like in the summer, but in the winter under forty inches of snow there are parts that undulate and parts that disappear dramatically from view. Good skiers take it all in their stride. They come zipping past fractionally checking their speed with a turn, skis parallel as if attached fore and aft; their weight shifts visibly from one ski to another and small muscled behinds twitch and blink and disappear into the white mist. Half a hundred rabbits grit their teeth and get off the ground and try again.

There comes a moment when the legs ache with the sheer weariness of unaccustomed movements; the ribcage burns, head is numb from falling and rising and taking in the words of the instructor ... and looking down the mountain there is nothing but a huge expanse of snow with never a St Bernard or a brandy cask to offer relief.

Captain Scott described Titus Oates's walk to his death in the snow as the action of a gentleman. I was prepared on that third day to walk off into the snow never to be heard of again. It would not have been gentlemanly so much as opting out.

I last noticed the shallowness of my desire to live at battle exercises in the Army of Northern Ireland. Racing around with a bayonet, while the duty corporal shot bursts of machine-gun fire over our heads and the sergeant major shouted, 'Lie down, Freud; you're a casualty (sic)', I noticed that I had no desire to rise again.

So it was now.

We had food in the restaurant after the third descent. The photographer ordered eggs and bacon and cheese and cake and wine and coffee. Christian ate risotto. I skulked behind a glass of redcurrant juice. I could not find it in my heart to speak to the instructor and used the photographer as my intermediary. 'Tell him to meet me at the hotel at 8am tomorrow,' I said. The photographer told him.

We now pass smoothly to the fifth day of my crash course in the gentle art of gliding across the snow. When people ask me on what day I broke my record it was Day Five.

We had gone up the mountain once again, the skis were now one metre thirty. We had come down once with Christian shouting, me sulking, Dmitri the photographer saying when he was a boy in Zermatt all the girls were beautiful and the men handsome and where had they all gone? Also, when we got to the restaurant could he have some Linzer cake with cream …

The second time, Dmitri and I skied down together. The sun shone and if there had been birds they would have sung. As it was the *edelweiss* rustled.

The third time, Christian came down with us; or against us. 'Now look,' he said, singing rollmeover; he went off on one ski, hopped on to the other. He skied with greater balance and control than anyone else I saw on the mountain. It was just after 2pm; Dmitri had been by my side and was now skiing towards some virgin slope; I went the well-skidded path of the learners, turned and seeing a small hill of ice I turned again and felt my left ski go into a hole, stop, and my ankle broke.

I lay there quietly thinking of Cheltenham's National Hunt Festival and Tyne-Tees Television who would miss me … and the various pains that had gathered about my body left their whereabouts and gathered together just above my left foot.

Dmitri came up and essayed a picture. Good, he said, excellent light. Are you all right? I said I was not. Christian came stalking uphill after about ten minutes. Get up, he said. Whatsematterwithyoupickingflowers…?

I have broken my ankle.

He said: 'No. Look, I'll help you. Get up,' and I got up and for the first time he helped me put on my ski. Feeling bone grind against bone I took it off and sat down.

It took us another ten minutes to persuade Christian to go off downhill and telephone for an ambulance sledge. But he finally departed giving a farewell hopping, jinking run as he rounded the bend.

I lay back on my skis and Dmitri said, the light is perfect you could not have fallen in a better place unless you could just move round a little this way and look up … that's marvellous.

Accident procedure on a Swiss mountain is entirely admirable. It is true that they treat broken-limbed humanity a bit like empties at an off-licence, but this is a question of familiarity breeding contempt. I was the third that day, said the SOS Parsenn man who came down with an ambulance sledge. Last Tuesday we had sixteen. I felt suitably humble and was moved with charm and skill from my seat on the skis to a padded sleeping bag on the sledge with leg in splint, cushion under knee, hot water bottle in stomach and finally having been zipped up and strapped to the sledge my skis and sticks were fixed to the sleeping bag. Like a warrior returned to the gods of battle I descended head first down the mountain behind the admirable ambulance man who skied off to the next station down the line bathing my head in a fine spray of powder snow at each pace-reducing manoeuvre. And so at length we reached the platform where an emergency operation was carried out to remove the rail ticket from my ski trousers; then on to the stretcher and down to Davos station and a waiting ambulance.

At the hospital skiing accidents are as commonplace as drunks at a wine tasting. There is an orderly procedure whereby you are shunted from ward to ward, give your name, age, place of birth, name, home address and Davos address every ten minutes and in the course of an hour or so you are undressed, X-rayed, plastered, dressed and given a bill – which they were rather surprised I did not pay on the spot. The hospital receptionist grudgingly telephoned for a taxi, lost interest, and if the taxi driver had not taken my wheelchair, pushed me out and fed me into the back seat of his cab I might still be there. As it was the driver even returned the wheelchair to the reception hall for the next customer. They are an orderly people, the Swiss, in a sort of sado-efficient way best demonstrated by my chambermaid who would daily put the top of the Maclean's toothpaste tube on to my Ingrams shaving soap and *vice versa* so that I spent the five days tasting shaving cream.

At the hotel I was pleased to learn that there was a message for me. It was from the Parsenn ambulance service ... a bill for 75 francs; also a large drink with the compliments of the management who had opened up their crutch cupboard and found for me the best pair of crutches upholstered in uncut moquette. I said it was a super hotel.

Christian telephoned later that night.

Whatsematterwithyou?

Broke my ankle, I said.

It wasn't my fault? ... he asked tentatively.

I assured him it could not have been; after all, he had been nowhere near me when it happened.

9
FREUD
ON HIS TRAVELS

'I like trouser-presses, for which I have found interesting sub-uses – like warming up a ham sandwich and pressing newly washed underpants between towels. (Of course you do not do these things simultaneously.)'

So I phoned and asked for Miss Oda ...
Daily Herald, **24 September 1963**

IF, IN THE years to come, I am asked about Zagreb I may well admit to a passing acquaintanceship with the city: 'Spent a day there in 1963 ... or was it 1964? – Jill was pregnant at the time ... with Matthew ... or was it Lucy?'

But I'm afraid it is likely to be a very long time before I shall be as objective as that.

JAT is short for Jugoslovenski Aerotransport. Our return flight was booked in Tottenham Court Road through the offices of a man called Pittock.

'JU216,' he said, 'departs Dubrovnik 7am Sunday. Arrives London 11.10, a direct flight.' While my back was turned he wrote 'report town terminal 5.30am' on the underside of the ticket.

A seasoned traveller, I, after only a short stay on the sun-soaked beaches of the Federal People's Republic, went to the JAT office to confirm my return flight as instructed in small print on the folder. JAT, in the person of a young woman wearing three plastic flowers, were kind and helpful.

Thank you, your name not on list. We confirm your confirm with Belgrade. You phone tomorrow. Ask Oda.

Miss Oda?, I asked.

She bared her teeth in assent.

I rang the following morning from the telephone on the cashier's desk at the beach restaurant. I asked for Oda.

Oda, they said, out. Who was I? What did I want?

My name, I said, is Freud. I am awaiting confirmation of my return flight to London on Sunday. I spoke slowly and distinctly.

You spell, said the voice on the other end.

Freud, I said. F ... like in France.

Where you going please, France? Where in France?

I was very patient. My name is Freud ... I am going to London. You spell ...

F ... I said. F like in four ... one, two, three ffffour.

How many ticket?

Two, I said.

You say four. Now two. What is your name please? You spell.

That evening we went back into town to see Oda. She had received confirmation of our reservations; there was just one thing, please. She attacked Pittock's 5.30am, and deleted the .30. Bus, she said, leave very punctual.

At 4.45 on Sunday morning we arrived at the terminal, checked in our luggage and on the dot of five, as exclusively forecast by Miss Oda, we were away. Four Dutch ladies, my pregnant wife and I streaking along the mountain pass that leads to the airport, in a 48-seater bus.

At the fourteenth sharp bend my wife said to me in a very small voice: 'I think I'm going into labour.'

Enchanted with the possibility, I began composing the announcement for the Births column of *The Times* ... a daughter, suddenly, in a bus on the outskirts of Dubrovnik ... I held her hand comfortingly and promised her London at 11.10. On reflection, she said, it might be indigestion (we had had breakfast at 3.30).

We reached the airport at 5.35am, an hour and 25 minutes before the scheduled departure of flight 216.

We had coffee.

At eight o'clock, with the runway full of planes and the lounges packed with the flower of British tourism, the flight was called.

At 8.15, three and a half hours after reporting to the terminal for a four-hour flight, we were seated in the Caravelle, sucking aniseed balls in anticipation of the take-off.

Twenty flying minutes later we were fastening our seatbelts for the landing at Zagreb. A fifteen-minute stop, said the hostess. Please to leave the plane. The restaurant is open. My wife, still unsure whether it was indigestion or our fifth infant, said she would like to stay aboard.

The hostess said, please.

My wife said, thank you.

The hostess said, please, no; leave plane.

My wife said, Oh, I see; left plane and joined the rest of us in the restaurant of Zagreb airport; we drank lemonade.

Twenty minutes later we were back in the plane. When I say we, I mean us, the pleasant, upright, original travellers from Dubrovnik, now joined by the usual rabble of people you tend to get midway on any flight, or bus or train.

As there were clearly one and a half times as many people as the plane could take, a steward came to inspect our tickets. The engines warmed up.

A stewardess came round to give us aniseed toffees for the take-off; another steward appeared and said everyone off the plane, please. Troubles; and as an afterthought he added that the airport restaurant was open.

We left the plane and had another lemonade. Jugoslovenski Aerotransport, mumble, mumble, mumble, said a voice in Serbo-Croat to the eighty English passengers.

After repeating her message, she gave it to us in English: 'Indefinite delay of flight 216 due to engine trouble. The restaurant is open.' It was 10am.

When I said earlier that I had spent a day in Zagreb, I really referred to the next seven hours.

We, the passengers, were split into two factions: the indignant and those who insisted that 'the poor dears were doing their best.' The waiter charged 100 dinars for coffee; rumour had it that a spare engine was coming by air from Belgrade.

I informed the waiter that when passengers are held up, food and drink should be provided by the airline. Four whiskies please. He gave me four whiskies, asked for 2,400 dinars (24s.). He said, please pay; only coffee is free.

I told him that, if he gave the coffee money back to the other passengers, I would then decide whether or not to pay for the whiskies.

He said, I call controller.

I said, I've been here two and a half hours. I would enjoy seeing the controller; quite apart from the whisky he might care to explain what is holding us up.

Rumour had it that a spare plane was coming from Split.

The controller did not come, but several people had gin and refused to pay. Rumour had it that a spare engineer was flying in from Skopje any moment now.

After a few more rounds of gin, some of the 'let's be nice to the Jugos' brigade joined the 'let's drink them out of house and home' group.

Now rumour had it that the plane was all right but they had run out of sweets for the take-off. It was 1.30; the hostess said that buses were on the way to take us to Zagreb for lunch.

At the International Hotel in the city, we sat at twenty tables of four, guests of the airline, poor relations who were not paying for their meal as far as the waiters were concerned. Lunch was leisurely; after it the hostess said we could sit on the terrace. We sat. I ordered coffee.

The waiter said, Turkish coffee?

I told him, no; espresso coffee; without sugar.

After a few minutes the waiter came back and said, please, no espresso coffee: you just become Turkish.

I refused. It had been hard enough becoming British.

The buses arrived at the hotel at 4.15. Back at the airport we returned to the restaurant where the waiter flinched when he saw us. Bus-sick and travel-weary, no one ordered whisky. At 4.45 there was an announcement in Serbo-Croat. We awaited the translation breathlessly.

Jugoslovenski Aerotransport announced that the following people were required by passport control. Rumour had it that if you went, you were never heard of again.

At 5 o'clock they said that the Caravelle was all right in Serbo-Croat and confirmed this in English. I am not at all sure how, but this time when we boarded there were only just enough people to fill the plane.

So if there is, somewhere in Zagreb – or held in a Jugoslav dungeon – a gaggle of Englishmen who had booked a flight on last Sunday's JU216, they may be interested to know that the rest of us made London Airport by 7.35pm.

Pittock and Miss Oda, please note.

* * *

In 1969 the Daily Mail *staged a transatlantic air race, starting at the Post Office Tower in London and finishing on the 86th floor of the Empire State Building, to mark the fiftieth anniversary of Alcock and Brown's first Atlantic crossing in 1919.*

'To broaden the appeal of the affair,' recalled Freud in his 2001 autobiography Freud Ego, *'there was a passenger category, open to anyone making their way from one eyrie to the other using commercial airlines. Aer Lingus of Ireland sponsored the £5,000 first prize – then equal to what I was paid for 250 instalments of* Just a Minute *– and as their rules demanded a stop-over at Shannon, where not too many non-Aer Lingus New York-bound planes stopped, this was probably done to make the prize self-financing. It seemed my sort of contest. I sent off for the full rules.*

'In London, the top of the Tower was then a Butlin-owned revolving restaurant that was losing money: waiters tended to mislay their customers who had spun 90 degrees between giving their order and chef fashioning their soup. For the air race there was to be a desk with a time stamp for competitors' cards. A similar machine to be installed at the top of the Empire State Building, and the winner would be the one whose card showed the fastest journey.'

My £5,000 air race victory
Sun, **10 May 1969**

NEW YORK, FRIDAY.

I am sitting in the drawing-room of a suite at the New York Hilton wondering whether it really happened and thinking up ways of spending the £5,000.

The money is, I hope, my transatlantic air race prize for the fastest crossing via Shannon on a commercial airline flight. When the air race was announced about a year ago, I studied form carefully and decided that the Shannon category gave competitors the least opposition.

In the eight days of the *Daily Mail* race there were only two flights with fast connections at the western Ireland airport: EI049 leaving London at 4pm on Wednesday, and the same flight at the same time on Thursday.

With a small gulp and a large cheque, I booked myself and one child on each of these flights.

Here was the plan: competitors had to leave the Post Office Tower and reach the London Airport rendezvous by 3.50pm – not a second later – to catch the plane.

Working backwards, my time from the airport helicopter landing pad to the rendezvous was ninety seconds on a fast motor-bike; the helicopter flight from a wheat barge moored in the Thames took seven and a half minutes; Surrey Marine had a motor-boat which made the trip from Cleopatra's Needle steps, on the Embankment, in one and a quarter minutes, including getting into the chopper.

It was therefore essential to be on the Embankment by 3.38 and a half, leaving a fifteen-second margin for disaster.

Now come the snags. Lifts leave the top of the Post Office Tower at irregular intervals and take between one and two minutes to reach ground level.

The journey from Tower to Embankment depends on traffic lights and occupies between three and nine minutes.

It was therefore decided to send one boy from the Tower six and a half minutes before the deadline, send me one minute later, and dispatch the second boy a minute after that.

The Freud timekeeper on the river – it was Mrs Freud – would give the go-ahead for the speedboat to make for the barge at the appointed second with me, ideally the second boy, or, in his absence, the first boy.

At New York I had arranged motor-bikes to take us from Customs to Kennedy Airport's heliport, a helicopter to whisk us to 30th Street heliport in the city and an ambulance to beat the evening traffic to the Empire State Building on Fifth Avenue.

And so, on Wednesday, with everything working like a well-oiled dream, I achieved the fastest time, and my junior colleague, ten-year-old Dominic Faulder, failed by less than half a minute to come second.

I left him with friends in New York, flew back on Wednesday evening, had a quick glance at Templegate's racing column and set out for my second attempt on Thursday with my ten-year-old son, another Dominic.

I did not have to go. I could have bitten my nails, believed the Met. Office forecast of unfavourable weather on the Atlantic route, and relied on my Wednesday time of 8 hours and 4 minutes to keep my lead.

This would have been the action of a miserly coward – also boy No. 2 was longing to join boy No. 1 in New York.

I have had some odd sensations in my life, but this was one of the strangest. Flying across the Atlantic realizing that a tail wind would involve me in another speculative split-second bike-helicopter-ambulance-lift trip which might lose £5,000 I already considered mine – while a head wind would let me amble into the city in a rickshaw.

On Thursday my Post Office Tower departure was beaten only by a Navy entrant.

I had worked out that as the enemy had left the top of the Tower at

3.34pm he had to reach the 86th floor of the Empire State Building by 11.38pm British time to beat me.

The final leg from Kennedy Airport takes a minimum of twenty minutes, the immigration men in America having this endearing habit of looking up everyone in their time-consuming black book. This meant that if we were still on the plane at 11.18pm I could start celebrating.

I spent the flight discreetly going to see the captain, asking for progress reports. This was tricky, since he was grimly determined to get there quickly while I was terribly happy to take the journey at a leisurely pace.

How is it, Captain?

Great. Eight minutes up on yesterday's flight.

At 10.45 we were over Deer Park, a seven-minute run from Kennedy.

The previous day we were over Deer Park at 10.50, but had to wait fifteen minutes for landing permission.

We expect to land at 11.05, said the captain. On Wednesday, in spite of forecasts to the contrary, we had landed at 11.14.

I went through the drill with my son: Jump down the steps. Race to Immigration. Look responsible, Republican, submissive, and call him Sir.

The moment he gives the word belt through Customs, declare a toothbrush and a passport, and jump on the motor-bike. Have you got it?

Yes, Dad.

At 10.55 came the announcement: This is your captain. New York have advised us that there is a delay and we are circling at 23,000ft awaiting landing permission.

The Navy man gritted his teeth. I let mine out about two notches.

We commenced our descent at 11.14, giving the enemy 24 minutes for the last leg. Down we came, with a medium bump.

Navy and I regarded one another grimly.

The plane taxied.

Twenty-two minutes to go – then the plane stopped.

'This is your captain ... I hope you have enjoyed your flight. We have stopped to let another plane cross the runway.'

The other plane took its time and when the doors opened the Navy man had eleven minutes to go.

Nine minutes when it was his turn to get out. Eight when he got to Immigration. Five as he jumped on his motor-bike.

My son Dominic and I looked at each other and decided to tell our motor-cyclists to drive slowly and request the helicopter to fly over Central Park and Coney Island for a treat.

It would seem that the Aer Lingus £5,000 prize is safe, although news has filtered through that the runner-up is considering an objection to my use of an ambulance in New York.

I used an ambulance solely because I could not find a fire engine and, as everyone knows, taxis in New York are at a premium.

The objection by 'the Navy man' came to nothing.

* * *

In early 1971 Freud competed in another and much more demanding contest, the yacht race between Cape Town and Rio de Janeiro. He served as chef on the Ocean Spirit, skippered by Robin Knox-Johnston, who had recently sailed round the world single-handed.

A dispatch from the galley
Daily Telegraph Magazine, **30 April 1971**

IT WAS NOT always going to be fifteen men, our crew. We had toyed with the idea of having thirteen men and two women. Two soft, non-women's lib women, preferably placid, hardworking, short-sighted nymphomaniacs, if that combination of quality

277

exists. That way they could do the washing up and the cleaning and embroider our towels with our crests. It never came to that.

By nature I am not one for communal segregated living. I joined a London club – mostly to have after-hour cheque-cashing facilities and free newspapers; for the rest I am uxorious.

As I do not go much for japes, or pranks, and I do not enjoy doing press-ups, I was quite honestly a shade apprehensive. There was no need for this. The crew were pleasant and helpful to a man, and it was amusing to see that of my galley slaves – I was given a man to square up the galley after each meal – the English worked like winners of the Charwoman of the Year Competition. The South Africans, who have servants queuing up for jobs, simply had no idea how to wash up even a cocktail stick.

There was no gambling, no excessive drinking, little petulance and no shows of temper. There was a lot of sunbathing, though nudity was more a uniform than a way of life. I think you would have been proud of us.

Two main aspects had concerned me prior to leaving London for Cape Town and the ocean. What provisions and things should I buy? How were we going to pay for them?

On the first count I recalled that throughout my military career people had said, 'Thank God we've got a Navy.' So I telephoned the Ministry of Defence, explained who I was and what I was about to do and asked if they might send me a list of the average man's requirements of food and drink per day on the high sea. I envisaged a buff form which would split up the consumption, by weight, into fat, cereal, protein, etc. and provide the average liquid intake per man at differing temperatures.

The Press Officer at the Ministry said he understood what I wanted and promised that I should hear from him. He was as good as his word; I did not actually hear from him … but I heard from nearly everyone else. In the course of the next few weeks I was telephoned by people from Plymouth and Pangbourne, Greenwich, Portsmouth and Greenock.

I am not complaining. I had some very lovely conversations with people to whom I would not usually have anything to say ... and I even got one list Xeroxed from an Olde Original Liste stating that the average sailor required one-eighth of an ounce of custard powder a week, a statistic that I personally would take with a pinch of condensed milk, as custard powder consumption is entirely dependent on a person's predilection for the sauce. In the end I asked Robin to give me a weight allowance for food and drink and did my own sums.

Financially, it was worked out that the race would cost around £8,000 – this being made up of wear and tear of sails; repayment of mortgage on *Ocean Spirit*; food and drink for crew – on the way to Cape Town, racing, and returning from Rio. Add to this sizeable insurance premiums, harbour charges, running repairs, flying out Robin and me; flying back Robin, his partner Leslie and me; add the cost of this to the price of the odd bacon butty and cup of tea and the change from a £10,000 note is light indeed.

We had decided to ask the racing crew to contribute towards their cost of living ... which would still leave £5,000 to be found. The answer to this came in a flash ... sponsorship would provide. A good public relations firm and then thanks to a couple of illustrious names like Knox-Johnston and Freud and the written guarantee of us both that we would win the prestigious Cape Town–Rio race ...

When it came to public relations firms we decided that what we needed was a small hungry company who needed us rather than a large fat one to whom we would be unimportant. We found a small firm. From time to time we went to see them ... In the end, after five weeks of high hopes, we emerged from the sponsorship race with a letter promising us ten cases of Heinz tinned food.

Once in South Africa, I found that by way of ships' chandlers at which I would be able to fulfil the demand of my six-page shopping list the classified directory listed a dozen ... while the information kiosk at the Cape Town Yacht Club dispensed Messrs Woolworth wholesale catalogues.

My shopping list by now had grown handsomely. I kept it by my bed and nightly I woke, said chocolate for chocolate sauce, wrote it down and went back to sleep, only to waken, mumble icing sugar, sleep, dream of running out of wine and jerk into complete wakefulness at the recollection that I had no corkscrew on my list ...

Sending for the other ships' chandlers' lists and comparing them with Woolworth's I found the prices substantially similar. My liberal principles bristling, I selected a small independent firm represented by a tall young South African with a bandaged hand and a small inscrutable Chinaman called Jackson ... Norman Jackson. Together we travelled around the city, inspecting their products and buying the odd pieces of hardware that they did not stock.

I ordered meat and fish; tins of jams and fruits and vegetables and stews. Sauces and spices and pickles and herbs, condiments and dried fruit. I made a reasonable freezer out of the boat's galvanized storage cabinet which was lined for me with polyester.

With Jackson and his single-handed colleague I went to the butcher and I showed him how I wanted to have my chickens portioned, my meat cut, my rumps peeled ... I went to the fruit market at Epsom and showed them the quality of the fruit I required ... green bananas, yellow oranges, white grapes.

I made a list of all the available storage spaces on board *Ocean Spirit*, measured each space, decided what would go where and made an order-of-unloading list so that the stuff would come off the truck in order.

People were deeply impressed by my planning and it would all have gone off like a charm but for the fact that as the lorry came alongside the boat, the sky opened up, the rain plummeted down, the four men who were to help me crashed everything on the deck and into the cabins and went away, so that my foolproof plan for knowing what was where became a three-week thimble hunt, some of the food only coming to light as a result of decomposing under a bed.

My drink ration was two cans of beer per man per day; three cans of soft drink; half a bottle of wine – I found an excellent South

African red wine called Nederburg Cabernet Selection for about 35p a bottle – and two large tots of spirits.

Now my galley – which is what they will insist on calling the kitchen on a boat – was small by land standards, rather large for a caravan or boat. It had a stove that gimballed – that is to say it rocked sympathetically with the waves – and a static stove with four flames fed by Calor gas. There was also an oven which was not as yet fitted but was useful for storing things. On the morning of our departure I spent the hours arranging things prettily. I also decided that for dinner we would have a crown of lamb – the butcher, an Englishman, had sent it as a going-away present or possibly as an apology for cutting the chickens with a grapefruit knife. Then thinly sliced potatoes and onions cooked in broth and browned under the grill; a salad of Mediterranean-type tomatoes followed by individual cream caramels set around sultanas steeped in brandy. Our last lunch was eaten in the yacht club. Then there was a rush of hoisting sails and casting off and Robin diving down to remove the propeller …

We started in a great gust, slowed to half a knot a week for an hour and suddenly took on some more wind and screeched away. Come the friendly twilight and I went below.

And here was an odd thing. The galley, which I had arranged tidily in calm Cape Town harbour, was at an angle of 45° to the way I had left it. Fortunately the cupboards were closed but it was noticeable that when I opened those on one side the food was trying to climb up the back wall; on the other it came towards me like a huge unhomogenous missile … cream, frankfurter sausages and mushroom caps hitting me in the face, while the lighter cheese biscuits and gelatine packets formed the second line of attack.

I found it absolutely astonishing that in a year of preparation, including a good four months of discussion and note-passing, nobody had mentioned that the galley went up and down and was liable to remain sideways for days on end.

By 7pm two members of the crew had been sick, we were racing along at a very fair speed in a force 5 wind, the crown of lamb was in the oven and every ten minutes I opened the oven door to find that the force 5 wind had extinguished the gas. At 7.15 a large sideways movement took the potato-and-onion pan and drove it across the floor. Soon after the oven door opened and spewed out the cream caramels sitting in a water bath at the bottom.

I sat down among it, swabbing away, wondering what had caused me to accept the offer of 'a trip across the South Atlantic'.

At about 8pm, having taken the crown from the oven, cut it into chops and fried them in very shallow oil, I served these with gravy and boiled potatoes and tomato salad. On deck there was a considerable amount of surprise that I was still alive and well, let alone cooking. Few were hungry, but Robin and Leslie ate heartily as did one Pete who turned out to be one of my best customers.

After we had been at sea for about a week, when we had eaten roasted venison, barbecued chicken, boiled mutton with caper sauce, moussaka, rump steaks, turkey with cranberry sauce and boeuf bourguignon, I asked Robin what, had I not come with them, he would have got in the way of victuals, fresh as opposed to tinned.

He thought for a while and said a joint of meat and half a dozen chickens.

I felt happier after that, like a dying boxer who is told his opponent is not likely to live either. 'If you don't like my food,' I practised saying, 'Robin would have given you tins after the second day.'

Cooking is an unpleasant job on board a ship. The watch system means that you have staggered meals, sometimes staggered over a period of over an hour. The heaving and tossing of the boat makes preparation difficult, actual application of heat hazardous, deep frying out of the question; any liquid in a saucepan, if it reached higher than halfway up, is likely to join yesterday's trifle and this morning's porridge on the floor on the way to their destination under the sink.

On deck there is almost always some breeze, even in the South Atlantic where the day breaks at 80° and creeps gradually to 90°.

The galley is the hot seat and it is not only hot; it receives all that is on offer in the way of smells. In the manner of early Victorian designers who pushed all menial and disgusting places into one location, the architect of *Ocean Spirit* had put the engine (which smelt of diesel) opposite the lavatory adjacent to the galley – and as it was at the rear of the boat, the hatch faced a rail over which washing was hung … so that my view was only medium.

However, I came to love the place … and loved it especially after the Sandhurst General's ADC had cleaned it up. If promotion is ever awarded for expertise in plate polishing and floor washing, Captain William King-Harman RA will be the youngest field-marshal in the Army.

> *After four weeks at sea, recalled her cook in* Freud Ego, *'Ocean Spirit was the first to cross the line, to win what is called "line honours"; on handicap a boat that arrived a couple of weeks later was declared overall winner.'*

* * *

The witching hour is 9.15pm
Daily Telegraph Magazine, 23 October 1970

JIM AND ELOUISE gave a party for me on my last night in Lincoln, Nebraska. They live a few miles out of town on the north shore of an artificial twenty acre lake that freezes over in winter, and thaws for spring and summer, so that residents have to buy snowmobiles *and* yachts.

On the way to Jim's house I pointed to other dwellings: 'I like the one with the marble tiles in the car-port,' I said. 'One hundred and fifty thousand dollars,' said Jim. He guessed most people knew what most people paid for their houses.

The party was a 'bring food, we've got drink' affair. Jim buys hard liquor by the case, picks up ice in 25lb plastic bags at a dollar a bag plus tax. Elouise gave me a typed memo with the names of the guests and their professions: 'our very excellent dentist', attorney, architect, president of life assurance company, head of department at university. With every man there came a wife. Elouise said they were all lovely, friendly people.

They were all lovely and friendly and very very 'square'. They would take 'square' as a compliment. I talked to the architect about Le Corbusier; the architect had not heard of him.

'Listen,' said a man, 'if there is anything at all that I can do for you ...'

I asked him what business he was into.

He said, 'Wholesale welding'.

I promised to let him know.

We arrived and had cocktails like treble gins, with hardly any vermouth and some ice. 'I reckon ice spoils it,' said a man, 'but it lets you stand on your feet longer.' The husbands came right into the 'lounge' overlooking the lake and took their drinks – and the wives hustled their pots and pipkins into the kitchen recess and told the hired woman (who had arrived in a large shiny Chevrolet) how to serve it or reheat it. The women laughed and said Why Arnold and Well Jim, and told each other how darling their outfits were and did they have the chicken pie in the fine restaurant at Miller and Paine's department store? It appeared they all had.

Steadily did the drinks get poured into us, and dish by decorated dish the dining table became laden with guests' offerings: a Virginia baked ham; Southern fried chicken with a chilli sauce; a roast round of rump; a best end of lamb, boned, rolled around a fillet of pork and baked on a rack (the main joy of this seemed to be that the creator could ask people to guess what it was and receive 100 per cent wrong answers).

There was tuna fish and noodles, brought by Jim's daughter-in-law, who apologized on the grounds that it was student rather than rich folk's food. There was a dish called Buns with Loose. Buns were sesame seed buns halved and spread with mustard; Loose was minced beef with salt, pepper, catsup and a little beef stock.

This, said a woman, is a real mid-West dish. We call it yonki. Everyone gathered round and said Yeah, yonki. I asked how it was spelt. G-n-o-c-c-h-i ... yonki.

And someone had brought something called Dilly Bread. I asked whether this was Biblical – like give us this day our dilly bread and they said it was bread and literally ten minutes later a woman turned to me and said I've just gotten your joke about dilly bread. Great joke. Funniest I've heard in months.

A man turned to me and said: 'I know what you've come to Lincoln for; but, well, if you were to write that we drink too damned much and we eat too damned much, you wouldn't be too damned wrong.'

By this time we were out of gin, so five of us killed a bottle of vodka.

Earlier in the evening one of the more distinguished guests had said to me: 'In this town we play it straight down the line.' And I had told him that I had noticed. At about 9.30 he turned to me, pointed to a matron with blue-rinsed hair and what must have been a whalebone corset, and said: 'That woman, she is one grade A super performer; take it from me.'

I reminded him that in Lincoln they played it straight down the line and he winked and said sometimes, at weekends, in Omaha ...

It was no easy matter getting to the gastronomic heart of Lincoln. I was asked to the house of what might be the richest inhabitants ... and got nut cutlets because the family were on a health kick. I dined at the sorority house ... and was served roast beef and Yorkshire pudding and was asked whether this did not make me feel all nostalgic.

The University, which is the main industry of Lincoln, has dining halls and restaurants and special rooms where the football team get steaks and eggs and fruit and advice. Cinnamon pancakes are popular at breakfast. A Denver sandwich consists of fried eggs on a base of ham and peppers. Custom Cut haddock fillet tasted like any other haddock fillet, but sounded better, and for puddings there is a permanent selection of peach and watermelon balls, golden glow salad, fruit Jello, lime delight, lemon chiffon pie and frosted raspberry dessert.

The influence of the University upon the catering establishments of Lincoln is considerable, because people work their way through college in just about every place in town. At the Country Club, male students are dressed in white gloves, war heroes wear doilies on their heads. Both call members Sir and Madam and treat the two Jewish members (who got in during the Depression) with the same courtesy as all the others. 'I guess,' said my host, 'that we'll have to have another depression before we get any more Jewish members, but the Jewish community in Lincoln is a fine community. Fine people; they apply for membership regularly twice a year.'

The University Club is at the top of the Stuart Building, which is to Lincoln what the Empire State Building was to New York. There is a lounge with leather chairs and bar service, attractive, inefficient, friendly students closely watched by professional uglies. The dining room is panelled, and on special nights they ship in oysters and clams and lobsters and stand in line at the buffet and everybody wonders how *those* people got in. The tables are set with knives and forks and coffee cups and people order their drinks three at a time because service is slow.

'Listen,' I kept asking newly acquired friends, 'where is the typical restaurant?' I went to Tony and Luigi's – Tony's name is in bigger print on the shop front because he recently bought out Luigi. The food was standard Fulham Road *trattoria*, with pizzas and escalopes and tomato paste and dancing which was square, as opposed to square dancing. 'It's the sort of swinging place to which kids take their parents,' was a fair description.

The Cornhusker Hotel has a flourishing banqueting scene. I went to a luncheon of a club that raises money to buy comforts for deaf children. We met at noon. Soup, powdered and hastily resurrected, was followed by a piece of fried chicken; creamed sweetcorn and baked potato; ice-cream, butterscotch sauce; coffee. Lunch was over by 12.55; there were two speeches.

At 1pm the waitress came in to clear the tables and the men went back to work. The cashier said, 'Hi fellers,' as we left. My hosts said, 'See you.' They do not drink with their food at lunchtime, though they have cocktails for special occasions and beer in some restaurants.

Perhaps the typical Lincoln eating place is the Legionnaire Club managed by Bob Logsdon. I went there one night and received friendly service from a professional waitress who looked after me like a mother and served me with the best steak I have ever eaten.

It was very large, entirely tender without being artificially tenderized, and was called a New York Strip Sirloin (which I had thought was going to be the cabaret). The price was 30s. All around me people danced; not just young people but old people and middle-aged people and the band was live and I learnt that the word 'veteran' included people who had served in the American forces and all their friends and families. It is very difficult to be ineligible for the Legionnaire Club.

The students of Nebraska University go to a cinema and make their way home via a Kings Food Host restaurant. There are a number of these in Lincoln with identical menus and varying standards of cleanliness. You can go in and buy food to eat there or take away. The popular move is to drive into one of the numbered parking lots, roll down the window, inspect the illustrated snack menu, pick up the telephone and say: 'Lot number 24, one foot-long hot dog; a fishwich and a broncoburger; also three root beers.'

In God's good time a student dressed in white overalls appears and pitches your order through the car window. It is a very handy way to eat and in the spirit of research I tried the fishwich. It is a large fishfinger – more like a fishpalm – between two slices of bread garnished with tartare sauce. The price is 2s. 6d.; a broncoburger, which is a close relative of a Wimpy, costs 5s.

By way of trendy places there is the establishment of the Brothers Lebsach – said to be the oldest continuing beer licence in Nebraska.

Lebsach's is seedy and comfortable and the customer is usually wrong. A long bar seats men, some of whom spend their lives buried in the sporting pages of the paper; a television set is switched on to the local channel 10, and there are a number of tables at which you get served if you wait quietly.

The menu is chilli soup, bean soup or vegetable soup; lean beef and cheese sandwiches. The lean beef is brisket and swims in a broth which later becomes bean soup and the bread is rye bread, fresh and fragrant. The Brothers Lebsach are elderly and do not care too much and if anyone asks for coffee they are told to 'go to some high class joint.' Lebsach's do not serve coffee and are proud of it. They serve beer on tap. And they talk football; football is the single most unifying force in the state of Nebraska and the stadium on match days is the third largest city of the state, with a population of 65,000.

I should put the witching hour of Lincoln at around 9.15pm, with a strong likelihood of turning into a pumpkin before 10.30 ... but there is one exception. Way down on the main street, the longest main street in the world, there is an all-night café called Millie's.

Millie is a tough lady who sits at the cash desk counting money out of all proportion to the rate at which it comes in. Millie, it is rumoured, never forgives, and there are those who are denied admission as a result of some foolish, youthful episode forgotten by all but the hard-hearted proprietress. Here students and professors mingle with travelling salesmen and junkies.

The food is standard all-night-café food – with good coffee, bottles of something called 'Family Catsup' and insufficient people to mop up tables. If there were any hustlers in Lincoln, this is where they would hang out ... but as one of my new friends said: 'When I was a kid we had two prostitutes in town but they were driven out by amateur talent.' That is Lincoln hospitality for you – generous to a fault.

* * *

It was always 'If only you had said'
The Listener, 17 December 1981, based on the talk 'Interpreting the Mandarin' on BBC Radio 4

I HAVE ALWAYS had an enormous love and admiration for China, so in 1978 when I went with a parliamentary delegation to Japan and had an open ticket, which meant that I could come back any way that I wanted, I thought it would be fun to return via China. I went to the Chinese Embassy, where they were awfully nice, and the girl recognized me.

She said: 'I've seen you on radio,' and I was pleased.

I had tea and she said: 'Can I help?'

I said: 'I want to go to China.'

She said: 'You must come back.'

I went back, every day for a fortnight, and, in the end, forty-eight hours before I was due to leave for Japan, I said, very, very amiably, that I really had to know whether or not I could come back via China. They told me to leave my passport with them. I said that I couldn't because I was due in Strasbourg the following day.

They said: 'Bring your passport tomorrow.' I got the most attractive stamp in the passport, which I took very quickly to the Foreign Office. They said: 'Yes, it's the right stamp and you've got all the best things in it.'

So, after my two weeks in Japan, I arrived at Peking Airport. I was met by my own small team, an elderly diplomat lady whose husband had once been Ambassador in France, and an interpreter, who was young and female and fairly aggressive.

We got into the car and I said: 'My passport,' and they said: 'Don't worry.'

I said: 'My luggage!' and they said: 'It will be at the hotel before you're there.'

And we drove through the night. I arrived at the Peking Hotel.

My luggage was there, my passport was not, but they said it was nothing to worry about.

Food in the hotel was served in a number of dining-rooms, each one seating about fifteen people. Breakfast is a set meal: you have a breakfast soup and you have breakfast vegetables and you have coffee and you have breakfast rice and you have breakfast fish. For everything there is a slip of paper, and if you say that you don't want something because you're not a great breakfast eater, you are given three slips of paper, one ordering it and one cancelling it, and one which you have to sign to show that you were offered it but didn't have it.

My interpreter and my diplomatic guide said to me one day: 'Today we are going to the Great Wall.'

'Oh, good. I've got a map of the Great Wall.' I opened up my map and said, pointing to a spot: 'I'd like to go here.'

They said, pointing to another spot: 'No, you go there.'

I said: 'But everybody goes there, I'd like to go here.'

They said: 'You can't go there.'

I said: 'But I *want* to go.'

'If only you had said,' was the answer.

It was always 'if only you had said', and I saw the Great Wall of China as has every European visitor. I met on the Great Wall of China more members of the House of Lords than I had ever met in the Palace of Westminster. I met somebody with whom I was in the Army. I met several people who recognized me from American television shows. There were no Chinese visitors. And although they say that the Great Wall of China runs for 2,500 kilometres I don't think any European has seen more than the same 800-metre stretch.

There comes a time in China when everything is so smooth and everything is in such a low key that you long to see a bit of aggro. One day I saw that in Peking there was to be an international football match – the People's Republic of China against Malta – and I went along to it with my interpreter. Now Malta is not a very good football side, but nor is China, and it was really rather refreshing to see the Chinese utterly disenchanted with their own side. It was like going back and watching Plymouth Argyle and the good people from Home Park shouting their disgust when the team lost yet again, 0-1 at home to Swindon. Actually, China won because the Maltese fullback scored through his own goal, but there was a great feeling of comradeship among people who didn't love their own football team either.

Perhaps the overriding misery of the pro-Chinese Englishman who is there to see whether all his dreams haven't actually come true, all his political ambitions haven't been realized, is that however much you trust *them* they never quite seem to trust you. For instance, I said that I was interested in prisons, and they said: 'Ah, if you'd only told us.'

'You have prisons in China?'

'No,' they said, 'we don't have prisons.'

But on my third or fourth day there was a story about a prison in one of the papers, which the Secretary at the Embassy showed me, so I said: 'You do have a prison.'

'Oh, we have a very few prisons, it's very recent.'

In the end, after a lot of argument, I was allowed to see over a prison, which they said would be very different from our prisons. They showed me a prisoner, who had obviously been got together specially for me or for tourists. I asked: 'Why are you here?' He looked very ashamed and said: 'I committed a terrible crime. I was a bus driver, I was thinking not carefully enough about the thoughts of Chairman Mao and I drove my bus on to the pavement and hit some people who were waiting at the bus stop.'

I said to my interpreter: 'Will you tell him that in our country you would not go to prison for that unless you were drunk?'

The interpreter got very angry with me and said: 'Of course he wasn't drunk.'

So I said: 'Would you tell him that in that case in our country he wouldn't have gone to prison?'

The interpreter said: 'No, it would serve no useful purpose.' One was very much in the hands of the interpreters.

But my prototype visit as a representative of the British Parliament was to go and visit specific places, and I would go to a school. The school was apprised of my arrival, the car would turn up, and the officials of the school would be waiting to meet the car. I got out and they all applauded. When they finished applauding I applauded them; that is Chinese courtesy. We then went upstairs, where there was a long table, and all of them sat opposite me and my diplomat and my interpreter and nothing was said until we got tea. After a while I said that I would very much like to see a class. It had all been arranged. We walked down corridors and when we got to the end of one I saw someone at the far end disappearing to give the signal that the distinguished visitor was arriving. At length, we went into a classroom where the thirty pupils or so and the teacher pretended not to notice us arriving. The teacher was giving an English lesson.

She said to her class: 'The Works Convenor is laughed at by the workers. How did he feel? He was not *humiliated*, he was *hurt*. Do you understand? Comrade Chong?'

'He was not humiliated, he was hurt.'

'Good. Comrade Chan?'

'He was not humiliated, he was hurt.'

'Good. Now our foreign visitor would like to speak to us.'

They all applauded and I walked to the front of the class, where I said I was so grateful to be allowed to come there. I was immensely impressed by so much of what I had seen and I hoped very much that in the not too distant future they would be able to come to our country and see what it is that we do. And, whereas at the moment in China everything was black or white, good or bad, in my country there was much which was grey, there was much which was not all good but not all bad either. I hoped very much that they would try to understand the way I was trying to understand their philosophy.

I turned to one of the pupils and said: 'Do you understand?'

He said: 'Yes.'

'What, in a sentence, have I said?'

'He was not humiliated, he was hurt.'

So I turned to another pupil and said: 'What did I say?'

'He was hurt.'

The Chinese inner man I found very easy. My hotel served very bad hotel food, very reminiscent of England, but, by comparison, when I was asked to Chinese banquets I found the quality absolutely astonishing. Course followed course. The banquets are usually held in hotels, in a dining-room just next door to where as a hotel guest you would get cabbage soup and pickled cabbage. But perhaps the best meal which I had in China was with a friend who worked at the Embassy. It was in a restaurant which had once been an imperial palace, which they deplored for its elitism and its decadence. The whole meal was based on the awful, labour-intensive, rich, hideous food which they used to have in the grand days. They brought you this magnificent food and said: 'Look at this – how disgraceful, how could people have eaten this?' They had prepared it with love and care and it was one of the best banquets which I had ever eaten. But, of course, politically, they kept their heads high above the water by denigrating every dish as it came. 'Decadent!', they said. 'That's what this is – decadent!'

My position, politically, diplomatically, afforded me an interview with the Fourth Prime Minister of China. I think that there are five or six altogether and I was some one-third of the way up the totem pole. I said: 'Prime Minister, I have such a feeling of well-being in your country. There are very few countries in the world, apart from my own, in which I could bear to live, but with one or two exceptions I think that this is a country very much after my own heart.'

'What exceptions?'

'Oh, very small things, niggly things.'

'What niggly things?'

I explained that the night before I had been to the cinema and I had terribly minded the people spitting because one couldn't hear anything for the spitting noise. I said: 'But, obviously, one gets used to it the way one gets used to any other personal habits.'

The Fourth Prime Minister then gave me a lecture on what they had tried to do to educate the public when it came to health care, to environmental health problems, to spitting, to the dangers of pollution by spitting, and I kept trying to say: 'But you don't understand. I love your country. I was saying this simply because you asked me what it was that I didn't care about.' But I'm afraid that as far as he was concerned I was just another knocking foreigner.

Perhaps my most lasting memory of China occurred on my last day. I went into my hotel room and there were three of the staff sitting on their haunches, watching my television set. I tiptoed in, sat at my desk and started writing. Each of the three watchers in turn saw me and tiptoed out. I gave no more thought to it, but in the next ten minutes three hotel officials all came, having been told by their staff what they had done and how they had been caught, and I got three completely different explanations of what had happened: 'Ah, those were television engineers. I believe you complained about the quality of the picture.' 'Oh, they thought you had gone and they were checking the television set for the next people,' and so on.

I left China with feelings of great affection, enormous love, though I am not sure that when I left China they didn't feel that there goes another of these foreign knockers. I hope I meet again all the people who were so kind to me, and I hope that, one day, without interpreters, I will be able to explain to them how we live, because I have a pretty good feeling and a great admiration for the way that they live.

* * *

Who, I wonder, eats damson jam for breakfast?
Saga Magazine, October 1995

MY FRIEND TOMMY Docherty is author of the phrase 'Do unto others and run like hell.' I spent the last few months staying in more hotels than usual and have encountered a lot of this philosophy ... or perhaps it is just hotel keepers getting their own back for the years of our jokey removal of shoes left for cleaning and changing breakfast orders hung on the bedroom doors from 'Tea for one at 8.30' to 'Six pairs of kippers at 7am.' In the era of 'as you would be done by' hotel managers spent one night every few months in each room of their hostelries – which is eminently sensible: restaurateurs eat in their own restaurants, wine merchants drink their own wares, why not hotel keepers spending a night in the rooms they let, possibly trying them out with the housekeeper, if the wife is understanding.

What I found much of ... and what cannot be very hard to put right ... are bathroom taps mounted directly above the plughole so that if you want a bath you have to perch for a minute holding the plug in place, alternatively dribble in the bath water as if it were oil on the way to becoming mayonnaise.

Loo-paper rolls attached to the walls in such positions that only agile contortionists are able to reach them without rising from their seats are commonplace. And then there are bathroom fans that go into action when the lights are turned on and go on whirring for twenty minutes after the light is switched off. In Edinburgh during the recent Festival I learnt the fan's funny ways soon after arrival; that evening I went to the theatre, had dinner, watched a stand-up comedian, came home and did my ablutions in darkness before going to bed; remembering I had not taken my pills, I instinctively switched on the bathroom light and lay there cursing. My pills say I should be asleep in fifteen minutes. The bathroom fan had other ideas.

It is important to bear in mind that some things which appear 'wrong' are carefully calculated money-spinners: like NOT having the telephone number of your hotel printed on the room phone. It is done because hotels charge four or five times the going rate for calls and if you had the number at hand, you might ring home and say, 'I am at ... ring me back.' To date they have not discovered a way of making you pay for incoming calls.

At Ipswich the other day I arrived late, asked the night porter if I might have a bottle of wine in my room and he informed me that this had been seen to by the manager. In my room there was an ice-bucket, glasses, and a with-compliments slip telling me to enjoy my stay; no wine.

A friend who spent much of his working life as a floor waiter says that nicking fruit and flowers and complimentary bottles of champagne is an almost entirely safe crime. No one complains about what they did not know they were to be given; he says a professional would never have left an ice-bucket.

I love staying in hotels, especially when they don't pretend that they are 'home from home'. I have a home. I look to hotels for diversion; large bathrooms, preferably with a fish or a boat with which to play in the bath. I am keen on lots of soft towels, wooden nail brushes, a choice of shampoos.

Also I like trouser-presses, for which I have found interesting sub-uses – like warming up a ham sandwich and pressing newly washed underpants between towels. (Of course you do not do these things simultaneously.) A kettle is useful. I travel with a bottle of Calvados, for medicinal purposes, and a glug of the apple brandy to an envelope of brown sugar, cup filled with boiling water, is a peerless goodnight drink.

Television is essential: if you have thin walls and noisy neighbours it is surprising how soon they lower the decibel-output when you give them the late night movie, on full blast.

I fear breakfast is where hotels have it hardest, for the better the breakfast the more people eat, the less money is made; hotels have a vested interest in the service of bad breakfasts, were it not for the fact that customers might not return to eat microwaved croissants, orange juice from cardboard boxes and soft butter in gold envelopes to go with the mini-portions of ill-conceived preserves. I mean, who eats damson jam for breakfast? In Inverness I stayed in a small hotel and the owner, too preoccupied to perform the niceties of her trade, provided a pot of tea, a loaf of bread, a toaster, a pound pot of marmalade and a packet of Anchor butter and apologized for not doing more but there would be herrings baked in oatmeal in ten minutes. She should open an academy of breakfast cookery.

10
FREUD TALKS FOOD WITH THE FAMOUS
(but not with Boy George)

'"These vodkas are exceedingly kind."'

In the early 1990s the series 'Gut Feelings', published in the weekly Saturday Review section of The Times, *recorded Freud's encounters with various celebrities who spoke to him about the place of food in their lives, and included in each was the recipe for a dish which Freud would consider appropriate to each interviewee. Around the same time the* Radio Times *started a similar weekly series under the title 'The Clement Freud Interview', but without the recipes.*

A taste of life's trial and error: Stephen Fry
The Times, 4 April 1992

I THOUGHT IT appropriate to take Stephen Fry to dine in the Grill Room of the Hyde Park Hotel. It is a serious eating place staffed by waiters who are mature and caring. The menu is honest, the wine list safe. Jeeves, on his day off, might have come to the Hyde Park Hotel grill.

Fry arrived early – I had arrived earlier. We sat in the bar. He ordered a screwdriver and a waiter brought us a dish of chipolata sausages in a Worcesterish sauce. The menu arrived and Fry chose Ogen melon with tea sorbet ('I've never had tea sorbet') then shepherd's pie, which was a dish of the day. We drank an Australian Chardonnay followed by a bottle of absolutely delicious Château Pavie 1982.

Fry was born in Hampstead in 1957. Father was a technical director of Hoover on the A40, mother Austro-Hungarian Jewish. When he was six the family moved to Norfolk, where father bought a large house, built a laboratory at the back and was then, as he is now, known as The Inventor. Fry's first gastro-memory was the discovery of a deep aversion to custard, which 'in common with anything made with hot milk makes me cat.'

I looked askance.

'*Stalky and Co.* Cat equals retch.' We discussed Kipling, whom we both admire although we have reservations about his politics.

The parental home in Booton, near Norwich, was large and Victorian, with a big, high-ceilinged kitchen that had no sink – there was a series of sculleries with sinks; the young Fry thought people who had sinks in their kitchens were very odd.

His sister's nanny, Mrs Riseborough, was in charge: a good, plain cook in the best sense of the phrase. The fare was regulated by deliveries: fish came on Wednesdays in a horse and cart from

Cromer; sausages on Fridays. Her best dishes were puddings: apple crumble and treacle tarts 'topped with crisp cornflakes for my brother, soft breadcrumbs for me, comfort food'.

He was sent to prep school in Gloucester. 'Meals were institutional, liver with piping; I was a creepy boy who hung around the kitchen and led night raids on the scullery.' He aimed for the jelly, which he ate raw: raspberry, blackcurrant, whatever. He brought a tuck-box to school containing Mrs Riseborough's Dundee cake, which was cleared out by the second day of term.

Uppingham at twelve. The quality of food depended on luck; on whose house you were in. He was unlucky but he made the sixth form at fifteen – at which age he was also expelled. He had been given a weekend's leave to attend a meeting of the Sherlock Holmes Society. Expected back on Monday evening, he returned on Thursday night, having discovered the cinema. For the school this was the final straw. Father came to collect him in his car, and said: 'We'll discuss the whole sorry business when we get home.' He was good about it.

Father cooks the way scientists cook, drawing on knowledge of molecular structure, knowing why soups thicken, what causes potatoes to go floury. Father's 'thing' is capers: caper sauce is considered the perfect accompaniment to most food.

Fry was sent to a direct grant school, ran away, committed a credit-card fraud, stood trial and was sent to prison at Pucklechurch in Avon. 'The food there was standard British institutional; anyone who has been to a public school recognizes and has no trouble with prison and its regime.'

He minded about plates that had indentations for meat, vegetables, potatoes; was put to work in the machine shop painting model soldiers, graduated to polishing floors, which he loved, for there is something satisfying in a well-polished floor.

Mother came visiting, brought *Times* crosswords – which he always finishes, sometimes as quickly as he can write the words. He had trouble with cocoa – the hot milk. His pay of 49p a week went on tobacco: a quarter-ounce of Old Holborn and a packet of HM Prison cigarette papers. Another prisoner showed him how to roll these and advised him to leave them to dry on the radiator; he went for association, came back and found them gone. 'I had to keep remembering that all my colleagues were fundamentally dishonest.'

After three months he was out, went to Norwich City College, achieved three As in A-levels ('Prison had made me concentrate') and got a scholarship to Queens' College, Cambridge, to read English.

The food at Queens' was not bad; he missed the really bad steward in respect of whom someone had written 'Carter must go' on the college lawn in Paraquat. Fry acted; in view of his height – he is 6ft 4in – and the depth of his voice, he played Volpone, Oedipus and heroes in tragic and bombastic plays. He attended three lectures in three years, drank wine ('I was never good with beer') and had a friend whose mother sent him cases of Taittinger champagne.

In his last year at Cambridge, he got a 2:1, was in the Footlights and went to the Edinburgh Festival; was filmed by the BBC. The company consisted of Hugh Laurie (president), Tony Slattery, Emma Thompson and Fry. He has not looked back a lot: actor, director, author, scriptwriter, master fundraiser for charities, all done with skill, style, humour and a tall, gangling dignity.

After university he lodged at first with the friend whose mother sent the champagne, moved to a flat in Chelsea and ate at the Villa Puccini, discovered L'Escargot in Greek Street, where Elena, the great maître d', recognized him the second time he went, which impressed him a lot. In his salad days he had spent a summer as waiter in a Norfolk resort hotel, learnt silver service, can manipulate a spoon and fork in one hand, hates that sort of thing. He likes places as much for the atmosphere as the quality of the food, particularly enjoys the Caprice and Kensington Place, where silver service is considered secondary to the customers' contentedness.

At about this time we had cheese from a good cheese trolley and Fry got hiccups. I cured them. We then had some pudding served by a waiter from Dortmund, to whom he spoke in good German; with the pudding we drank excellent Italian dessert wine.

Fry has a house in Islington, where he never cooks, and a manor house near King's Lynn, Norfolk, which is old and has seven or eight bedrooms, also a great kitchen where he spends much time behind the Aga stove. An honoured guest might get gazpacho, followed by a casserole of braising steak with shallots and a reduction of different vinegars, amended from a recipe by Raymond Blanc: 'There are at least three good butchers in King's Lynn, which is helpful.' He can do crème brûlée and brown bread ice-cream.

We finish dinner and he drinks black coffee, sips Hine brandy and we discuss his all-time favourite dishes: foie gras comes high on the list. 'There was great excitement when I realized that this was not pâté but whole liver which melts in your mouth.' He is extremely keen on oysters, first encountered on tour in Australia; he eats them fresh or with Mornay sauce or Kilpatrick – which has a sauce rather like the one we had on the chipolatas.

He loves properly roasted spring lamb, is 'not bad on steak', and speaks of memorable quenelles of pike served at the Waterside Inn at Bray. We leave the hotel at 11pm; he has a 6am start in a film studio the following morning. The screws at Pucklechurch would be very proud of their most distinguished old boy.

The recipe headed 'Clement Freud prepares a dish for Stephen Fry' was for quenelles of scallops with oyster sauce.

* * *

Ice-cream tubs on the Rocky road:
Sylvester Stallone
The Times, 27 June 1992

IT IS 11.30AM at the Halkin Hotel in London. Your very first impression is: 'How can anyone that size portray a heavyweight boxer?' Then you think: 'How can anyone that famous be so totally punctual?' Then you shake hands and thank him for giving up his time.

He is 5ft 10in, weighs fractionally over 11 stone, wears moccasins, blue jeans, and an emerald-coloured silk shirt.

Sylvester Stallone was born in Hell's Kitchen, New York, in 1946. Father was a beautician, mother was a cigarette girl in Billy Rose's Diamond Horseshoe bar in Manhattan. 'She says she was, like, a singer, but she was a cigarette girl.'

Soon after he was born, he was farmed out to a Mrs Hanson in Jackson Heights. She had three children of her own, and took in kids during the day while their parents were at work: 'I was a lifer, served four years.' It was a meat and potato household, nothing memorable.

At the age of five he was back in Hell's Kitchen; mother was working nights, and looked after him and his younger brother during the day: 'Home was a cold water flat, the lavatory doubling as a sink and a trash can; for fun we played with the mice.' I ask whether his mother had been a good cook.

'She was a horrible cook; everything tasted like tin foil – we later found out that everything *was* tin foil.'

For his birthday there would be a cupcake with a used candle stuck into it or a match, whatever burned. 'I don't recall pony rides.' He did get sent to a day camp, where parents gave an extra $5 so that the birthday child got an extra scoop of ice-cream and the biggest hamburger.

Father moved to Maryland and developed a few beauty parlours, and bought some polo ponies.

'Was the family close?'

'Like the Croats and Serbs in Yugoslavia.'

At sixteen Stallone quit school for three or four months to become a cosmetologist. He was deterred by 'great ugly broads who looked like burn victims and wanted to become beautiful', and resumed his studies at Deveraux College doing liberal arts. 'And I was quite athletic.'

I ask what had been the best meals of those times; he says that meals did not figure. 'At night I had beef and potatoes. I believed in heavy-duty protein and really went for junk food. At Twinkies I ate hostess cupcakes in abundance and was keen on juju fruits – a basic plastic lozenge, like eating ice.'

At seventeen he got a sort of athletic scholarship to a college in Switzerland, did boxing and taught physical education to girls, if girls turned up; his working knowledge of boxing was minimal. An ex-Rhodesian policeman, Dudley Pringle by name, came to the gymnasium and said: 'How about a fight?'

'He beat the shit out of me; in fifteen seconds I had knocked him on his arse, which was the last time I saw the man; for the rest of the time I just felt the leather in my face.' He had eleven stitches in his lip, and the name Dudley Pringle remains in the memory; there was no lasting physical damage.

At nineteen he enrolled as a drama student at the University of Miami. 'As far away from mountains as I could get.' Two years later, three credits short of a degree, he dropped out, got a job in New York as an usher at the Translux movie theatre: 'Just stood at the back and watched the films over and over; Indian films like *Shakespeare Wallah*. I was the worst usher in Manhattan, everyone got in free.' His favourite film of all time is *The Lion in Winter*. Stallone considers Peter O'Toole the greatest actor in the world and the one who has undeservedly received least recognition for his brilliance: no Oscars, no awards, and he reels off the O'Toole films from *Lawrence of Arabia* onwards.

His first acting break came in 1972 in *Lords of Flatbush*; he was cast to play Stanley, a big, leather-clad street-bully, for which part he increased his weight from 160lb to 220lb 'by eating six quarts of ice-cream a day and becoming blob-like; it takes years to take off the subcutaneous fat which is always lurking there waiting for any opportunity to mug you.'

Having watched his *Rocky* movies (in which he does his own stunts), I suggest that if one could achieve that level of fitness, elegance of footwork, speed and accuracy on the punchball, one would be tempted to give up acting and go for it.

He had thought that also, tried it in the ring against Larry Holmes and Tim Witherspoon, also some others: nothing. One just cannot give away that much weight, not for real.

Stallone, who was a hyperactive kid back in Hell's Kitchen, does a fair stint forty years on: he plays polo – having learnt to ride in Maryland – and golf; on the previous day at Wentworth, in the course of an hour and a half, 'Sandy Lyle showed me the total uselessness of the $50,000 I had spent on golf lessons.' And he runs and works out …

Steering him back to food, I ask if there was a time when he could afford to eat anything he wanted and changed his diet.

He said no; 'Good food just came, I don't enjoy eating that much.'

He says he likes simple stuff like that which they serve at Planet Hollywood, the restaurant he owns in New York – pizzas and pastas, salads heavy on carrots, with oil and vinegar dressing. His very favourite food is parmesan cheese, so long as it is Reggiano 91. His eating pattern is to breakfast like a king, lunch like a prince and dine like a pauper, and he talks of 'gigantic breakfasts, frightening in size, really obscene – needing an hour and half in the gym to work off; I would really love to weigh 400lb.'

And become a sumo wrestler?

He says yes, sumo men are much maligned, and agrees with me that it is a great sport and a wonderful spectacle.

We discuss the cooks in his family: wife number one 'was not bad: McDonald's would have hired her.' Wife number two 'had never heard of cooking, thought food was brought by the tooth fairy,' and mother's cooking 'was horrible, like eating turf.'

Does he cook?

'Actually, I'm not a bad cook for the sort of food I need: eggs, pasta, meats. I understand food mixing, how to get the best out of my body.'

Around the time he was a cinema usher in New York, he also worked as short order cook at Dober's, on 57th Street and Lexington. 'I could cut sturgeon so thin you could read through it.'

Has he eaten goose liver, wild mushrooms, beluga caviare?

It transpires that he is a gastro-innocent; last week he ate his first olive: it was black, small, shrivelled. I tell him of plump, juicy olives marinated in oil and coriander, cumin and garlic; he listens politely. When we talked about boxing, polo, golf, sumo and cricket – I mention Peter O'Toole's passion for cricket – he hung on every word.

> *The recipe headed 'Clement Freud prepares a dish for Sylvester Stallone' was for oysters with white alba truffle.*

* * *

Deadpan whose favourite line is pungent: Paul Merton
The Times, 5 September 1992

I HAD READ an article about Notarianni in Battersea High Street: Festival of Britain décor; pizza, pasta and ice-cream served by the sons of the house, while dad, who had been there, done that, now sat around, smoked and watched. I had forgotten that one must always beware places where the décor, the ease of parking or the floral arrangements are praised without mention of the quality of the food.

When Paul Merton agreed to a lunchtime interview, and explained that he lived in Battersea, but had no fave places, I suggested we met at 12.30 on Wednesday at 142 Battersea High Street.

I arrived early: marble tables, art deco chairs not made to be sat on; a poster stating that Senior Service Satisfy, a Bill Haley and the Comets playbill and a clock with green back-lighting. On my table was a vase containing a silk rose on a plastic stem and I sat there wondering whether this should be washed or dry-cleaned. I ordered a tomato dough stick to while away the time. My guest arrived punctually.

To say that service at Notarianni is haphazard would be over-kind. But there is service and if the hands of the clock were not so egregiously green, we might not have noticed that mineral water took fifteen minutes to arrive; other items, being specially prepared, took longer.

Merton was born in Parsons Green, southwest London, in 1957. Father was a train driver on the Underground, mother a nurse; they shared a council flat with grandfather who, when mother went back to work, looked after him and his younger sister. The only meal he remembers is roast chicken after Sunday Mass.

I had ordered antipasto, Merton tagliatelle; both eventually arrived, and when I asked for bread to go with my salami, an elderly lady was dispatched to the baker to obtain this. She was only an average shopper and slow with it. Merton's pasta was cooked – how shall we put this – without flair.

When he was eight years old, Merton's father was transferred to Morden, where Paul attended the Roman Catholic primary school. Lunch is recalled because it was served in another building: 'Form a crocodile, walk for five minutes.' There was swede for lunch. At home, food was not important; father cooked when mother was at work – mince and mashed potatoes – and for holidays they went to mother's family in Waterford, where there were huge plates of beans and chips.

He failed his eleven-plus, attended Wimbledon College just

as it became comprehensive, took sandwiches to school – 'Quite nice, cheese and tomato, John West salmon, also Mars bars' – and achieved two A-levels. He did not want tertiary education and signed on. 'There were less than a million unemployed at the time, so being on the dole was quite exclusive.'

He had always wanted to become a comedian, became a civil servant, worked at Tooting employment office in charge of training courses – telling punters which of the mainly available courses were most apposite to the work they were seeking.

He left home at twenty-two, bought a ramshackle maisonette in West Norwood, south London, with John Irwin, a school friend with whom he still writes comedy material. They cooked 'basic dishes and we bought a sack of potatoes every week, did fried onions and tomatoes, also courgettes wrapped in pastry'.

In 1982, he phoned the newly opened Comedy Store, where alternative comedians were put on show. He lied about gigs he had done and was offered an engagement.

'The Comedy Store was a bear pit of drunks, had a tiny stage and when I went on at 2.15am the audience was tired and emotional. While I had no confidence in being funny, I knew that my material was well written.'

Similar work followed. He read *Time Out*, learnt of places that had recently opened and rang them for work. 'I have done the Comedy Store' was an open sesame. He did a good gig at the Earth Exchange in Archway, north London, a vegetarian curry restaurant with acts on every Monday evening.

In 1987, five years into a career that kept him close to the breadline, he hosted *Comedy Warehouse* for Channel 4, then did *Whose Line Is It Anyway?*, and a couple of years later he got his big break: a one-man fringe show at the Edinburgh Festival.

The opening night was a triumph. 'Go and see this man' was the headline above the ecstatic review the next day. It was advice that could not be taken because the following afternoon, playing football, he broke his leg. The show was cancelled. Merton lost the

£3,000 he had paid up-front for the theatre, and would have been in even more serious trouble had the Comedy Store not held a benefit for him.

The leg took a long time mending, hospital food was dire, he got hepatitis A – 'as a result of the food, the doctor told me' – but friends came to visit and brought him dishes from the local Indian takeaway. Biryani was his favourite, but food was really a necessary inconvenience; he thought this was due to the unimportant part it had played during his adolescence.

His girlfriend at the time was spectacularly bad in the kitchen, had no inclination to make anything and, having taught himself to make pancakes one Shrove Tuesday, he sometimes made those.

His girlfriend took him to Australia, where he became fond of white Chardonnay and his leg healed. He left her, returned to England, married Caroline Quentin, with whom he lives in Battersea in a flat with a large kitchen in which they spend much of their time.

Do you entertain?

'We had a party for fifteen people.'

What did you eat? He thought trout, and when I looked doubtful he said it might have been salmon – anyway a large fish which was cooked in the wedding-present fish kettle. Caroline, when she has half an hour to spare, makes pasta with her machine. He loves garlic bread above all things, and his best meal ever was in Kuala Lumpur on his honeymoon: chicken satay. 'I always liked chicken, although now I am quite keen on duck.'

We ordered chocolate brandy fudge cake, £2.70. It was deeply disappointing. And, for the next twenty minutes, we waved at the staff to try to get a bill.

Whose Line Is It Anyway? goes on; *Have I Got News For You* is about to get another outing and *The Paul Merton Show* returns this year.

He and his school friend write the scripts – in longhand, everything carefully considered, not much rewriting. He is a great

311

believer in travelling to work, keeping good hours like 10 to 4, or 10 to 6 if it goes well. There is a break for lunch: baked potatoes and tuna fish.

I wondered about tipping: being a coward, I left 10 per cent, on the strength of which we tried to say goodbye to the staff, but they were busy, locked in conversation with each other.

The recipe headed 'Clement Freud prepares a dish for Paul Merton' was for chicken biryani.

* * *

The cook, the star, his mash and her diet: Helen Mirren
Radio Times, 12-18 December 1992

SHE PLAYED CLEOPATRA at the National Youth Theatre aged nineteen and was acclaimed 'a star' in every sensible newspaper; gave a glittering performance in *Age of Consent* with James Mason; was one of the reasons for Trevor Nunn's knockout successes in his heyday at the RSC. Helen Mirren is the woman most men want to take out to dinner; it is her blend of beauty, warmth and humour.

Radio Times decreed that I was to invite her to lunch; my life has been like that – teetering on the fringe of success; as long ago as 1950 I arrived at a party ten minutes after Brigitte Bardot had left.

I thought I might cook Miss Mirren something special – like a breast of pheasant marinated in Calvados, sliced and baked in cream and wild mushrooms in a scooped-out Catriona potato, which I would then glaze with egg yolk. After that, Poire Belle Hélène, which is a plump dessert pear simmered in Sauternes, served with best vanilla ice-cream and a rich, hot chocolate sauce. I telephoned her and asked whether she liked game. She said yes, she did, but was on the Hay diet, which demands consumption of either protein or carbohydrates at one sitting; while she loved pheasant, she was quite especially keen on mashed potatoes, actually keener on mashed potatoes than anything.

We settled for an all-carbohydrate lunch; she arrived punctually, only puffing a bit after all my stairs, and we sat down to eat.

I had bought rosemary focaccia, which is currently my favourite bread, made vichyssoise soup, boiled corn on the cob, cut into 2in pieces and lavished with butter; and prepared pasta with truffle oil and a grating of white truffle. The main dish was large King Edwards, boiled and ready to be mixed at the last moment with hot single cream, Maldon salt, butter and some scrapes of nutmeg, followed by bread and butter pudding, which I would brûlée when the time came. We drank a white Châteauneuf du Pape shipped by Paul Jaboulet.

Three hours later there was not a scrap of food left, the wine also had been drunk; inroads were made into a bottle of Delamain brandy. I had a substantial pile of washing up and a new friend.

Journalism is a very desirable occupation.

Helen Mirren was born in London after the war. Father was Vassily Petrov Mironoff, one-time viola player with the London Philharmonic, wartime ambulance driver and 'by the time I knew him, a driving instructor'. Mother was Scottish. Their first home was a big gloomy house in Westcliff-on-Sea, then a smaller, nicer one in Leigh-on-Sea. There was an older sister and a younger brother, not much money, no fridge till she was ten so food was bought every day and butter was kept in the meat-safe in a dish of water.

Her mother cooked wonderfully well on limited resources. 'We had spaghetti before anyone else, were the first people in the street to eat yoghurt and she baked her own bread, made fruit jellies and bespoke cakes for birthday teas.'

The young Helen attended the local primary school, played the Virgin Mary in her second year, wearing a blue veil and stars; it was such a good performance she was taken to present herself in all the other classrooms: 'I thought I had died and gone to heaven.'

313

Her next school was St Bernadette's Convent, an odd choice for a child from a socialist/atheist family, and from there to grammar school via the 11-plus.

Were there incentives to pass?

'My parents were classically good, they said: "Do your best."'

I asked about school meals.

She said, 'There was a slow-eaters' table and I sat at the top of the fast-eaters' table. I am not very choosy; I like food too much to be picky.'

She went to see Terry Scott in *Out of the Blue* at the theatre at the end of Southend's pier and saw chorus girls dressed in powder blue and pink veils, 'who made me want to be an actress. I thought it was the most beautiful thing I had ever seen.'

There were no outings to restaurants, though a Russian uncle – dearly loved as a consequence – took her to a pub in Guildford: 'Very glamorous, we had prawn cocktail with lettuce and mayonnaise.'

She got A-levels in English, Art and Spanish; went to teacher training college, spent three years in Hampstead 'treading water until I could be an actress', living in a bedsit. Her first paid job was at the Kursaal in Southend, blagging: 'Roll up, roll up, see the bearded lady.'

Back in London she played Hermia in the National Youth Theatre's production of *A Midsummer Night's Dream*, then Cleopatra: 'I became a fat little star; I was fat you know, young and fat, and I snuck on and walked off with the show. After that I made the biggest mistake of my life. I stayed on at teacher training college.'

She had a boyfriend, they dined in Indian restaurants on 'one cheapest dish and two plates – they were so kind. We were very into food, looking at menus trying to decide where we would go if we had money.'

Six months in repertory in Manchester, living in digs, and then the RSC during Peter Hall's last year. 'I wanted to be a proper actress, which meant playing all the major parts.' Trevor Nunn cast her in *Miss Julie, The Two Gentlemen of Verona*, many more Shakespeare plays ... and she got her first and best screen part with James Mason, in Vienna, where she drank her first champagne cocktail, ate her first oyster, and liked both a lot.

She has had a succession of serious relationships, but never married. Had she been the other Cleopatra, the one who appeared opposite Richard Burton, she says she would have had four husbands ... 'anyway, Cleopatra did not marry all her men, either.'

She now lives in Hollywood. I nodded, making a mental note to impress the cleaning woman with the information. What took you there, I asked.

'Love took me there.' She lives with Taylor Hackford, director of *An Officer and a Gentleman*. They tend to go out for dinner, occasionally eat in: buy a piece of tuna and grill it, plain, without sauce.

I asked what parts she still wanted to play.

'Hamlet, Richard III, Henry V, Macbeth, Uncle Vanya.'

Othello?

'No.' We talk of *Prime Suspect* and I go on a bit about the brilliance of her performance. I am wrong; anyone could do it. It was all down to the writer [Lynda La Plante], everything Helen Mirren did was in the script. I had not realized it was that simple.

At 4pm a car comes to collect her. At 4.30pm I get withdrawal symptoms. I miss her.

* * *

Spaghetti-like figure with a Rye sense of humour: Spike Milligan
The Times, 2 January 1993

AT RYE STATION I got into a taxi and asked for the Casa Conti, and after a minute or so the driver said: 'Have you come far?'

'London,' said I.

'All that way for lunch at the Casa Conti?'

He had a point. The restaurant has half a dozen tables and 25 dishes from which to choose – a bad sign. But they did have San Pellegrino water, and when my guest arrived, punctually, quietly, limping a bit, looking a respectable Home Counties septuagenarian, he explained that this was the only place around where they turn off the piped music when he arrives.

The waiter beamed. He and Spike Milligan conversed in advanced phrase-book Italian. I believe I caught 'I would like a room facing the sea ...' There were certainly lots of 'benes'.

The menu, as I have intimated, is voluminous and, uniquely, the last page lists the 38 tapes of its music centre so that you could have, say, spaghetti con vongole with number 36 – the *1812 Overture*. There is also a wine list.

Milligan ordered melone followed by minestrone. Did he want ginger with his melon? No. Parmesan cheese with his minestra? No. He is seriously thin and, as he ate less than half his soup, no pudding or coffee or tea, and only sipped at a small glass of Orvieto, our luncheon did nothing to make him less so.

He was born in India in 1918; father was regimental sergeant major in the Royal Artillery.

'Tough, hard bastard?', I suggested, remembering those who put the fear of God into us junior officers.

A delightful man, said the RSM's eldest son. Mother, the daughter of the trumpet sergeant major, organized life in a huge bungalow set in the Maidan. 'We were fourth-generation gunners.'

Cooking was done by ayahs, as was child-minding and preparing the banana sandwiches the boy took to his first school: a convent in Poona, where the fathers of the other children were 'whisky-swigging colonels who spent most of their time falling off polo ponies.'

Did he have a favourite food?

Prawn and egg curries, the hotter the better, jalabi, everything cooked in a mud stove on coal, lots of lemonade – no real favourite.

Birthday cake? 'No.' Presents? 'Father was insane on cowboys and Indians, and I got guns, holsters, headdresses.' Father was also – uniquely I should think among class-one warrant officers – tremendously keen on the stage; had won a tap-dancing competition with a first prize of a week's engagement at the Queen's Theatre, Poplar – but *his* father would have none of it, put him in the army at fourteen.

In 1932, the Labour government of the day reduced the strength of the British Army by 10 per cent. Father was forced to retire, and the Milligans travelled to England and took up residence in an attic in Catford, east London: father, mother and two sons with the stove in the bedroom.

What did they eat?

'Straightforward British meals: ox heart, cod's roe, pigs' trotters, faggots, suet puddings; nothing was favourite.

'I went to Brownhill Road Boys' School, learnt to masturbate; teacher stood over us while we did it.'

The occupants of the other tables at Casa Conti, who had been listening raptly to our conversation, now made rhubarb-rhubarb noises like a well-rehearsed rabble. 'It seemed like that,' Milligan said. The crowd noise subsided.

School meals? 'No: banana sandwiches wrapped in greaseproof paper.' He passed no exams: 'I was a duffer, although I won an essay prize.' Father got a job on the photo desk of Associated Newspapers and wrote articles on dressage, for he knew a lot about horses, and obtained for his fifteen-year-old son a job with Stones Engineering of Deptford. 'Military nepotism – I got 13 shillings a week.'

Was there a canteen?

'I took banana sandwiches to work; thought they should be produced in pill form – to be taken three times a day.'

At work, he made things he did not understand, such as long pieces of webbing with three holes in the end, and he fell in love with Lily Danford of Brockley, took her to St Cyprian's Hall, had egg and chips – thought that this was the big time.

The Milligans moved to Honor Oak, in southeast London. 'Father was very strange, he would not buy a house, and the war came and broke up the family: a good family. We were never together again after that.'

He became a gunner – would eat 'any bloody thing, army food has the charisma of an out-of-work phone box'.

His break came after the war in Italy, where he and two soldier friends played in a group: 'Bill Hall, a superb cockney violinist, with Jock on bass and me on guitar. After our first public performance – we were the hit of the night – an officer booked us for the Bellini theatre in Naples – got a year's contract at £10 a week, fell in love with a prima ballerina who took me to good restaurants.'

His previous Italian restaurant experience had been when Sergeant Bullock said: 'Stick with me, men, I'll show you the good restaurants.' They walked down a street and he said: 'That one, men, they have white tablecloths and knives and forks.' The waiter came to take their order. Bullock told him: 'Quattro egg and chips.'

He married June in 1952, and has three children: Laura, Sean and Silé, 'with an accent over the e'. He lived in Highgate, divorced, and married Paddy – another great cook. They had a house in Finchley. He is now married to a third good cook, Shelagh, who the previous day had made him Dover sole bonne femme; she uses fennel and makes wonderful fish pies. They drink Hügel Tardive Gewurztraminer 1974, Orvieto Abbocato and 'bloody marvellous shiraz. If Australia were in the Mediterranean, the French would have a hard time competing with their wines.'

They are mildly attracted by Rye: cobbled streets, wall-to-wall traffic, but a good place to go for a walk at one o'clock in the morning.

While he recorded the *Goon Shows* he, Peter Sellers and Harry Secombe would go to a restaurant in London's Edgware Road, 'now part of Saudi Arabia'.

These days his London home-from-home is the Trattoo in Abingdon Road, 'where they don't have canned music, the salmon is cut so thin you can see the plate through it and they serve Corvo Rosso – a mafia wine with blood on the labels.'

The recipe headed 'Clement Freud prepares a dish for Spike Milligan' was for tortelli di erbette.

* * *

Were those the gags that were?: Sir David Frost
The Times, 23 January 1993

IT MUST BE said that there are not many folk in the highest reaches of public life who attach to a Gut Feelings interview the same importance as do I, who conducts them.

As a consequence, unless my guest is quite particularly early (I arrive fifteen minutes before the agreed time) I sit in the location not just drinking in the atmosphere and assessing the menu, but contemplating replacements should the invited guest do a Boy George, and fail to show. I also work on my opening speech. 'Welcome, and thank you for coming. This won't hurt; if there's any aspect of your life that you wish to bypass, it's all right by me.'

I was doing that in the breakfast room of the Carlton Tower Hotel at 9 the other morning. It is an agreeable, cared-for place with pleasant views over Cadogan Gardens. The menu lists Chelsea buns at £2; an extra £2.50 gets you butter and jam. At the next table a couple of young men were selling each other launderettes. The head waiter came to ask whether I would like tea while I waited for my guest, at which moment my guest arrived: the newly knighted Sir David Frost, exuding bonhomie, pleased to see me, pleased also to see the head waiter. How was I?, he asked. How was my wife, how were our children ... and within

319

minutes he had ordered orange juice, wet scrambled eggs, coffee, and reminded me of a joke of yore about a Trappist monastery.

In the mid-Sixties, when he had become one of the best-known faces on television, a journalist wrote: 'Frost rose without trace.' I traced him: he was born in Tenterden, Kent, in 1939. Father was a Methodist minister, mother a fantastic support to him at home and in church. There were two sisters – fourteen and sixteen years older than he. 'I was an afterthought, an accident; they had sold the pram.'

Father was moved to Kempston in Bedfordshire when his son was one; to Gillingham, Kent, seven years later, then to Raunds, Northamptonshire, and finally Beccles in Suffolk. 'He loved the small towns of England and his parishioners loved him; elected him as chairman of councils and societies; enjoyed his sermons which were based on personal experiences.'

I asked about gastro-memories. 'The main thing I remember is that we never had dinner – what others call lunch. We had high tea and a light supper; cereal, and Smith's crisps from packets inscribed "Founded 1922 at Brentford", which also contained small blue envelopes of salt; chocolate cakes made with biscuit crumbs, and fantastic Sunday roasts which we had on Saturdays. Sunday was for going to church – three times.'

Food was plentiful – something of a miracle, given that a Methodist minister's top salary was £750 per annum. He was not conscious of their lack of money, never remembers them skimping, 'although they must have'. There was chicken at Christmas, fruitcake for his birthday – 'Mother was a superb maker of icing; I did not like marzipan, so it was thick icing. The family was totally teetotal; the only alcohol I had pre-Cambridge was beer after the game at Beccles cricket club.'

Holidays were spent in boarding houses at Llandudno and Lowestoft, with ice-cream the main holiday treat; they also went to Methodist guild homes at Sidmouth and Swanage: 'Terrific – sixty or seventy people in country houses; all Methodist, young and old.'

At eighteen he went up to Caius College – his first year living in, subsequent years at 1 West Road, Cambridge, 'which had useful French windows'. College food was good, especially the crème brûlée, and he and friends founded a dining club called The Cabal which met at the Garden House Hotel for 'right royal dinners by our standards – mostly English and centred upon meat.' He never liked Indian food, 'although I would defend to the death their right to eat it.'

We went back to the Trappists: the head monk, impressed by lotteries, decided to hold one annually: the prize a dispensation from the vow of silence to make one statement. Father Gabriel was the first winner – Gabriel who had not spoken for twenty-nine years. He stood for a while, then said: 'The porridge is always cold.' A year passed. Father Dominic won the lottery, blushed, said: 'The porridge is always lumpy' and silence reigned for another twelve months.

At the Carlton Tower, Frost's eggs arrived, softly set, upon a piece of soggy toast. I pointed out that had the bread been fried in clarified butter, his breakfast dish would have benefited. Frost thought soggy toast was an integral part of scrambled eggs.

After university he came to London, lived in Churton Street – a short thoroughfare housing four dental repair services; he did cabaret, first at the Royal Court Theatre Club (proprietor C. Freud), then at the Blue Angel. He hitchhiked home for the weekends, paid off his Cambridge bills. Ned Sherrin, about to launch a satirical television review, selected him to present *That Was The Week That Was* and Frost became the name on everyone's lips.

He was seen eating ulanovas (caviare and sour cream on prawn crackers) at Bensons in Beauchamp Place, bought a house in Egerton Gardens where a Spanish woman called Luisa cooked for him for twenty years. On television there was *The Frost Show*, *Frost Report*, *Frost on Sunday*; he squired well-known actresses and singers, interviewed presidents and prime ministers, married Carina and has three sons, a house in Chelsea and another in Hampshire.

A Portuguese cook makes really good vegetable soup, steak and kidney pies, chicken fricassées, chocolate-chip cookies and cauliflower cheese, with the emphasis on cheese. In London he eats at the White Tower, for the roast duck; at Nico At 90 (onion tart) and in New York at the Four Seasons, to catch up with a lot of friends. Does he cook? 'No.' Nothing at all? 'Nothing.' It was time to go; he was toying with his first Romeo Y Julieta cigar of the day; he thanked me, left.

In the Trappist monastery, Father Raphael won the third annual lottery and announced that he was leaving the order. The Reverend Father, stunned, asked him why, permitted him another sentence.

'I can't stand the bickering over the porridge.'

> *The recipe headed 'Clement Freud prepares a dish for Sir David Frost' was for cauliflower cheese, with extra grated cheese 'for emphasis'.*

* * *

'Fish and chips is a cliché; it is so beautifully quiet here': Timothy Spall
Radio Times, 9-15 July 1994

I WILL START at the beginning, for there are people who begin reading articles at the end; to do so with this would give an altogether false impression of my subject's character. I had telephoned Timothy Spall to invite him to dinner; he said that he would be pleased to come. I asked what he would like to eat. He said curried prawns and Dover sole, grilled chicken was one of his favourite dishes and such green vegetables as he had discovered since leaving home – which included everything except peas and cabbages.

Puddings? Actually savouries, cheese.

Wine? He mentioned an esoteric white burgundy, a prestigious claret. I felt as Mrs Thatcher had when she first encountered Mr Gorbachev; here was a man with whom I could do business.

Punctually at 8pm on the appointed day the front doorbell rang and I pressed the entry buzzer shouting, 'Right to the top.' A minute or two later he appeared: 'Far king stairs,' he said. 'How do you manage?'

I told him the stairs might be the reason I was still alive; they provide the only exercise I take.

He gave me a bottle of champagne, also the carrier bag in which he had brought this; the champagne was good grand cru. He was neatly dressed in a suit with a black shirt and a tie bearing a strange device – the sort of thing Wardrobe give you on a bad day. We shook hands and I noticed that his are exceptionally well cared for. He is plump, which makes two of us.

We shared a bottle of champagne from the refrigerator, he took off his jacket, as I had done for it was a warm night, and I found him excellent company: discerning, in that he found the wine good, which it was; amusing while we discussed Arsenal and Danny Baker, Comic Relief, after-dinner speeches and being famous.

I had boiled some chicory in white wine, cut these into quarters, placed them on a buttered oven dish and anointed the leaves with strips of sizzled streaky bacon and a rich cheese sauce, baked this in the oven until golden.

As the champagne bottle was dead, I opened a bottle of Cloudy Bay Sauvignon, which is a wonderfully complex New Zealand wine. Timothy liked it a lot, sipped it while I prepared prawn curry – and as this took seven or eight minutes and the bottle was empty, I opened another.

Before embarking on the grilled chicken, we had some frozen lemon vodka. At pretentious banquets they serve sorbets before the main course – to cleanse the palate. Frozen vodka performs this task much more efficiently.

With the chicken we drank a bottle of 1991 Boillot Pommard, a Burgundy of quality. We agreed about the quality and when we finished it and there was vodka left, we finished the vodka.

He liked the matured cheddar a lot, seemed only medium fond of brie, cutting himself a dry thin sliver from the peak of the triangle; as neither of us feel strongly about coffee I invited him to bring his cheese and port to the far end of the dining table, where I had a pen and pad. This, I explained, is the working part of the evening – the interview.

He asked if he could first have a cigarette. I explained that this was a non-smoking apartment, noticed his disappointment, suggested we sit on the stairs outside the front door and have one there. This was fine by him. He had cigarettes, did I have matches? I did not, so lit the grill and rolled a page of the *Guardian* to make a spill which I could run down to where he would be sitting, smoking.

As I was fanning the griddle, he decided he did not really need a cigarette; more vodka would be all right.

Timothy Spall was born in 1957, in Lavender Hill, London. Father was a scaffolder when he was born, became a postal clerk. Mother was a home hairdresser. He is the third of four brothers. No sisters.

What were your early gastro-memories? 'What?' Favourite childhood food? 'None.' How did mum cook? 'She didn't. She knew the ingredients of rabbit stew and pearl barley. She is brilliant, wanted me to become an actor.'

How old were you then? 'I was seventeen.'

I explained that I was trying to get his life into chronological order; we were currently on his childhood. Food was the theme of the interview.

Were there treats? 'Fried bread and pearl barley (or he might have said Pearl Bailey) and we went to the Lake District and had dinner at Miller Howe.'

How old were you then? 'Last summer.'

What was the first restaurant to which you went? 'An Indian in

Eastbourne and thought it lovely and gorgeous and twenty years later I went back and realized, retrospectively, that it was piss.'

As we had run out of frozen vodka, we drank some at room temperature. Primary school was at the end of the road, food was fish-fingery things; after that Battersea County comprehensive where he and his friend John sussed out the catering and found the stores and ran amok among the jellies.

Were you a good scholar? 'Useless. O-levels failed. None.' Girlfriends? 'Only post-marriage.' Holidays? 'Butlins in Bognor or Clacton.' He left school, worked at the National Youth Theatre, lived at home. 'Mother kept me, gave me a shilling or two'; says this in a Rex Harrison voice.

What sort of food did you get? He gives me a vacant stare. Fish and chips?, I suggest. 'Fish and chips is a cliché; it is so beautifully quiet here.' I asked how he got into the Royal Academy for Dramatic Art. What age were you? 'I was nineteen. I got in because I was a good actor.'

What was your audition piece? 'Falstaff. I was seventeen, full of myself, so I did Falstaff.' I thought you said you were nineteen. 'I was. I forgot.' Who won the gold medal in your year? 'I did. The gold, the Bancroft. The best actor.' Did you go out and celebrate? 'Had five slices of toast served up by my Ma.'

He never cooked, not ever, except the day before he came to dine with me when he made breakfast for his children: 'So horrible, so astoundingly horrendous I wouldn't do it again.' I asked how old his children were. 'Nineteen, eleven and eight; these vodkas are exceedingly kind.'

I asked about his wife; when did you get married? 'In 1987 or something. I have to go soon.' What did your wife do? 'She married me.' What is her name? 'Mrs Spall. A gorgeous geezer. Live in SE23, wife and three children aged seventeen, eleven and six. They might cook eventually.'

Were you always fat? 'No.' When did you start putting on weight? 'Yesterday. I must go now.'

I ask whether he would like to ring home and tell them he is on his way; dial the number he gives me, hear him say: 'Hello, my darling. I love you. How are you? Love you. It's your dad. See you in half an hour.'

I fetched his jacket but he was putting on mine; we sorted it out. Halfway down the stairs he slipped, landed at the bottom and the heel of his shoe, which had come off, landed on him. I helped him to his feet and gave him his heel. He insisted it was not his. We argued a bit about that until the taxi arrived and we said goodbye.

It occurred to me that it would be proper to telephone his wife and explain that he was en route and might need some assistance when he got home; re-dialled the number to which he had spoken. It was an answerphone. I told it I loved it.

* * *

'I am not that fussed': Jeremy Clarkson
Radio Times, 23-29 March 1996

I TELEPHONED JEREMY Clarkson and invited him to dinner. He said, 'Yes please,' and I asked what he would like to eat. 'Anything.' What is your favourite dish? 'I am not that fussed.' What sort of restaurants do you like? 'Ones where they let me smoke through the meal.'

This was difficult. I don't smoke. I am not good with people who smoke, can't function in smoke-filled rooms ... and I explained and he said, 'All right then, I won't smoke.'

What shall I cook you? He said, 'I don't have a lot of palate left but am into textures and I like spicy food and game and savouries rather than puddings.'

He was punctual. My younger daughter had said, 'Dad, you will either like him a lot or hate him; he is worthwhile.' She did not say that he was tall. He stands tall and he sits tall and we got on quite well though, like Cilla Black's less successful couples, we are unlikely to see each other again.

For the record, I considered making him a jellied soup, a velvety stew with crisp potatoes, followed by deep-fried camembert cheese: after careful consideration, I cooked him an acceptable Thai kind of spiced dinner. He said he enjoyed it. I worried about his yearning for a cigarette.

Jeremy Clarkson was born in Doncaster in 1960. Father was a rep for a timber company but gave it up to join mother's business.

Mother created a three-dimensional interpretation of Paddington Bear and when Jeremy's school called in an educational psychologist because his work had dropped off, the shrink blamed the role reversal in his family.

Home was a 400-year-old farmhouse with ceilings so low that he hit his head on them. I suggested that a ceiling would not have to be that low …

He said, 'That was when I was fourteen and only 6ft tall.' He has a younger sister, she does not appear to have been hugely important to his life.

Earliest food memory is a picnic on the way to Manchester airport and peeling an egg when he was about two.

The best food memory is halibut, new potatoes and parsley sauce with his grandfather who was a general practitioner, playwright and author. That was the happy side.

Who cooked at home?

'Father cooked; he was a superb cook, was and still is the best cook I have ever encountered. School friends would want to come over to eat and father was unhappy unless I brought home twenty of them. He spent two days cooking cakes for the birds.'

How about mother?

'Mother rustled up puddings; mother ate out of a tin.'

Explain.

'It is not important. Being the source of Paddington Bears was important; at fifteen I was a successful bird-puller because of the bears.'

Mother had been a schoolmarm with a sideline in soft toys and early in the seventies produced Paddington. He has clearly told this story before.

'No, we did not have marmalade sandwiches, not at home, but I was partial to halibut and peas, and raspberries and cream – had a large garden all given over to raspberries.'

The interview was beginning to get out of hand, kept reverting to halibut and raspberries and grandfather: 'Built a house by a railway line and everyone said he was mad; then he bought the spur line.'

He was drinking wine and I was making a Welsh rarebit – grated mature cheddar and Red Leicester with strong ale and Colman's mustard and cayenne pepper and beaten egg yolks, spread on wholemeal toast and cooked under a medium grill so that the mixture blended before the top coloured.

Clarkson family holidays were spent in Padstow, either in a hotel or a rented cottage. Father cooked, a couple of times they went to France, where he encountered langoustines 'and started a love affair with shellfish that pertains to this day – oysters are one of my favourite foods.'

I considered asking why he had not told me. Decided against it. 'Sydney,' he said, when I asked about Australian oysters, 'is just like Birmingham.'

At prep school in Doncaster he was very, very, very bright ... and remembers meat pies: a sweet taste seeped in pastry, disgusting. At thirteen, because of the role reversal, he stopped working, scraped into Repton, had five fantastic years there before being expelled.

Why?

A constant series of misdemeanours: smoking, walking across the ruins (it was a rule not to), listening to David Bowie instead of doing prep.

How was the food?

'Steve was the cook. He is now cooking either at a prison or on the *QE2*. I was spoilt by father's cooking, though even if I had been brought up in a Little Chef I would have been disappointed with

Repton food. Grease. Water. Chicken bone, air, skin. They should have been set free. Meat-free birds.'

I ask about restaurants: there are memories of the Gingham Kitchen in Hallgate, Doncaster, where they had gingham tablecloths. He went with his grandfather and was very proud because everyone knew him and talked to him. There was 1492 in Marlow 'which was very expensive, and I ordered strawberries and cream. I was into lobster thermidor ... went to the Newton Park Hotel which smelled of Brussels sprouts cooked for some time; when you reserved a table they asked, "What vegetables?" so that they could start cooking.'

After leaving Repton he worked on the *Rotherham Advertiser*, lived at home, Rotherham being near Doncaster. I did not know that. 'Rotherham had no restaurants because they had a Labour council who wouldn't have them; they had pubs.'

With all his friends at university, Doncaster became lonely and he moved to London and flogged mother's Paddington Bears from Hamley's to Harrod's, living in a hideous flat.

Did you cook?

'Eggs, could have done boiled, fried, scrambled.'

Where did you eat?

Mostly drank, like at the White Horse in Fulham.

In 1993 he married Frances, who comes from the Isle of Man, counselled people who were made redundant: 'Oh yes, she cooks very well, comes from a family of great cooks.' They have two children.

Do you cook for them?

'I did the other night: bought pork and pasta and peppers and lobbed in mange tout peas as an afterthought; my Yorkshire blood: waste not want not.'

His favourite restaurant is La Lacanda del Santa Offici in Asti, where he drinks a very dry, iced Asti Spumanti. At home in Oxfordshire he goes out a lot: pizzas and much wine. I offer him a brandy. He says he thinks Armagnac is out to get him.

My daughter asked whether I had liked him; I told her I am still not quite sure; it could have been to do with his wanting to smoke, or me trying to get the meal over so that he could ...

On reflection, it was mostly to do with quizzing a man on a subject that genuinely did not interest him. Had we gone to a pizza bar and discussed women, or motor cars, or practically anything over a double magnum of Italian wine, we might now be inseparable.

* * *

Showing up at the culture club: Boy George
The Times, 14 November 1992

IN EPERNAY, SOME years ago, the directrice of a champagne company said: '*J'aime l'Angleterre et j'adore le bois George qui est si beau.*'

I told her that we had many lovely English woodlands, although this was one I did not know; she replied that *bois* was a singer.

Since then I have thought of Boy George as *bois*, and some weeks ago rang George's manager to ask if his client might care to meet me for an interview. The singer's manager said he would put it to him.

The following day I had a call from Eileen of Virgin Records to ask whether I would give an assurance that, if she arranged a meeting, my subsequent article would plug George's new single, Toxic Thingy. I was unable to give a firm guarantee, told her that I was as close to being a fan as someone who did not have a gramophone could be. She said she would let me know.

Two days later Eileen rang to say that George would consider it if I would do my best re Toxic Thingy and he could approve the photographer. I hastened to tell her that photographs did not feature in 'Gut Feelings' – there would be a picture, like that which I had faxed her: I had sent Michael Buerk's portrait to persuade him. George, it appeared, would not like to have a picture done. No photographer, no interview, said Eileen.

I told my daughter about George and me, I mean no George and me, and she said he is really nice, unpretentious, intelligent, easy to get on with. 'If you rang him personally, I am sure he would love to have lunch.'

I rang him – one has ways of finding telephone numbers – and a voice said: 'Leave a message.'

Three days later George telephoned: really nice, said lunch on Thursday would be fine, how did one o'clock at Blah Blah Blah in Goldhawk Road suit me?

I told him that Blah etc. would be good, did he know which number? He said he would ring me back.

Blah Blah Blah is listed in the London business directory as a vegetarian café. It is at the Shepherd's Bush end of Goldhawk, just beyond the railway bridge: glass-fronted, black and white tiled floor, old film-studio lights with barn doors on the ceiling; the letters BYO – bring your own (wine) – on the door.

Several shades of beige adorn the wall and there are four tables for four, three for two. When I arrived there was one customer, taking soup from a large rustic bowl.

The menu is chalked on a big blackboard; most things cost between £2.50 and £4.50. A smaller board suggests that you have your Christmas party at Blah Blah Blah.

An agreeable Australian wearing bleached, frayed shorts asked whether I would like mineral water and bread; brought both at the right temperature. With the warm bread came two slabs of butter, garnished with a sprig of greenery.

I had gone to Goldhawk Road from an editorial meeting, where a colleague told me that he had interviewed George some years ago: a really nice guy, easy, pleasant, intelligent, no side to him; he is surprisingly tall and has huge hands – really big. I think his brother is a boxer.

I sat at a table facing the door. Goldhawk Road is worth watching, hardly a dull moment, lots of very small people walk past. The Australian waiter was also quite small, perhaps it was something in the air; I was not going to have any trouble recognizing my guest.

At 1.20 I told the waiter that if my companion did not come in another ten minutes I would start. He said: 'You people are so polite.' I said: 'All right, I'll start in five minutes.' And soon after that he brought a Greek salad, redolent with best feta cheese and good basil vinaigrette.

Two girls came in, walked to the counter and asked for two cups of coffee. Nothing else?, said the Australian. They said no. He said all right and they took the table next to mine, pulled out cigarettes, saw my look, moved to the other side of the room; and smoked.

At 1.45 a man came in with a ham sandwich and asked if he could have some mustard to put on it; the Australian said sure, go ahead. They would not do that at La Gavroche. A van pulled up outside to deliver goods: Salumi and Formaggio was written on its side. I have never eaten Salumi.

At two o'clock I recalled a saying of Confucius: it is a mark of insincerity of purpose to seek an emperor in a low-down tea shop. It also occurred to me that Blah Blah Blah was an extraordinary place in which to be stood up; the Savoy would have been so much more convenient.

Byron (the Australian waiter who was also the owner) came and joined me. I asked whether he knew Boy George. He did. George was in at the end of last week, a really nice guy, gentle, unassuming, you'd never think he was a great star; easy to get on with and eats a lot; on Saturday he had six portions of spring rolls.

Was he alone?

No, there were four.

At 2.30 I ordered a chocolate and banana trifle, which they spell triffle; took one mouthful, discovered it to be full of desiccated coconut, left it.

'You didn't like it,' Byron said.

I said: 'Well ...'

He said: 'You people are so bloody polite. Why don't you just say "I hate it"?'

I explained about me and desiccated coconut, also tobacco smoke and Dr Scholl sandals. He asked if I was a journalist.

I said I would be if George had arrived. 'Nice guy, George,' Byron said once more.

When I got home there was a message of abject apology and the promise of a bunch of flowers, via Eileen. Where I had gone wrong was in not booking George through Eileen; she reminds him of things, without her he would never be anywhere – although he is a really pleasant, down-to-earth guy.

There was no recipe accompanying the Boy George article. Instead: 'Clement Freud does not cook anything for Boy George. He will wait to see whether he turns up, then send out for a takeaway.'

Index

Freud on Food
Clement Freud

All his life Clement Freud was passionate about food. In his
first ever full-length book, originally published in 1978, recipe
and anecdote jostle each other for the reader's attention. It
contains numerous irresistible recipes for dishes as varied as
Billybi, Cider Duck, Boiled Leg of Lamb with Caper Sauce
and Strawberry Romanoff, and brims all the while with his
hallmark wit and humour.

Freud on Food is divided into sections that take the reader
from starter to main course through a variety of fish, poultry,
game and meat dishes, to garnishes, sauces and vegetables and
finally fruits and 'sweet talk'. Unusual suggestions for special
occasions such as dinner parties, picnics, Sunday lunch and
weekend breakfast also abound with advice served up in
inimitably dry and deadpan humour.

Freud on Food is a book to be dipped into or read from cover to
cover and, either way, is a heart-warming reminder of Clement
Freud's great zest for life and love of good food.

9780552776547